Maps of Reconciliation

MĀNOA 19:2   UNIVERSITY   HONOLULU
                    OF HAWAI'I
                    PRESS

Maps of Reconciliation

LITERATURE

AND THE

ETHICAL

IMAGINATION

Frank Stewart

EDITOR

Barry Lopez

GUEST EDITOR

Kapa master Puanani Kanemura Van Dorpe
presents traditional burial kapa to Les Kuloloio.
Honokahua, Maui
Photograph by Franco Salmoiraghi, 1990

Editor   Frank Stewart

Managing Editor   Pat Matsueda

Production Editor   Brent Fujinaka

Associate Editor   Brandy Nālani McDougall

Designer and Art Editor   Barbara Pope

Fiction Editor   Ian MacMillan

Poetry and Nonfiction Editor   Frank Stewart

Staff   Jennifer Larson, Maureen O'Connor, Gabriel Prince

Corresponding Editors for North America
Barry Lopez, W. S. Merwin, Carol Moldaw, Arthur Sze

Corresponding Editors for Asia and the Pacific
CAMBODIA   Sharon May
CHINA   Howard Goldblatt, Ding Zuxin
HONG KONG   Shirley Geok-lin Lim
INDONESIA   John H. McGlynn
JAPAN   Leza Lowitz
KOREA   Bruce Fulton
NEW ZEALAND AND SOUTH PACIFIC   Vilsoni Hereniko
PACIFIC LATIN AMERICA   H. E. Francis, James Hoggard
PHILIPPINES   Alfred A. Yuson
SOUTH ASIA   Sukrita Paul Kumar
WESTERN CANADA   Charlene Gilmore

Advisory Group   Esther K. Arinaga, William H. Hamilton, Joseph O'Mealy, Robert Shapard

Founded in 1988 by Robert Shapard and Frank Stewart.

Reprint permissions can be found on page 226.

Mānoa gratefully acknowledges the continuing support of the University of Hawai'i Administration; the support of the University of Hawai'i College of Languages, Linguistics, and Literature; and grants from the National Endowment for the Arts and the Hawai'i State Foundation on Culture and the Arts. Thanks also to the Mānoa Foundation.

NATIONAL
ENDOWMENT
FOR THE ARTS
A great nation
deserves great art.

Mānoa is published twice a year. Subscriptions: U.S.A. and Canada—individuals $22 one year, $40 two years; institutions $40 one year, $72 two years. Subscriptions: other countries—individuals $25 one year, $45 two years; institutions $40 one year, $72 two years; air mail, add $24 a year. Single copies: U.S.A. and Canada—$20; other countries—$20. Call toll free 1-888-UHPRESS. We accept checks, money orders, Visa, or MasterCard, payable to University of Hawai'i Press, 2840 Kolowalu Street, Honolulu, HI 96822, U.S.A. Claims for issues not received will be honored until 180 days past the date of publication; thereafter, the single-copy rate will be charged.

http://manoajournal.hawaii.edu/
http://www.uhpress.hawaii.edu/journals/manoa/

CONTENTS

Editors' Note————————————————————————————

Maps of Reconciliation

                In the opening years of a new century who wishes to think of the final years? And yet, the old ways—war, the colonies—are worn out. What once served, or, truly, what once served only a few, is no longer feasible. The siren song of technology, to be sure, still courts an audience, the dazzle and promise of its solutions continue to make a plausible case, and its acolytes, with just a flicker of condescension, ask us for more time, more leeway.

The old ways, the path of the pirate and the conquistador, are worn out but, still, we acquiesce. Who will say no when effective new drugs are guaranteed, just there in the wings? When the elected and successful say it's time to move forward, who will say the game is over? With so many bets on the table, who wishes to say no to another roll of the dice?

The elders. As if with one voice, eerie as a solar eclipse, from Tibet to Tierra del Fuego, these historians of the workable now speak the same words. What are the words? What are their prescriptions? Without a book, a program, a charismatic—at the very least a crude map—how are we to know?

The neurologists and paleoarchaeologists tell us something happened fifty thousand years ago in Africa—perhaps it was the dawn of imagination—and hunter-gatherers became, overnight, something else. Us. We then moved swiftly, more swiftly than any driven animal before us, toward our destiny—the Hanging Gardens of Babylon, T'ang dynasty literature, the Constitution of the United States of America, Birkenau, the artificial heart. Then there were too many of us, and there was too much stuff— though, horribly, not enough for everyone. And those who said there was not enough, not enough of whatever it might take to make even more for anybody, were asking to be stoned by those who saw themselves as our enlightenment, who cursed the doubting.

And then the climate changed. And in the protracted and preternatural silence that followed, as if the unexpected slumping of a road had pitched a busload of children into the steep walls of a deep canyon, it was time to

Salt crystals on lava
Ka Lae, Kaʻū, Hawaiʻi
Photograph by
Franco Salmoiraghi, 1991

think through our destiny all over again, this time without words like *profit, conquer,* or *killing fields.*

Someone will have to make an outline, draw a map and pass it around, with a pencil and an eraser and no thought of ownership. The voices of individual authorship and the duly elected will need to give way to the repositories of community wisdom. For the first time in centuries, wisdom will need to be seated beside intelligence, a second light to cut the deep and unknowable dark.

Where once we might have begun the pursuit of another destiny with more (justifiable) war and additional (reluctant) enforcements of will, with vetted doctrines and the ruthlessness of reason, we might now begin with reconciliation. And with a capacity for reverence. In place of direct confrontation, the humility and unfamiliar courtesy of reconciliation. In place of a single belligerent epistemology and the self-assurance of its promoters, reverence for all that lies beyond human control. In place of indifference, compassion. In place of a brave army, courageous people.

The true test of usefulness for the human imagination now is in the invention of a life never before lived. The creation of a way in the world to which no one now, anywhere, is privy. We begin with the scraps of what seems right, and with the hope that what is now invisible is in fact possible, even if not likely in our lifetime.

We start with our instinct for reconciliation, to address the war in ourselves, the war in our kitchens, the war in Sudan.—Barry Lopez

Acknowledgements

For help and advice, the editors wish to thank Jocelyn Fujii, Dana Naone Hall, Adrian Kamaliʻi, Edward and Pualani Kanahele, Puanani Kanemura Van Dorpe, Charles Kauluwehi Maxwell Sr., Davianna Pōmaikaʻi McGregor, Māhealani Perez-Wendt, Franco Salmoiraghi, and Homer Steedly, Jr.

The editors give special thanks to producer and director Meleanna Aluli Meyer for permission to use portions of the script from *Hoʻokuʻikahi: To Unify As One,* a film written by her and John Keolamakaʻāinana Lake, available on DVD from Native Books / Nā Mea Hawaiʻi (www.nativebooks hawaii.com/).

Hōnaunau, Hawai'i
Photograph by
Franco Salmoiraghi, 1991

The Ice Is Melting in the North _____

The following statement reflects the position of the Traditional Circle of Indian Elders and Youth and was delivered by Oren Lyons, Faithkeeper, Turtle Clan, Onondaga Nation, to the Millennium World Peace Summit of Religious and Spiritual Leaders, held at the United Nations, New York, in August 2000. It is reprinted here with his permission.

Leaders of the World,

Neyaweha-scano (thank you for being well). Today I bring you greetings from the Indigenous Peoples of North, Central, and South America. Indeed, I bring you greetings from the Indigenous Peoples of the world.

We are the keepers of the traditions, ceremonies, histories, and future of our nations. We are the ones who escaped from your proselytizing. We survived with the wisdom of the Old Ones.

And we are pleased to add our voices to yours in this great effort for common sense and peace among nations.

Leaders of the World,

I bring you a most urgent message that was brought to our twenty-third annual gathering of the Traditional Circle of Elders and Youth. This message was brought by a runner from the north, from Greenland, and he said:

The ice is melting in the north!

He informed us that some fifteen years ago they noticed trickles of water coming down the sheer face of Glacier Mountain. That trickle has grown to a roaring river of ice water pouring out of this mountain into the Atlantic Ocean.

He informed us that Glacier Mountain has lost four thousand feet of ice in these past few years. And the melt continues to accelerate.

This is an alarming message that requires your absolute attention.

Leaders of the World,

We are a collective voice of Indigenous Peoples. We have joined this great mission for peace. We add our presence in support of this great effort for reconciliation between peoples and nations.

We agree that there must be parity and equity between rich and poor nations, between white people and people of color, and rich people and poor people, with special attention to women, children, and indigenous peoples.

We, in our collective voices, add to this: that there must be a reconciliation between peoples and the natural world, between nation states and the forests that sustain us, between corporations and the resources they mine, the fish that they catch, and the water that they use.

Leaders of the World,

Indigenous nations and peoples believe in the spiritual powers of the universe. We believe in the ultimate power and authority of a limitless energy beyond our comprehension. We believe in the order of the universe. We believe in the laws of creation and that all life is bound by these same natural laws.

We call this essence the spirit of life. This is what gives the world the energy to create and procreate, and what becomes the ponderous and powerful law of regeneration—the law of the seed.

We, in our collective voices, speak to this to remind you that spirit and spiritual laws transcend generations. We know, because this has sustained us.

Religion and spirituality are vital to survival and moral law. It is a faith that has sustained our human spirit through our darkest hours. It has sustained our human spirit in times of crisis during the times we suffered through the grinding measures of inexorable persecutions that have spanned generations and continue today. Yet here we are, today, adding our voices to this plea for sanity in leadership and responsibility to the future generations whose faces are looking up from the Earth, each awaiting their time of life here.

Leaders of the World,

We believe that reconciliation should begin here because peace is an inclusive term, and peace and reconciliation are the purpose of this summit.

Peace is dynamic and requires great effort of spirit and mind to attain unity. Leaders of peace must step forward and take responsibility for a paradigm change in the direction of current lifestyles and materialistic societies. The human species has become the most voracious and abusive consumer of Earth's resources. We have tipped the balance of life against our children, and we imperil our future as a species.

Leaders of the World,

Despite all of our declarations and all of our proclamations, no matter how profound they may be:

The ice is melting in the north.

We see the acceleration of the winds.

We see the fires that are raging in North America.

And we see that the sun's rays that provide us with light, energy, and the very essence of life now are causing cancer in people, blinding animals, and killing the plankton and krill of the sea.

This is only the beginning, and already we are helpless. We will now see the real spiritual powers that govern the Earth.

Leaders of the World,

There can be no peace as long as we wage war upon Our Mother, The Earth. Responsible and courageous actions must be taken to realign ourselves with the great laws of nature. We must meet this crisis now, while we still have time. We offer these words as common peoples in support of peace, equity, justice, and reconciliation.

As we speak, the ice continues to melt in the north.

Dahnato (now I am finished). *Neyawenha* (thank you).

The Leadership Imperative:
An Interview with Oren Lyons

Oren Lyons, seventy-six, is a wisdom carrier, one of the bearers of a variety of human tradition that can't easily be reduced to a couple of sentences. One reason he—and the tradition for which he is a spokesperson—isn't more widely known is that he doesn't actively seek forums from which to speak. If someone asks him, however, about the principles behind the particular Native American tradition of which he has, since 1967, been an appointed caretaker, he is glad to respond. He chooses his words carefully, and these days, there is occasionally a hint of indignation in his voice, as if time were short and people generally willful in their distraction.

In an era of self-promotion, Oren Lyons represents the antithesis of celebrity. When he converses about serious issues, no insistent ego comes to the fore, no desire to be seen as an important or wise person. His voice is but one in a long series, as he sees it, and the wisdom belongs not to him but to the tradition for which he speaks. His approach to problems is unusual in modern social commentary because his observations are not compelled by any overriding sense of the importance of the human present. In place of a philosophy of progress, he emphasizes fidelity to a set of spiritual and natural laws that have guided successful human social organization throughout history.

The appeal of his particular ethics in the search for solutions to contemporary environmental and social problems can become readily apparent. It is, however, not a wisdom anchored in beliefs about human perfection. It's grounded in the recognition and acceptance of human responsibility where all forms of life are concerned.

Oren is a Faithkeeper of the Turtle Clan among the Onondaga people of western New York. He sits on the Council of Chiefs of the Haudenosaunee, or the Six Nations as they are sometimes known. (In addition to the Onondaga, these would be the Seneca, Cayuga, Oneida, Mohawk, and Tuscarora.) The people of this "Iroquois Confederacy" share a philosophy of life given to them a thousand years ago by a spiritual being they call the Peace Maker. (He was named so partly because his instructions and warnings ended a period of warfare among these tribes, but his teachings about peace are understood to refer principally to a state of mind necessary for good living and good governance.)

When the Peace Maker came to the Haudenosaunee, he instructed them in a system of self-governing that was democratic in nature. (Benjamin Franklin and others, in fact, borrowed freely from this part of Haudenosaunee oral tradition and practice in formulating the principles of government upon which the United States was founded.) He emphasized the importance of diversity in human society to ensure sustainability and rejuvenation. And he urged a general tradition of thanksgiving.

The Peace Maker is sometimes called simply "the Messenger," someone sent by the Creator. The clan mothers among the Haudenosaunee, along with sitting chiefs such as Oren, are regarded as "runners," people responsible for keeping the precepts handed to them by the Peace Maker regenerating through time. As a council chief, Oren is said to be "sitting for the welfare of the people" and to be engaged in sustaining "the power of the good mind" in discussions with others on the council, all of whom are exchanging thoughts about the everyday application of the wisdom given them by the Peace Maker.

Oren has spoken often, recently, about a lack of will among international leaders, a failure to challenge the economic forces tearing apart human communities the world over, and the Earth itself. His response to the question of what society should do to protect life, however, is rarely prescriptive. Frequently what he says is, "It's up to each generation. There are no guarantees."

The Peace Maker's advice included an important warning for the chiefs and clan mothers. Some of his instruction, he said, would apply to life-threatening situations that would develop before the Haudenosaunee were able to fully grasp their malevolent nature. While the insights needed to manage such trouble would emerge among council members, the people might initially adamantly reject the council's advice. As decision makers, he said, the chiefs and clan mothers would have to be prepared to absorb this abuse. Oren recounts these words of the Messenger: "You must be tolerant [of harsh critics] and must not respond in kind, but must understand [their fear], and be prepared to absorb all of that, because it is not all going to be coming from your enemies. It is going to be coming from your friends and families. This you can expect."

In public, Oren Lyons carries himself with the unaffected manner of elders in many of the world's indigenous traditions—unpretentious, understated. His physical presence in a room, however, radiates authority. In conversations, you quickly sense that he takes life more seriously than most. He is an articulate and forceful speaker when it comes to discussing the worldwide movement toward civil society, a movement that would marginalize the sort of governance and commerce that today threaten life everywhere.

Oren Lyons, long a professor of American studies at the State University of New York at Buffalo, is the publisher of *Daybreak,* a national Native American magazine. Before being appointed to the Onondaga Council by the clan mothers in 1967, he was successfully pursuing a career in commercial art in New York City. An All-American lacrosse goalie while a student at Syracuse University, he was later elected to the National Lacrosse Hall of Fame in both Canada and the United States, and named honorary chairman of the Iroquois Nationals lacrosse team. He is the recipient of many national and international awards, and for more than three decades has been a defining presence in international indigenous rights and sovereignty issues.

Barry Lopez   Why is sovereignty such a crucial issue for Native American people today?

Oren Lyons   Well, sovereignty is probably one of the most hackneyed words that is used in conjunction with Indians. What is it, and why is it so important? It's a definition of political abilities and it's a definition of borders and boundaries. It encapsulates the idea of nationhood. It refers to authority and power—ultimate and final authority.

It's such a discussion among native peoples in North America, I would say, because of our abilities at the time of "discovery"—and I use that term under protest, as if to say that before the advent of the white man in North America, nothing existed. Where does that idea come from? Well, it comes from the ultimate authority of the pope at the time. I'm talking 1492. The Roman Catholic Church was the world power. Now it's my understanding that in the Bible, both the Old Testament and the New Testament, there is no mention of the Western Hemisphere whatsoever—not the least hint. How could they miss a whole hemisphere?

So here we were in our own hemisphere, developing our own ideas, our own thoughts, and our own worldview. There were great civilizations here at the time. In 1492, Haudenosaunee—which is better known as the Iroquois by the French, and Six Nations by the English—already had several hundred years of democracy, organized democracy. We had a constitution here based on peace, based on equity and justice, based on unity and health. This was ongoing.

As far as I know, all the other Indian nations functioned more or less the same way. Their leadership was chosen by the people. Leaders were fundamentally servants to the people. And in our confederation, there was no place for an army. We didn't have a concept of a standing army, and we had no police. Nor was there a concept of jails, but there were of course fine perceptions of right and wrong, and rules and law. I would say that in most Indian nations, because they had inhabited one place for so long and were a people for so long, the rules and laws were embedded in the genes of the people more or less, in the minds of the people certainly, but not written. Plenty of law, almost on everything, but unspoken. Unspoken unless transgressed. There was always reaction to transgression.

Across the water, in Europe, our brother was engulfed in great crusades. If you look at their histories and what is in their museums, no matter where you are—whether it's Germany or France or England or Holland or whatever nation—in their great halls you'll see paintings of battles. Always. That must have been a terrible way of life. Now I speak of Europe because they are the ones that came here. And when they came here, the pope said, If there are no Christians on these lands, then we'll declare the lands *terra nullius*—empty lands—regardless of peoples there. And the question arose almost immediately, Were the aboriginal people indeed people? That was the big discussion. Why? Well, you can say a lot of things, but the issue is land—always has been and always will be.

The ideas of land tenure and ownership were brought here. We didn't think that you could buy and sell land. In fact, the ideas of buying and selling were concepts we didn't have. We laughed when they told us they wanted to buy land. And we said, Well, how can you buy land? You might just as well buy air, or buy water. But we don't laugh anymore, because that is precisely what has happened. Today, when you fly across this country and you look down and you see all those squares and circles, that's land bought and sold. Boundaries made. They did it. The whole country.

We didn't accept that, but nevertheless it was imposed. They said, Let's make us a law here; we'll call it the law of discovery. The first Christian nation that discovers this land will be able to secure it, and the other Christian nations will respect that. What does that do to the original people, whose land of course they are talking about? We just weren't included. They established a process that eliminated the aboriginal people from title to their own land. They set the rules at the time and we were not subjects, we were objects, and we have been up to this point. That's why indigenous people are not included in the Declaration of Human Rights of the United Nations. We are still objects in common law.

In today's courts, in New York and Massachusetts and Pennsylvania, they talk about the pre-emption rights of the law of discovery. Today. Land claims are being denied on the basis of the law of discovery. It has not gone away whatsoever. You really have to get the case law and look at it, because they not only say that we don't have land tenure, they say that we have only the right of occupancy.

And they don't have to pay us anything, because we're part of the flora and fauna of North America.

No wonder Indians wonder about what sovereignty is.

BL   Native elders are often credited with being informed about the environment, or knowledgeable about spiritual issues, but rarely credited with expertise when it comes to governance. Why aren't native elders sought out for their wisdom about a good way to govern, a good way to serve people?

OL   Well, to put it simply, our worldview, our perspective, and our process of governance are contrary to private property. Private property is a concept that flies in the face of our understanding of life, and we would say of the reality of life. Private property is a conception, a human conception, which amounts to personal greed.

And then there's the spiritual side that you mention. You can't see the spiritual side…well, you get glimpses of it. Any hunter will tell you, you see it in the eyes of the deer, that bright spark, that life, that light in his eyes, and when you make your kill, it's gone. Where did it go? It's the same light that's in the eyes of children, or in the eyes of old men, old women. There's a life in there, there's a spirit in there, and when you die, when your body gives up the ghost, as Christians say, spirit leaves. We believe that.

We believe that everything we see is made by a Creator. Indeed that's what we call the ultimate power. Shongwaiyadisaih. The maker of all life. The giver of life. All powerful. We see the Creation—everything—as what the giver of life has produced here. And if we believe that, which we do, then we must respect it. It's a spiritual Creation, and it demands that kind of respect. So when I see people, they are manifestations of the Creator's work, and I must respect them. It doesn't matter what color they are—anything alive.

A thousand years ago, when the Peace Maker brought to us the Great Law of Peace, Gayanahshagowa, he set as our symbol for the confederation of Haudenosaunee a great tree, and he said, "This is going to be the symbol of your work and your law: a great white pine, four white roots of truth that reach in the four directions of the world. And those people who have no place to go will follow the root to its source and come under the protection of the Great Law of Peace and the great long leaves of the great tree." And then he admonished the leaders and the people, and he said, "Never challenge the spiritual law. Never challenge it because you cannot prevail." That's a direct instruction to leadership.

BL   It seems to me that the federal government in the United States is reluctant to invite Indian people to the table because, as you've just said, you can't have effective leadership without spiritual law, and you can't talk about good governance without environmental awareness. Yet we need—all of us need—the counsel of minds that successfully addressed questions of social justice long before Western culture, arguably, complicated them with the notion of industrial progress.

OL   After the Peace Maker gathered five warring nations—the Mohawks, the Oneidas, the Cayugas, the Senecas, and the Onondagas—and after great efforts and great cohesive work, the power of the unity of the good minds brought together this confederacy based on peace. And after he had taken the leaders and sat them under this great tree on the shoreline of Onondaga Lake and instructed them on the process of governance, on the principles of governance, on the importance of identity and the importance of rule and law, he said, "Now that we've planted this great tree, in your hands now I place all life. Protection of all life is in your hands now," and when he said all life, he meant literally, all life.

And it's an instruction that we carry today. We feel responsible for animals, we feel responsible for trees, and responsible for fish, responsible for water. We feel responsible for land and all of the insects and everything that's there. And when he spoke of the four white roots reaching in the four directions, I think he was talking to all people. Not just Haudenosaunee. This is an instruction for all people.

But after all of that, a woman said to him, "Well then," she said, "how long will this last?" And he answered, "That's up to you." So it's completely up to us if we want this Creation to continue, and if we want to be involved in it, a part of this whole recycling, this whole regeneration of life, and we want to be celebrating it, and we want to be enjoying it, and we want to be preserving it, carrying it on, protecting it for future generations.

In one of his many instructions he said, "Counselors, leaders," he said, "now that we have raised you here, now that you are who you are," he said, "when you counsel for the welfare of the people, then think not of yourself, nor of your family, nor even your generation." He said, "Make your decisions on behalf of the seventh generation coming. You who see far into the future, that is your responsibility: to look out for those generations that are helpless, that are completely at our mercy. We must protect them." And that's great counsel in today's times, if we want the seventh generation to be here, and to have what we have.

BL   What do you think is the great impediment to the implementation of that wisdom?

OL   Human ego is probably the biggest impediment—the amazing ability of any human to perceive themselves as almighty powerful, no matter what. That is a big problem. We were instructed long before the Peace Maker to be respectful, to have ceremonies, to carry out thanksgivings for everything. We have an enormous amount of ceremony and thanksgiving still going on in North America. Indian nations across the country are still carrying on those ceremonies in their languages and through their dances. We're trying.

And we're told, as long as there is one to speak and one to listen, one to sing and one to dance, the fight is on. So that is hope. To not give up. To try, and to use reason. Peace Maker said, "I'm going to throw your weapons of war into this hole." He uprooted that great tree and instructed all the men to bring their weapons of war and to cast them into this hole. That was the first disarmament. And he said, "I'm not going to leave you unprotected and helpless." And he gave us the great tobacco plant. And he said, "This will be your medium to speak to me when you need to." And he gave us a very special plant, which we still use, still speak to him with.

We believe. And I think as long as we're doing that, there is a chance.

BL   When you meet with people—Desmond Tutu for example, Gorbachev, other people who've sought your counsel and the wisdom of the Six Nations—do you sense a possibility that these cultures that are driven by issues of private property, social control, and capitalism can be guided by your example of how to conduct a civilization without warfare?

OL   Indian people have as much dissension among themselves as anybody. I think that our understanding is simply that dissension begins with each individual. You don't need two people to have that tension; you have it within yourself. As a human being, you have a spiritual center, and if you go too far to the right or too far to the left, you're out of balance. And that occurs every day.

In the creation story that we have, we talk about the twin brothers, one good, one evil, and we talk about the battles that they went through, enveloping the Earth itself. It's a story to the people, to explain that within each of us we have these tensions, and that on any given day any one of us can be the world's worst enemy.

And that's why you have councils, and that's why you have rule, and that's why you have community and law, because that is part of humanity. And there is no ultimate authority. But of course over time, people have found standards of moral right, and I think that's where the real law lies. It lies in morality. A balance.

The only thing that you can do is have custom in usage, and a good example. That's why grandpas and grandmas are so important. They are the transition people. They move the children into the next generation. Peace Maker said, "Make your decisions on behalf of seven generations." He's telling you to look ahead, to not think about yourself. If you can stop thinking about yourself and begin thinking about responsibility, everything is going to get better. Immediately everything will change. But that is not the makeup of the human mind. There's always the evil twin. And there's always the good twin. It's a daily battle.

BL   My own problem at the moment is a frustration that my fate, the fate of the people I love, and the fate of my family are in the hands of men who see no reason to listen to counsel from outside the circumscribed world of their own knowledge. I live in a country in which people take pride in never having had any kind of experience with other cultures, who believe that they have perfected the ways of life to such a degree that forcing them down the throats of other people is an act of benevolence. They don't want people who speak for the integration of spiritual and material life to be at the discussion table because these people are disruptive when it comes to issues of consumerism, economic expansion, and international cooperation. To me, this is fundamentally not only unjust, but stupid.

OL   I see it that way too. We're being placed in an untenable position by greed and force and authority. If I was sitting on the moon looking back on North America, on the democracy that was here when Haudenosaunee was meeting and the Peace Maker was bringing these ideas to us, I would have seen this light, this bright light. I'd see it grow. And then in 1776, when the Continental Congress came as close to Indian nations as they ever would in their style of thinking, that light was growing again. The idea of democracy and the idea of peace were there.

But it began to dim almost immediately, as the government began to take away peoples' rights in the Constitution of the United States. The Constitution institutionalized the idea that only men with money or property could vote. They said it was OK to have a slave or two or three or ten or twenty. The light began to dim. Haudenosaunee chiefs shook their heads and they said, "You're courting trouble." And then it really got dim in 1863, and –4 and –5 and –7 and –8, when they had a great civil war in this country over the issues of power, authority, slavery. That was a very intense war. That was brother against brother.

And so it goes on, this idea of private property, this idea of accruement of wealth. And now we have corporate states, corporations that have the status of states—independent and sovereign, and fealty to no one, no moral law at all. President Bush has said, "Let the market dictate our direction." Now if that isn't about as stupid as you can get. What he said was to let the greed of the people dictate the direction of the Earth. If that's the basis of a country, then it's really lost what you would call a primary direction for survival.

This is really the danger today: this empty, senseless lack of leadership. But it doesn't mean that responsibility isn't in the hands of the people. To come down to the nut of the whole thing, it's the people's responsibility to do something about it. Leadership was never meant to take care of anybody. Leadership was meant to guide people; they take care of themselves. People should be storming the offices of all these pharmaceutical companies that are stealing money from them. They should be dragging these leaders, these CEOs out into the streets, and they should be challenging them. They're not doing that. They're just worried about how they're going to pay more.

It's the abdication of responsibility by the people. What was it that they said? By the people and for the people? That was the Peace Maker's instruction: *Of, by, and for the people.* You choose your own leaders. You put 'em up, and you take 'em down. But you, the people, are responsible. You're responsible for your life; you're responsible for everything.

People haven't been here all that long as a species on the Earth. We haven't been here all that long, and our tenure is in question right now. The question arises, Do we have the wisdom, do we have the discipline, do we have the moral rule, the moral law, are we mature enough to care for what is our responsibility? That question can only be answered by the people.

JULIA MARTIN

Wonderwerk _____

At the base of a hill near Kuruman in South Africa, in a place of grasses is the dark mouth of a cave. The cave is wide and very deep, extending far into the body of the hill. Until the first property owner built a farmhouse on this land, people had been living in the cave since the beginning. The roof is black from their fires, and the floor holds traces of their habitation.

The cave is fenced now and excavated. The fire is out, and the people who come to it are visitors. Yet the swallows return to their nests each spring, and climbing the hill you can see fine, tough plants still growing, and beyond, the blue rim of the world.

Like many other farms whose names evoke the joy of a longed-for home-coming—names like Weltevrede or Welverdient—the property was called Wonderwerk, a miracle. The first white owner, N. J. Bosman, lived with his family in the cave from 1900 to 1907 while their farmhouse was being built. After that, they used it for a stock shelter and a wagon house, and for several years in the 1940s, they mined a layer of prehistoric deposits and sold this as bat guano, used as fertilizer.

The first archaeological excavations of Wonderwerk Cave began when someone noticed bones and stone artefacts in the so-called guano. From the late 1970s onwards, the archaeologist Peter Beaumont and others worked at the site. I understand that their findings, as yet largely unpublished, will change some aspects of the way that the Stone Age is understood.

Passing through a gated entrance, Michael parks the car near a cluster of small face-brick buildings. Across the mouth of the cave is a big steel railing. I had not expected these: keys and a gate. But there has been vandalism, including graffiti, and the barrier is probably necessary. I interrupt the meeting in the little information centre a few metres away to ask for the key. Peter comes out and offers to escort us.

"I really don't mean to take you out of your meeting."

"Oh, there are various reasons why one might want to be out of a meeting," he says. "I can have a smoke for one thing."

"Well, we're really lucky to have a world authority as our tour guide."

"I don't know about that."

The cave is huge. It stretches 139 metres into the hillside, Peter says, and is about 17 metres wide, big enough to keep a fire. Inside the entrance, a single giant stalagmite stands like a guardian of the threshold. There are paintings, what is left of them, on the wall near the mouth of the cave. Painted buck, finger marks, wriggled lines, and stripes seethe ochre and white on the surface of the rock: traces painted over other traces, layer on layer, touch of hands on stone, successive generations.

Peter switches on the halogen lights, and the darkness beyond is illumined. The excavation of the site reaches as far back as we can see. Deep trenches lie on either side of the narrow walkway that leads into the hill, and the entire floor of the cave has been dug up and marked with string. This net stretches like a perspective drawing converging to a vanishing point in the distant dark, each square labelled with a small piece of paper. Looking back into the cave, we see that the space is hatched across with lit-up string squares that mark the darker regions of excavated earth, their bright labels gleaming in the light.

I give each of the twins a small box of juice. The layer of dust on the ground near the entrance of the cave is thick, and the twins want to pound about, to stir it up. Peter looks concerned.

"Don't do that," I say.

Peter tells us that Wonderwerk Cave is the only place in the world known to have been inhabited, whenever possible, from about 1.2 million years ago until the early twentieth century, when the last people to live there were the Bosman family. The information is so extraordinary that it is difficult to absorb. This cave is home.

Then he starts to show us Excavation 1, a great squared-off hole on the left side of the walkway, fenced with a steel railing. "As you go back into the cave, it averages day and night temperatures. It would have been warmer inside during an Ice Age…"

As the informal discourse takes shape, Sophie and Sky, having now finished their juice, disappear along the walkway between the trenches and run away into the gloom. Peter is talking enthusiastically, but I am beginning to feel panicky. Five years old, the twins have run far away into the dark, and I can no longer see them.

"I must just see what the children are doing," I say, then leave the conversation.

Back, far back in the dark cave, treading along the narrow path between excavated trenches and the deep pits left by the guano diggers, walking into the cavernous body of the hill, back, back into the fire-blackened cave, far into the prehistoric dark, I see my children. Colored with modern dyes, red corduroy and blue gleam in the darkness.

"Mommy, come! Hold hands, tight!"

The children are standing at the end of the walkway, gazing down into the pit. We look about the cave together, imagining aeons of mothers holding babies in their arms, little ones learning to walk, children playing hide and seek, mothers giving birth, people sleeping, singing, playing, making tools, making music, over and over again. And always there is the fire, and the fire-blackened walls.

Together we walk back to where the men are talking. Two small, warm hands rest in mine, two small, bright bodies, skipping.

"Look," Peter says, taking up the thread when we return, "you see that layer of ash down there. It's the fire ash: one million plus years old. We found thousands of burnt bone fragments with it."

This is the ash from their fires. This is the ash from their fires a million years ago. This is the evanescent ash from their fires. We are looking at the ash from their fires, pale ash buried deep. Light flame of life burned hot, here at the hearth where food was cooked and people sang and the fire burnt bones and flesh. Stories of bodies took shape and were consumed in the burning of this flame. And this is the ash from their fires.

While other beings may make tools and create sociable forms, only we have learned to burn. And this is the ash from the fire that makes us human. This is the beginning of burning: wood, coal, fossil fuels, combustion. And this is the hearth, the deep, long, buried continuity of our kind, pale ash in the ground, fire ash soft as a pigeon's back, light ash from their fires, this hearth.

"We know that they made grass bedding," Peter continues. "There's a bedding layer at 400,000 BP, silica traces from the grass. When you look at the hand axes under a microscope, you can see that some of them were used to cut grass."

He turns to me then, his face lit with delight. "Can you believe that at 200,000 years we found actual grass, quite preserved, like ordinary grass? The cave is extremely dry, so there's incredible preservation."

The people used stone tools to make grass beds, and here is the womb of the years that holds the layers of transient grass. Archaeologists like Peter, who dig in the deep loam of habitation, unearth the actual grass layers where people slept, grasses cut with worked stone tools, light grasses growing on the hill. There was love in this place, and sleeping bodies, human people curled together within the sanctuary of the cave. Each stalk recalls the imprint of their sleep and the warm crush of their desire, fragrant bodies brief as grasses on the hill.

"It's like a pyramid—it preserves things," Peter says. "We found that porcupines were living here 10,000 years ago, at the end of the last Ice Age. When you crush the droppings, they still smell of porcupine—10,000 years later.

"There was also a horn core from a sort of blesbok and bones of *Hipparion,* the three-toed horse from the Middle Pleistocene. It's really dry in here. Really dusty too. No matter what mask you're wearing, everyone's coughing up black dust after half an hour of excavation."

For Peter the vertical cross-section of excavated earth is layered as years: stratigraphy read as a map of time. In this cave, he says, a centimetre equals one thousand years.

He says, "I brought some gardeners here from the museum one day, wanted them to see where I spent all my time. I showed them the excavation, the layers, and I said to them that in those layers a human lifespan takes up about one millimetre. One man said, 'You mean my life's only that much?' And I said yes, that's what it is."

"How did the dust get here?" I ask. "I read somewhere about aeolian sands. What a beautiful name—it reminds me of Coleridge."

"Yes, the wind-borne sands, blown in from the Kalahari. But here it seems to be something different. It's quite sheltered inside."

"Maybe they walked it into the cave," Michael says. "I remember as a child living at Clifton. If we hadn't got all the beach sand off our feet when we came into the house, the floor would soon have been covered with the stuff. It was a basic rule: get the sand off your feet before you come inside."

"I think you could be right," Peter says, "about walking it into the cave."

"What do you think it was like for the people who lived here?" Michael wonders. "You've spent nights and days at the site in different temperatures. What do you think?"

"It was tough," he answers simply. "There were no Post Toasties."

"But, of course, they knew about the land and the plants in ways that we don't," Michael continues. "We would never know how to keep ourselves alive here, but hunting and gathering people would. I remember reading that during dry years in the Kalahari, when the farmers and cattle people went hungry, it was the !Kung San who helped them gather food."

"Yes, you're right," Peter says. "You know, the first time I went up to Border Cave, we were taken there by a young woman from the area. She was really thin, legs like sticks, and carrying a baby. I thought she'd never make it. Well, halfway up, there we all were, really tired and sweating, and she was fine—not a trace of sweat on her face. And I mean, we were fit!"

I ask about the squares of string marking out the excavation.

"It's the grid. When I began excavation here, instead of using the usual metre measures, I kept to the yard square grid system set up by B. D. Malan in 1943. I wanted our findings to be strictly comparable."

The grid. It is called the grid. Of course. Dug up by teams of archaeologists and labourers, in less than sixty years the unimaginably ancient cave became a space marked out in squares. Through this fieldwork—dividing, measuring, sieving, taking notes—the buried accumulations of human and nonhuman culture were turned into a collection of things in boxes, objects of study and forgetting on shelves and tables in museums.

As William Blake says in the story of Urizen, the Eternals formed a line and a plummet to divide the Abyss beneath…and called it Science. Perhaps Blake was not concerned with archaeology; yet his story is one of gates and grids—a locked steel gate and grids of labelled string. From the threshold of modernity, it is a story about the construction of systems and the making of knowledge, about discovery, conquest, and control, about enlightenment science and early industrialism and the organised religion of the orthodox Church. It is a story about the last brief dust of history, a story of pain and loss and the fruitless quest for some immutable truth.

Now if no more virgin territories are left, then digging deep into the dust may yet yield precious objects of information or knowledge. For a million years and more, people were here, and their fires gave some light and warmth in the unfathomable dark. And now, in the very brief now of the last thin layer of dust, the ancient cave is penetrated and hollowed out, its stones and bones and stories sieved and documented, irrecoverably.

And yet, and yet, Peter's voice is full of wonder. "Do you know we found ochre way down? And there were quartz crystals at levels dated to before 200,000 years and chalcedony at older than 350,000. They were pretty things—beautiful, non-functional, you see. People collected them from somewhere else and brought them here."

"Maybe from that farm where we were today," I say.

"Maybe."

Like us, they loved crystals. Like us, they bent towards the earth, collecting precious things. Like us, they looked for treasure to carry home.

"What goes beyond the excavation at the back?" I ask. "Is it the end of the cave?"

"No, there's a final tunnel. It's blocked by a rock fall, but you can crawl in and peep. There are thousands of artefacts around the entrance—Middle Stone Age. Beyond that, we don't know. There's a dolomitic cavern, a huge chamber continuing into the koppie."

"You must really want to get in there and have a look."

"Yes, of course. But there are difficulties with permits."

In all his excavations at the site, Peter has not found significant human remains. But this is the final tunnel, the dolomitic cavern, the last of the place to be discovered. Perhaps this is where they are, at the end of the cave, the undiscovered.

"Come, Mommy, come!" The children are pulling at my shirt. "We want to see the farmer's pants."

We leave the cave and walk to the little face-brick information centre a few metres away. Peter's meeting is over, and people are having tea in the midst of a collection of crystals in glass cases, lithic artefacts, and some archaeological and botanical information about the area. People joke about installing him as the local tour guide.

Near the entrance to the tiny museum, the gigantic pair of trousers worn by Peter Eduard Bosman is on display. A sign says that he was 1.98 meters tall and weighed about 200 kilograms. His hundred-year-old pants are made of good-quality tweed. I wonder whether he wore these pants during the seven years that he and his wife, Magdalena, and many of their children lived in the cave. When the family moved into the farmhouse, some of the fourteen children stayed in the cave, and it is recorded that the last child born in the cave after maybe a million years of occupation was Bosman's granddaughter, Cornelia or Girlie, in February 1914.

"Enjoy the rest of your trip to the Northern Cape," says Colin, the museum director, as we say goodbye.

"We really are enjoying it, thank you."

"It's the undiscovered province," he says, smiling.

We are spending the night in the small face-brick chalet that has been built beyond the ablution block not far from the mouth of the cave. Neels Lehule, a slender, soft-spoken man who lives at the site and tends to visitors, gives us the key.

"Would you like to see the cave again?" he asks.

"Later, please. We want to get things sorted out in the chalet first and feed the children, and then perhaps a walk."

Leaving Michael to make food for the children, I go for a small walk on my own. Full of loss and longing, I need the immediate exertion of climbing the hill above the cave, strata of dolomite and growing things. Climbing the hill that people have always climbed, I reach a place at which to sit and look.

My notes identify grasses, bushes, and healing plants. There is *Themeda triandra,* rooigras, for bedding and feeding animals; *Pellaea calomelanos,* a fern used for boils, for pimples inside mouth and nose, for asthma, for head and chest colds; *Rhus burchellii,* taaibos, the tough leaves chewed for chest colds, the berries edible; *Grewia flava,* the brandy bush, its red berries used for alcoholic drink; *Cyondon dactylon,* kweekgras, for healing sores and swelling; *Eragrostis lehmanniana,* knietjiesgras, for colic, diarrhoea, and typhoid fever. These plants grow here. These plants grow here still. These families of grasses, berries, leaves. Still here.

While the bones of the ancestors have not been discovered, excavation of the cave has shown that Stone Age people cut the grass to make their beds and burnt the trees as firewood. The old hill rests in quietness, the hill flows slowly in the flow of stone, ripple of rock, ripple of the small fern growing at the edge where a little water has collected in a crack. Breathing in and breathing out: this is the one breath passing from mother to child and on. In the hill, our bones decay to earth and grow again into trees and radiating grasses, into the small limbs of striped mice and the bright voice of a little bird who is watching me and singing to tell the others. My words are gone into the calling of this voice. The afternoon is warm. The clouds are white. Each leaf grows according to its pattern. This body sweats and breathes.

Then Michael calls my name from near the chalet, and he and the children climb the hill to join me, Sophie with a grubby Maltese poodle she is encouraging to follow her. Together we climb to the top and see the undulating flow of other hills, their tawny backs like the flanks of a great body at rest. Sitting and resting, we sit where others have sat before, each fold of land and rock known and named, each place remembered, and the wide sky reaching out and beyond to touch the slender blue edge of the world.

Michael explores, finds a few stone tools. Sky taps a rock with another stone while his sister plays with pebbles and cradles the Maltese poodle. Then the children come to my lap, drink some water, and have a biscuit. I tell them about the animals who lived here before guns and wire fences, and about the people, their fires and beds and pretty stones, and how their stories are forgotten and their bones are gone into the body of the hill. The world is quiet. Sky's tangled hair is blond as wild grass in the afternoon sun. Sophie's small, hard shoulder leans into my heart, her warm hand resting in mine. Flesh and bone.

Returning, we follow the path down towards the cave, taking turns to carry the dog, which now refuses to walk.

Once we are back at the buildings, Neels knocks at the door.

"You want to see the cave?" he says. "Kom."

I want to see the dark. I ask if he can switch off the lights.

Walking back, back into the darkness, we find the cave huge and silent, but not as dark as I would have imagined. Even at the furthest end of the tunnel, the late afternoon light still penetrates, and each small label on the string grid gleams clearly. Neels points out a small mud structure on the roof near the entrance of the cave. He smiles.

"Swaeltjies, swallows," he says. "They are gone now, but they come back every year. They like this place to have their babies."

"Lift us up! Lift us up!" the children shout. "We want to see."

"Oh! Look at their house," Sophie says. "Look at the tunnel. I wish I could see the little babies."

If it had been summer or even early autumn, we could have seen them. Wave a hand above a swallow's nest, and immediately the small bright-yellow beaks are up and open, shrilling for food while the parent birds fly about, anxiously watching. But now it is early winter, and the swallows are gone. Each year they leave and they return. Each year brings new babies and the long flying across continents and seasons. Dia!kwain said that the swallows are rain's things. He said our mothers tell us we must not harm them, for they come with the rain and the makers of rain.

To me they are small things whose comings and goings trace different routes from those of human traffic. They are tenacious things, communities of little ones that endure when other beings have disappeared, like the striped mice in the veld eating grass seeds and living in holes, or mouse bones in owl droppings, which archaeologists use to chart temperature change and to date human occupation—little bones chewed and swallowed and dropped into the body of a cave. Here on the hill, some of the small ones have remained. Mice and swallows live here still. Owls too, still here. How many years.

A man approaches us from somewhere beyond the ablution block where he has set up camp for the night. His eyes are blue and his brown face lined. He wears a knitted cap on his head.

"Good evening," he says graciously. "My name is Anthony, Anthony Simpson."

We smile and introduce ourselves.

"I've come here to play a bushman instrument," he explains, "my version. It's something I've adapted from the sort of thing they used to play. I'm going to be at the cave this evening to summon up the spirits. Around dusk, you know, when it's starting to get dark. I'd like to invite your family to come and listen."

While he is speaking to me, the children have begun to get irritable and are trying to hit one another. I thank him and quickly lead the children towards the chalet.

Later, with the first stars brightening and a big, almost full moon rising among clouds in the dusky evening, we meet at the mouth of the cave to listen.

"I've come to summon the spirits," he says again simply. "It's like a bushman instrument, but I've added my own variations."

The instrument is something he has constructed from a big tin and a piano string tightened with a guitar key. Sitting with us now at the mouth of the cave, Anthony begins to play. He plucks one string. One note, one sound, and all the harmonics. Big moon rising, first stars opening, and a thin string is plucked again and again. Sitting together, this one sound. Grasses, thorn trees, mice, dassies, a single string plucked. Sitting on the ground at the threshold of Wonderwerk Cave, we hear this sound. Ash, dust, grass, stones, fingers, sound. In the changing light of dusk, one sound and all the harmonics.

I remember William Burchell's story of the man who played the *gorah* for him in a rock shelter not far from here. Camped in the early nineteenth century at a location in the foreign wilds of Africa that later came to be known as Burchell's Shelter, he described the bushmen who lived there as the most destitute of beings, people of deplorable ignorance whose life was the same as that of wild beasts, their fellow inhabitants of the land. In the evening, after giving them food and tobacco, Burchell played on his flute as they all sat around the fire. And later one of the men brought his own instrument to play: the one-stringed *gorah*. Burchell recorded him in a sketch of a thin man seated on a flat piece of rock, elbows on knees, one forefinger in his ear and the other in his nostril, plucking the single string of a slender instrument, a light string stretched across a bow.

While Anthony plays now in the darkening night of moony clouds, a pale form appears, moving silently towards the cave from among the trees.

Neels, dressed in perfect white for the evening, has come to join us. Sitting together, we listen to the single string sounding, late-modern people assembled, the children cuddled against Michael and me, warm shawls drawn close against the cold.

The fire is out. Yet here where people sit at the mouth of the cave the repetition of this sound absorbs the rhythm of our hearts, fingers plucking the single string, one sound calling into the night.

Later, over a supper of couscous and vegetable stew in our chalet, Anthony talks about his childhood in Sea Point in the fifties and sixties. He is about Michael's age—probably went to some of the same parties—but whereas Michael grew up among writers and books, Anthony did not.

"I don't read, you see," he tells us. "I didn't go beyond standard seven. I was a rebel when I was younger, so I left school early. All I wanted then was to get out of school. But now I look back and think I must have missed out on some things, cultural things, because of not really reading. I'll have to do it in my next life."

To the sleepy children he says, "You're very lucky that your parents bring you around the country to places like this. I wish I'd had it. One day you'll be grateful to them. One day when you're older, you'll appreciate it."

We ask what he does for a living, and he explains that he makes instruments and plays them, travelling as much as he can. When at home in Zimbabwe, he lives more and more simply.

"Most of the time there's no petrol, so I use a bicycle when I'm there. My food is really basic: sadza and beans. I cook on a wood fire, no gas. In a way I'm living more and more like a Bushman. I don't mind. It's the way I like it."

He enjoys the food we have cooked, but eats less than we do. After the meal, he says goodnight. His smile is open and unencumbered.

In the evening when the children are asleep, Michael and I sit outside and watch the stars and the moon among the clouds, watch two human figures running in the dark and chasing each other among the moonlit bushes of Neels's house.

Again we try to call to mind some sense of the people who lived here before. This time we try visualising a long line of human beings walking, each person representing a generation, maybe twenty years each. The line of generations stretches from the past all the way to this hearth, home. And for a moment I see. Our flesh is made of theirs. Our bones are formed in their pattern. Our breath is their unbroken succession.

Later Michael says, "I felt them. I was lying on my back on the bed, and I felt the ancestors. I felt them walking through. They were treading on my heart."

I feel no spirits, but falling into sleep, I sense the ancient and persistent liveliness of the place. In my dreams the swallows come.

In the dream we are standing in the cave, the labels on the string grid shining in the gloom. Suddenly a dark shape flashes towards us, flies over our heads, out into the light. First one and then another and another and another. Neels, dressed in perfect white, smiles. *Swaeltjies.* Come, he says, I'll show you. Reaching up, he waves a hand in front of the nest, and two tiny, bright-yellow mouths gape at us, shrilling for food. Sophie and Sky say, Lift us up, lift us up, we want to see, as the small beaks open wide. And in the dream, the parent birds return, darting towards the nest and out again into the light, catching insects in the evening air beyond the cave, first stars brightening in the dusk. In the dream I know that soon the gathering swallows will leave for the long flying far away across the continent, flying across seas and generations, to return to the cave in the spring. In the dream, Neels smiles to the children. *Swaeltjies.* The baby birds are awake in the fire-blackened cave—frail, tenacious things, shrilling for food.

Next morning, cuddled in our bed, Sky says, "I wish our holiday never ended."

Almost incredibly, we have woken to the sound of rain, rain in early winter at Wonderwerk Cave.

"Look," he says, "it's a female rain."

We have explained to the children the differences between male and female rain. The kind now falling is the quiet rain for which the /Xam stories yearn, rain that touches on leaf and soil, the gentle rain soaking into the land, rain walking on rain's legs across the world. Recording the last stories of a group of desert people living temporarily in a Victorian house, the marbled notebooks of the Bleek and Lloyd Collection in Cape Town are full of rain and the longing for rain, stories of rain's things and rain-makers, of rain sorcerers, waters' people, and of rain's medicine people, who could call the rain by plucking a bow string and leading the rain animal across the land. Remembering, the stories tell of a string that is broken and describe the sadness of an irretrievable loss.

Now the face-brick chalet is filled with the breath of rain, beautiful scent of rain, the tender female rain that feeds the land. The veld is misty, quiet, and through the white mist and rain of early morning, you can see the great steel gate across the entrance to the excavated body of the cave. Above, the hill gleams green and fawn and dark.

When the rain is over, we climb the hill once more. Walking among grasses, thorn trees, tiny ferns, and lichens, the air is full of birdsong. Each particular thing is wet and alive.

Here where they came to cut this grass to make their beds, the air is clear and fragrant. Here among the earth and leaves and tiny animals that are their flesh and bones, here where they climbed in the utter liveliness of the hill, we climb. Sitting on the quiet summit where human beings have always sat and human eyes have seen the wide, wide reach of sky and hill and grassland stretching far away, we sit and breathe the air. The children are hungry again, as children are, and we feed them what we have, as parents feed their children. They sit on our laps, and we hold them in our arms. Their eyes are new, their warm skin soft and sweet.

For most of the year, the veld in this region is far drier than it is now: no rain for months and months. But this season of drought recalls the grace of growing things, of plants that wait until rain comes, for years perhaps, until the seeds can open. Here at the hearth, at the very place of burning and excavation, the fragrance of grasses is sweet and familiar. Perhaps this is what our flesh remembers across the generations: evanescent softness of our skin, light in our eyes, thread of breath, trace of joy that does endure and is not lost. In each particular thing this morning, even if buried or forgotten, the light of this liveliness seems ineradicably to gleam—germ that waits in the earth to grow and green again whenever rain returns.

In the cave, our life is just one millimetre of dust. The years of iron and steel and all of recorded history measure just a little more. Beneath and before, the deep cave floor extends in long accumulation of human habitation, long before race or history, a million years or more.

And for a moment, I see that beyond the brief small breath of our particular dust, the hill continues to flow. Months, years, lifetimes, hundreds of years, thousands of years, tens of hundreds of thousands of years, whatever it takes to heal, the tough joy waits to sprout and leaf and flesh and fur again—swallows calling, returning home.

Coming down from the hill, we meet Anthony drinking a cup of coffee outside the neatly equipped old Land Cruiser where he has spent the night, knitted woollen cap on his head. His clothes are hung out to dry on the thorn tree, breakfast mango pip tossed into the veld. He smiles and waves, then places his palms together. A little bow.

Behind him is the dark mouth of the cave. Beyond the steel gate are the grid, the excavation, and the place that has not been excavated yet.

They say the human bones have gone without a trace, yet here is ash from their fires. Here is dust carried in from their feet. Here are the grass beds in which they lay. Ash and dust and grass—the fragile, transient things remain. Beyond and above, the rocks of the koppie are wet with rain, misty Wonderwerk hill in the early morning, the layers of dolomite gleaming dark against the green, layer upon layer, deep before stories. In this place of habitation, our breath makes mist in the cold morning air.

As in every other quest for a story of origins, the scientists, writers, travellers, and tourists like ourselves imagine, measure, photograph, and describe the shape of that which was the beginning. But the feel of bodies living in a cave, the smell of dust, the stillness before our eyes eludes all metaphors. Perhaps one can simply gesture, perhaps a bow.

Everywhere the veld is alive in the fragrance of grasses and the particular lives of swallows and mice, continuity of the small.

Honokahua

For Hawaiians, as for people in many cultures, the remains of ancestors are to be treated with utmost care. Before and after Western contact, Hawaiians conducted burial rituals and protected burial sites with great reverence and secrecy. Desecration of the remains of ancestors was unthinkable. The bones (iwi kupuna) and sacred funerary objects of chiefs were often sealed in caves that were deliberately inaccessible. Other burials were in beach sands and dunes, unmarked but not forgotten by the succeeding generations charged with protecting them.

When outsiders began to carve up and develop the land, the iwi kupuna of Hawaiian families were frequently unearthed and scattered: taken by archaeologists, given to museums, sold as curiosities, or simply discarded. The anguish this caused the Native people was largely ignored.

In the late 1980s, however, a large burial site was disturbed during the building of the Ritz Carlton Hotel on Maui, and this time, Hawaiians came together to challenge the laws that allowed such sacrilege and to reaffirm their obligation, right, and responsibility to protect ancestral remains. Among the first individuals to draw attention to the Honokahua burial site were Charles Kauluwehi Maxwell Sr., now the Maui Burial Council chairman and president of the board of Hui Mālama i Nā Kūpuna o Hawai'i Nei, and Dana Naone Hall, a leader and activist with the group Hui Alanui o Makena. Hall has written of these events:

> Everyone must realize that Honokahua, as dramatic as it was, wasn't the first time that a concentrated burial site belonging to native Hawaiians had been disturbed; it had happened hundreds if not thousands of times before, everywhere in our island chain practically. But this was the first time anybody latched on to what was happening and stayed with it and slowed the process down enough so that we could really see and understand what was going on and other people could understand it, and the uproar could occur. Honokahua allowed for the final necessary element to be put in place, which is that the people whose culture it is were able to begin to make the decisions about what happened to these important sacred places.

*Hui Alanui o Makena
leaders Dana Naone Hall
and Les Kuloloio at the
Honokahua burial site.*

Photograph by
Franco Salmoiraghi, 1989

The dispute among the Native Hawaiians, the hotel developers, the Maui County Planning Commission, and the State lasted for three years. In 1989, an agreement was reached. One of the ramifications of this agreement was legislative revision of Hawai'i's historic preservation laws: Burial Councils on each island would review all findings of human remains. The following year, the Federal Native American Graves Protection and Repatriation Act went into effect.

One group that was formed to take the responsibility for repatriation and burial of iwi kupuna was Hui Mālama i Nā Kūpuna o Hawai'i Nei. In the words of the founders, Edward and Pualani Kanahele:

> Hui Mālama i Nā Kūpuna o Hawai'i Nei (Group Caring for the Ancestors of Hawai'i) was born December 1988 from the kaumaha (heaviness) and aokanaka (enlightenment) caused by the archaeological disinterment of over 1,100 ancestral Native Hawaiians from Honokahua, Maui. The ancestral remains were removed over the protests of the Native Hawaiian community in order to build the Ritz Carlton Hotel.
>
> The desecration was stopped following a 24-hour vigil at the Hawai'i State Capitol. Governor John Waihe'e, a Native Hawaiian, approved of a settlement that returned the ancestral remains to their one hānau (birth sands), set aside the reburial site in perpetuity, and moved the hotel inland and away from the ancestral resting place. Today, stone memorials and plaques mark the location of the re-interment site, a chilly reminder of the pain, anguish, and shame that could have been avoided if State and County officials and the private landowner/developer had only listened to those who demanded the hotel not be built, or at least moved away from the burial site of the Honokahua families, to begin with.
>
> In one sense Honokahua represents balance, for from this tragedy came enlightenment: the realization by living Native Hawaiians that we were ultimately responsible for the care and protection of our ancestors and that cultural protocols needed to be relearned and laws effectively changed to create the empowerment necessary to carry out this important and time honored responsibility to mālama (take care) and kūpale (protect) our ancestors.
>
> Moreover, we have been taught that the relationship between our ancestors and ourselves is one of interdependence—as the living, we have a kuleana (responsibility) to care for our kūpuna (ancestors). In turn, our ancestors respond by protecting us on the spiritual side. Hence, one side cannot completely exist without the other.
>
> *E hō mai ka 'ike, e hō mai ka ikaika, e hō mai ka akamai, e hō mai ka maopopo pono, e hō mai ka 'ike papalua, e hō mai ka mana.*
>
> Grant us knowledge, grant us strength, grant us intelligence, grant us righteous understanding, grant us visions and avenues of communication, grant us mana.

"It was because of Honokahua that laws were enacted and methods of [commercial] development changed," writes Adrian Kamaliʻi. Kamaliʻi is the president of Pae ʻĀina Communications, a consulting firm, and the grandson of Charles Kauluwehi Maxwell Sr. "It uncomfortably forced the government, developers and officials to recognize that a burial without an approved plot or without a headstone does not mean that person was loved any less, or that those individuals were not important as humans. Honokahua made clear that we as Hawaiians are born of these lands and that we are buried in them. It forced us as Hawaiians, as the progeny of these iwi, to take a stand, to take action; it required our vigilance."

As a result of long negotiations, the 13.6-acre burial site at Honokahua was set aside, to be used exclusively for Native Hawaiian religious practices. However, confrontations in the courts and in communities have continued to break out across the state whenever Native Hawaiian ancestral remains are disturbed by developers. The issue of a just relationship between the Native people and the Federal and State governments is unresolved.

The photographs in this portfolio help us recall the enormity of what happened at Honokahua and the complexity of each decision by the Burial Council. Dana Naone Hall writes:

> We realized that if the kūpuna were going to come out against their will and against our will, that we had a duty to stay with them, to comfort them as they were exposed. And that was a very difficult decision to make…and once we made that decision, then we had to engage in a process of working out exactly how the disinterment would occur and [if] you can imagine how painful and distasteful an experience that was, that we would have to concede that there were powers that were forcing us to engage in this process, perhaps you can begin to understand some of the difficulty.

Among the protocols necessary for reburial was the task of wrapping the iwi in traditional funerary kapa cloth. Unfortunately, the skills for making kapa were nearly lost over the past century—even though Hawaiian kapa was once the finest in all of Polynesia. Only in the 1970s was the art of making fine kapa revived. Principal among the artisans who rediscovered and perfected the technique—vital for religious practices as well as daily life—was Puanani Kanemura Van Dorpe. Having studied kapa-making in Fiji, she began working at the Bishop Museum in Honolulu, examining ancient kapa under a microscope to discover its properties, growing traditional wauke (paper mulberry), having traditional tools fabricated, and preparing traditional dyes. As she worked, she says, "I realized I had to have help, so I

Lehua Pali, here wielding a wooden hohoa on the softened wauke bark, was among the women who beat kapa every day for four months to prepare materials for the reburial. In the early stages of kapa-making, bark is soaked in ocean water to soften it; a wooden anvil is used for pounding the bark, and a stone anvil for making the watermarks.

Photograph by
Franco Salmoiraghi, 1990

Puanani Kanemura Van Dorpe soaks a sheet of kapa in Aimoku Pali's loʻi (an irrigated terrace for taro cultivation) in Honokōhau Valley. After soaking in hili kukui (dye made from kukui bark), the kapa is submerged in the mud of a loʻi for seven days; when retrieved, it is black, the color of greatest honor.

Photograph by
Franco Salmoiraghi, 1990

*Lehua Pali and Puanani
Kanemura Van Dorpe
gather the black kapa and
then rinse the sheets in a
nearby stream.*

Photographs by
Franco Salmoiraghi, 1990

began to rely on my 'aumākua, ancestral spirits. Two sisters are the goddesses of kapa: Lauhuki and La'ahana. One is for beating the kapa, the other for the decorating process."

The kapa-making for the reburials at Honokahua was painstaking and taxing. Fine kapa the size of a bed cover can take five hundred hours to finish, and there were many remains to be wrapped. Writer Jocelyn Fujii described the making of the kapa:

> As a witness, I remember how Puanani Kanemura Van Dorpe, the world's unparalleled master of kapa, the bark cloth of the ancient Hawaiians, gathered some strong Hawaiian women, had tools and implements made for them, and created with them over months, more than a thousand pieces of kapa to wrap each set of bones for a proper, respectful, traditional reburial. I remember, years ago, how Pua had scraped the inner bark from wauke trees with the sharp edge of an 'opihi shell, and how she bundled the bark in tī leaves and submerged it in the ocean in Lāhaina, secured under a rock for weeks, until the bark was pliable enough to pound. I remember the women of the hālau in their pareus, beating the bark in a small wooden building in Kapalua, their knees bruised and swollen from months of sitting on a hard floor, their pain empowering and ennobling their work. I can still hear the dreamlike rhythms of the beaters striking the anvils, reverberating through the village like a primal, centuries-old call from a time when such sounds were commonplace. When finally formed into sheets, some of the kapa was buried in the mud of a taro field, where the minerals of the soil reacted with the sun to dye the kapa black, the color of highest honor. I remember the stunned silence when the women were told they could stop, that there was enough kapa, that they had fulfilled their obligation to their kūpuna. I think of these women often, still, two decades later....their rhythmic beating like a tribal heartbeat, carried across the ocean by the winds....

Charles Kauluwehi Maxwell Sr. relates this story about the completion of the reburials:

> So we wrapped, we started to wrap the remains...so we would come like eight, nine o'clock at night and go home like three, four o'clock in the morning. For three and a half months we did that. And the last night when we buried the last remains here, was about 12 o'clock, we just was going to chant, all the torches were lit up here, and we just was going chant and we heard one slapping from the ocean...and Leslie say "Eh! hō'ailona [auspicious event]," and so we came on the edge of the cliff. When we looked down, we barely saw the outline of one koholā, the whale, turning on a side and slapping the waters, ceremoniously-like...poom...poom, just like you beat the pahu drum, you know.

For fifteen minutes that whale did that you know. We stood on the edge, cry and when we turn around they went down in the puka [hole, opening], had these owls, pueo that flew over, whooooo…and flew right…they scream and went right to the mountain…and only me and papa was on top the hill, because I couldn't go down. Everybody was dressed in their black malo, and so immediately, it was like I was so privileged, in 1990, looking into the past, a thousand years.

For the ali'i burials, the kapa pieces were dyed black and watermarked with the maka ūpena pūpū ("netted eyes of the fish") pattern.

For binding, coconut fiber was woven into sennit. Above, Puanani Kanemura Van Dorpe adds kapa to the other ceremonial offerings.

Photographs by
Franco Salmoiraghi, 1990

The Crow

1

The convict Liu Bing was coming home.

An old convict was tottering along behind him.

It was noon. The villagers were eating in the public square, where the sunshine warmed the weak autumn. Behind the village, black smoke from the brick kiln was rising straight up in the air. Yellow leaves were whirling in the sunshine as they fell. From the square, the sounds of talk and laughter were moving in all directions like rippling water. Just then, someone looked up and was briefly panic stricken. Then he let out a loud *Oh!* All of a sudden his gaze straightened and, like the long trunk of a green tree, rested stiffly on the entrance to the village. The villagers in the square all turned their eyes that way, their gazes colliding with one another. Dust fell from the light of their gazes.

They all saw the convict Liu Bing coming back to the village.

He was wearing faded blue and white work clothes. No doubt these were his work clothes from labor reform—old and serviceable, giving off a clacking sound like twisting sheet iron. He was carrying two bedrolls on a pole hooked over one arm. In his free hand, as if pinching a mud-black cotton flower, he held a crow with a broken leg that he'd picked up along the way. His other arm hung below his hip; in that hand, he carried a mesh bag holding a face basin, rice bowl, teapot—all stamped with his serial number—and various other things. Sticking out of the bag's holes, they looked as though they would fall out. His situation was clear to everybody. His face was dark green, as if a layer of ice were forming on it. Behind him was the old convict, whom no one in Liujia Gully recognized. He was wearing work clothes like Liu Bing's and carrying a bulging suitcase in his left hand. With his right hand, he leaned on a wooden stick that he'd picked up somewhere. The remaining nails and broken iron wires on the stick were reminders that it came from the labor camp's work shed or the scaffolding at a construction site in the city. The old prisoner kept walking behind Liu Bing, but the distance between them was lengthening. When Liu Bing drew close to the villagers, he waited—fixed in their blank gazes—for a long time before the old convict caught up. Only then could the people see that the old convict's kindling-thin face was thickly layered with sickly yellows and browns. He looked as if he had one foot in the grave and would die of weakness today or tomorrow. When he caught up, Liu Bing—still holding the crow—began leading him toward the vast expanse of the villagers' shocked gazes: it was like wading through a dense field of green corn. With his head high, he walked steadily, stepping on the villagers' gazes until they broke and crashed, as if he were trampling worthless weeds that weren't supposed to grow so densely on the ridge.

Amid the stiff sound of footsteps, the crow in Liu Bing's hand suddenly let out a cry of pain from being clutched too tightly.

The villagers saw the echo in Liu Bing's eyes. The rice bowls in their hands swayed violently.

Someone dropped a biscuit he'd been holding with chopsticks. The chopsticks also fell. On the ground, the chopsticks and the biscuit made a *pffft* sound.

The dust that Liu Bing kicked up as he walked was rolling up like a storm on the dark ground of the square. The villagers had colluded in sending him to labor reform. He was a notorious thief in the Balou mountain range. Three years ago, he had stolen things until the village was in turmoil. At night, everyone's doors and windows kept creaking. At dusk, the cattle were still eating hay at the trough, but the next day, they'd be plowing land in other villages and towns. Hens that had just finished laying eggs were clucking loudly at the gate, but in the blink of an eye, only chicken feathers would be left. In autumn, your corncobs hung on trees or under the eaves in your courtyard, their golden brilliance fragrant. But one day when you happened to turn around, you'd discover that the trees or eaves were bare of corn. It was all gone. Liu Bing not only stole grain, poultry, and cattle, but also the telephone wires and electric lines that the government had provided the mountain village, the copper screws from transformers, and the headlights from cars crossing the ridge. The only things he didn't steal were the weeds on his family land and the loess soil on his parents' graves. When he finally incurred the public wrath, the people took him to prison. He was sentenced to five years. If you think about it, five years is quite a long time: people could use those five years to recover from their wounds and fear. But when two years were barely up, the fears still present, Liu Bing was released early. Without serving his whole term, he had come floating back like a ghost. The villagers had no time to adjust. It was as if, when you were listening to singing in the warmth of the sunlight, thunder suddenly crashed overhead. In the blink of an eye, a frightening storm dropped frost, snow, and hail on the village. Everybody thought winter had arrived: they were trembling with cold. Liu Bing's footsteps thumped as if trampling over people's chests. The friction of his work pants sounded as crisp and white as ice cubes. Awkwardly and numbly, someone made up to him with a nod of his head. Someone else, flustered, stood up and said with a smile, "Bing, are you back?" But whether he didn't see them or didn't hear them, he ignored them completely and— head high, baggage on his pole—he charged into the villagers' gazes, stepping on their shock and fear. Step by step, he reached the village street and let the crow's strange caw fall to the ground through the cracks between his fingers.

It was the old convict's manner that gave the villagers some thin consolation. He looked apologetic, the way someone does when needing to borrow something. He stood next to the public square as if reporting to the people of Liujia Gully, then bowed from the waist and shouted, "Bing, kneel before the villagers! Kneel down, you!"

Liu Bing didn't kneel: he slowed down a little, stood there for just a moment, and then went on walking.

The old convict knelt down. He banged his head once on the ground, and then leaning on his walking stick, he staggered away in the gazes that Liu Bing had waved aside. Behind them was the crow's cawing, a sound that should accompany only the approach of death.

2

Unexpectedly, one blow had shattered life's tranquility. People wouldn't again forget to bolt their doors at night. No one would forget to check on the hens when they were laying. There seemed to be fewer footsteps on the village street than before. Children even stopped playing at the entrance to the village.

Everyone was waiting for something to happen.

Everyone was waiting for someone to be the first to say something had been stolen the night before. Life was like rough hemp rope being pulled through the villagers' hearts. No one passing by the thatched hut in the western part of the village could keep from taking a look. Someone would ask, *What did you see?* Another would answer, *The gate is still closed.* Someone would ask, *Isn't there even a little activity?* Answer: *There are some crow feathers in the front.* They said, *After this thief finishes eating crows, he'll have to eat chickens.* In the midst of this talk, Liu Bing's gate creaked, and the air on the street instantly became as wrung out as a piece of cloth caught up in a running wheel. The air didn't flow anymore. People saw Liu Bing carrying a rusty bucket to draw water from the well; when he returned home, he closed the gate again. *Creak.* The next day, people saw Liu Bing go to fetch water. The third day was the same. The fourth day— *boom!*—was different. The terrifying blood red that people had been dreading had finally arrived.

The Zhaos had lost a chicken. As soon as they got up, they saw chicken feathers drifting all over their courtyard like snowflakes. The eldest Zhao son grabbed a bunch of moon-colored feathers, the second son picked up a shovel and the third one a knife, and when the sun was fully red, they went to Liu Bing's gate.

"Liu Bing, come out for a second."

Liu Bing opened the gate.

The eldest Zhao son threw the chicken feathers in Liu Bing's face. "Did you steal this bird?"

Liu Bing's face turned black and purple. "Yes."

The second Zhao son slammed the ground with the shovel. "So what are you going to do about it?"

Liu Bing didn't say anything. He turned around and went back to the stove in a corner of the courtyard. The villagers heard a crisp sound, and then he came out again. At the door, with one foot in and one foot out, he threw something at the Zhao brothers. When the villagers looked down, they saw a carrot-thin section of a finger. It was a pallid greenish yellow. The section from which it had been hacked was bright red, blood seeping slowly from it. When they took another look at Liu Bing's hands, they saw that he'd balled his left hand into a fist and closed it tightly over his index finger: blood was dripping from his fist.

The Zhao brothers and the other villagers were speechless with fear.

They all heard the blood flowing like water on the village street and saw the blackish-red blood slide like red silk along the alleys and spread out beyond the village. In the blood, they saw the old convict in Liu Bing's courtyard. His face still looked sickly yellow, but he'd stopped using a walking stick. He stood there idiotically for a while. He didn't go out the gate or say anything, nor did he immediately bandage Liu Bing's finger. Instead, he went over to a tree and took two bricks off the battered basket sitting upside down under the tree, lifted up the basket, and let out the crow with the broken leg. He scattered a handful of corn kernels on the ground and then began sweeping the courtyard.

And so the incident ended.

The village was quiet again.

Day after day, life slid by like silk.

Farmers worked the land; tradesmen engaged in business. As soon as it was light, the farmers went to the fields with their tools. It was dusk before the tradesmen came back from town with their empty baskets. Other people fired bricks all day in the village kiln. Everyone had stock in it, and everyone could buy its bricks at the lowest prices. All the new houses in Liujia Gully had been built with bricks from this small kiln. So many people had been waiting to buy bricks that the villagers decided to tear down the small kiln and build a large one. While they were busy constructing the large kiln, they caught sight of Liu Bing and the old guy: they were like a relaxed and contented father and son. They neither got up early, nor worked overtime, though you couldn't say they were slacking off either. It was always about eight o'clock, when the sun had already risen, that—right on schedule and carrying shovels and pickaxes—they went past the villagers building the new kiln and on to the mountain across the way, where Liu Bing's land had been neglected for years. As though clearing wasteland, they dug and dug with the pickaxes. Then they broke up the clods of earth and moved the weeds and rocks away from the land. At about noon, they came back from the field. They rested after lunch, and then around two o'clock, they went back to the field. At about six o'clock, right on schedule, they came back again. People realized that they didn't vary their working hours by the season and that their hours were the same as those of laborers. At autumn harvest time, it was light at five o'clock in the morning and all the other villagers were already busy by then, but it was eight o'clock when Liu Bing and the old man set out. By five o'clock in the afternoon, the sun had set and the other villagers had quit work and were eating supper, but it was about six o'clock when—walking through the dusk—these two came back and cooked their supper. They were out of step with the villagers. They were like two workers living in the village and going to the factory. But they were tilling the wasteland just the same as the villagers plowed the cornfields. Squeezed between the autumn-ripe cornfields was a stretch of dark red oozing with the smell of new earth and brightly overwhelming the yellow smell of autumn. The smell crossed the ravine, irrigating the whole village like rainfall and moistening the villagers' breaths. The people who were exhausted from building the kiln loved to stand at the cracks of the kiln and look across the ravine at the land the two men were turning over. Looking at the dark figures working at an even pace and watching the crow walking in front of them, the villagers squinted and asked, "Has Liu Bing's father come back from his grave?"

Someone responded, "Hell, more like his grandfather!"

Someone else said, "Do you know what the old convict was guilty of?" He continued, "He's a murderer: two lives ended at his hands. At first he was going to pay with his life, but after he was sentenced to death, the sentence was suspended." He said, "At first, he was going to spend the rest of his life in the labor reform camp, but after forty years he was so old and sick that they released him." He said, "But releasing him doesn't mean he was acquitted; rather, his labor reform is continuing outside the prison." It was the most experienced villager who was saying all of this. He had just returned from the outside world. After the kiln was finished, he went to the city to get several truckloads of coal and bought a set of brick molds. People were just getting ready for the autumn harvest. All over the village, they choked and hiccuped from the rotten yellow smell of the corn, as though they had half a fried dough stick stuck in their throats. People were calculating how many days it would take to finish harvesting, how many days to plant the wheat, and exactly what date they could begin firing the first load of bricks in the new kiln. Like sunshine, the good days were warming all sides of the brick kiln. The future the villagers had longed for lay before them. Everyone heard the warm golden sound flowing among them. But just then someone had to say something like this: not only was the hardened thief Liu Bing in the village, but so was a convict who'd killed two people.

In front of the brick kiln, the villagers stood without moving.

They didn't have enough strength to go on clapping the dirt off their clothes.

They were all watching Liu Bing and the old guy leave their land—one in front, one behind: as the men went into the ravine and climbed the hill, the noontime sun shone as bright and clear over their heads as it did over the other villagers' heads. On the old guy's shoulder, the crow with the glossy feathers was like a ball of black glass. With each step, it had to spread its wings to keep its balance. Each time it did so, the sun glistened, casting reflections of the feathers on the sky, on the trees, and sometimes—with an ink-black pouncing sound—on the villagers' faces.

Someone called out, "Bing, come over here!"

The old convict went back to the house to cook. Liu Bing walked over.

"Who *is* that old man?"

Liu Bing didn't answer.

"I hear he took two lives."

With a roar, Liu Bing's face darkened.

"Tell him to leave. You have land in the village, but he doesn't."

Without a word, Liu Bing left the kiln. His heavy, hoarse breathing hammered the air like a wooden club. Even after he was far in the distance, the villagers still felt that the air around them was like sailcloth flapping up and down. An oppressive, heavy noise was hiding in the air. The people watched Liu Bing as he went into the village, turned into an alley, and closed his willow-wood door tightly. They were still standing at the brick kiln, taking in the sound of his heavy breathing. Right up until harvest time, the villagers could still sense the heaving breath.

Harvesting consumed only a fortnight. During this time, work on the brick kiln stopped. The villagers harvested corn, plowed, and then planted wheat. During this time, when the mountain range changed color and everything turned dark brown, and when the cornstalks had been carried back and placed on trees in front of each home, bundled up, and lined up in rows along the rear walls, when all the land had been newly turned over, when every place had the same earthy red, like persimmon leaves carpeting the world, when the smell of the fresh earth came in bursts like livestock kicking, trampling, and leaping, the villagers once more converged on the kiln and noticed a large expanse of green gleaming on the mountain slope across the way, as though a chunk of blue sky had fallen on the reddish-brown mountain ridge. The villagers smelled the faintly moist green scent coming from the wheat fields. Most people had just started planting. Some of the land still needed more plowing, but floating in the distance was an eye-catching delicate green. And all around that large expanse of green—along the gully, next to the road, and on the unarable wasteland on the cliff—every bit of land had actually been reclaimed. At the edges of the fields, rocks had been piled up as neatly as brick walls. Some of this waste-land was tender green, while some was the same as the villagers' land, the fresh earth color bright and so red it was like blood. People saw Liu Bing and the old guy planting on the cliff. Like an ox, Liu Bing pulled a plow by its handles and walked toward one end of the cliff, then retraced his foot-steps. The old guy held the plow and walked behind it. As he walked, he swayed back and forth, and the copper bell tied to the plow rang out: it seemed as though the whole region of mountain and wasteland was filled with the clear sound of the bell. The crow perched on the old convict's shoulder. Black and bright, it was as gentle and tame as a black pigeon. Now and then, it cawed, startling the villagers: only then were they reminded that the crow had always been an inauspicious bird. Then they noticed that, for some unknown reason, the crow was flying in circles in midair. But Liu Bing and the old guy—accustomed to this—weren't sur-prised or frightened. They went on planting, creating a scene beautiful enough for poetry and paintings.

Watching Liu Bing and the old guy, the villagers said, "Fuck!"

Looking at the vigorous green wheat fields, they said, "Is this convict now one of us?"

Looking at the crow that flew for a while and then came back to the vil-lage and alit on Liu Bing's rooftop, they said, "Where's the sun gone? Hurry up and get back to work."

And so they all moved bricks over to the new kiln.

After moving bricks for a while, two men went back to the village to use the toilet. When they came back, their laughter turned the world red and violet. At about noon, Liu Bing and the old guy walked back from their field with their tools. When they walked on the road behind the brick kiln, the violet-red laughter was still drifting like leaves in all directions. Not until the old convict and Liu Bing reached their gate did the drifting laugh-ter stop like a hawk that had been set free.

In that instant, everyone saw the old guy turn numb. Liu Bing also stopped all of a sudden. The hoe he was carrying on his shoulder began falling to the ground, but before the handle slipped from his hand, he quickly picked it up and shouted himself hoarse with a black-colored *Ah*. He spun around and began brandishing the hoe in the air, as though several wild dogs and hungry wolves were about to pounce on him from all directions. The villagers saw the hoe flash with a cold light, heard the whip-like sound of the hoe lashing the air, and smelled the thin, red blood of the crow flow like a brook behind Liu Bing. Then the laughter snapped. Disappeared. The villagers were out of their wits, but they all knew that a dense black calamity was approaching.

Everyone's gaze was fastened on the two men who'd gone to use the toilet. Under their gazes, dust dropped from the two faces.

But, in the end, nothing happened. It was as if there'd been thunder and lightning, black clouds and high winds, but no rain. The old guy was standing there, and then he took a few hurried steps and squatted at the gate. All of a sudden, Liu Bing stopped brandishing the hoe, threw it aside, and walked over to the old convict.

People stopped gazing at the faces of the two men who had gone to use the toilet.

The two of them were looking at each other. One said, "Can't be." The other said, "If it were a cat, would it have nine lives?" Then they both knocked off work. They both saw that Liu Bing's gate was closed as usual. The crow feathers—black and white—were like black clouds and sunlight stained with blood. The glutinous, thick blood smelled like worms crawling around in rainwater.

3

The crow was dead. The old convict disappeared.

The villagers loaded the kiln, sealed the opening, carried coal to it, and remained occupied at the kiln for about a fortnight. As usual, every day they saw Liu Bing finishing up the corners at the edges of his field across the way and filling in the spots where the wheat hadn't germinated. They didn't see the old convict and the crow go with him to the fields anymore, nor did they peer through the cracks in the gate and see the old guy feeding the crow. No longer was there the sound of the crow cawing in the village, nor were there the halting footsteps of the old guy. In the village, a sedate tranquility settled like springtime warmth over the main streets and alleys.

Once more, people began forgetting to bolt their doors at night.

They didn't need to check on the chickens and sheep or to count the animals when they came back to their coops and pens.

They didn't need to ride herd on their children, thinking that the murderer was going to blow his top.

The days were flowing ahead smoothly and calmly like water in a bay. None of the villagers mentioned the crow, the old convict, or Liu Bing. Even when Liu Bing walked past them, they ignored him. The kiln was firing bricks: every night, firelight towered at the village entrance. Half the world was alight; the stars and moon vanished from the sky. By the light of the fire, children played hide-and-seek all around the kiln. By the light of the fire, adults chatted about anything and everything. So many young lovers took advantage of the villagers spending their time at the kiln that trysts were as dense as a forest. The village drew up a distribution list for the bricks from the kiln. The people on the list went all over in search of laborers and negotiated the time for building new houses. Those not on the list impatiently estimated when it would be their turn. Because the kiln and the firelight were burning with such excitement, everyone smelled a sweet warmth in the days and listened to the dreams of fellow villagers. But just then, the old convict reappeared in the village.

This was the third day of the firing: the smell of sulfur had just begun fanning out from the kilns, and the air in the streets and alleys had just begun mixing with the red burning smell. People noticed that someone was hiding far away, standing idiotically in the field west of the village and watching the kilns. Then he went to the mountain ridge south of the village and watched the kilns. Finally, he went to a hill southwest of the village and watched the kilns until dark. At last, they figured out that where he went was where the dense smoke was being blown.

Someone walked toward him.

And realized it was the old convict.

Leaning on a small tree, he was absorbed in staring at the new kiln, the sound of his breathing pushing violently against the sunlight, as if he were a hungry man staring at a frying pan—hungry for the aroma of oil. Right until the villager walked up to him and called him a few times, he stared at the kiln, half stooped and half erect. His elongated neck was as slender and rigid as an iron rod; it held no hint of a wrinkle.

The villager clapped him hard on the shoulder.

The old guy was so startled that a white collapsing sound came out from his bones, and his body shrank into a small bundle. The wrinkled skin on his neck began piling up like folded clothes. When he turned around, the villager saw that he was holding the crow at his chest. The crow was still alive; it was just missing a wing. It looked like a house with a corner that had caved in. A black hole had sunk into its right side, which was covered by a few feathers. It was as if the crow had also been taken by surprise: as the old convict shrank back, the crow seemed about to caw, but it only opened its beak; it couldn't make a sound. The villager saw the crow's frightened, raspy breathing: like rough-split kindling, it fell to the wheat leaves at the old convict's feet.

"What are you looking at?"

The old guy gave a stiff smile of apology. "I'm smelling the charred, burnt odor from the brick kiln."

The villager said, "What's so great about it?"

The convict said, "I spent a lifetime in labor reform. I've smelled this odor for a lifetime. I'm kind of addicted to it, the way some people are to liquor."

The other man said, "If you intend to stay through the winter here in the village, you'd better not let people see you very much. All the villagers know that you murdered two people, one your wife and the other your child. Do you think Liujia Gully can tolerate a murderer living here for long?" At that, the old convict blanched and his hands trembled. The crow almost fell out of his hand. Then, silently turning his back on the burning smell coming from the kiln, he walked away from the village and circled around to Liu Bing's home. His footsteps were as light as falling feathers.

But he still wanted to go out and smell the odor coming from the kiln. He stayed in Liu Bing's home in the daytime, and at night while the villagers slept, he went out in the direction of the wind and circled around the kiln. When the wind blew east, he was in the east; when it blew west, he was in the west. When the wind was strong, he moved a little farther away from the kiln and stood there, half in light and half in darkness. When the wind was light, he moved closer to the kiln and hid himself in the darkness. Sometimes at midnight, Liu Bing also came out in the moonlight: the villagers didn't know whether he came to tell the old guy to go home and get some sleep or to keep the old guy company. This went on until the cold winter arrived and the brickyard was heaped with ruined bricks. Heaped with the anxieties of Liujia Gully. Not until then did the old guy appear openly in front of the villagers. Upon seeing him, the villagers stopped breathing. They couldn't move either: it was as if their feet were tied with ropes.

Altogether, they'd fired four batches of bricks: all were ruined.

The varicolored bricks were heaped up every which way like an abandoned city wall. In this heap of twisted purple and black, the sulfur smell from the kiln was coldly streaming: you could hear the clamor of the sick-looking stench spread in all directions like rainwater. At twilight, as the coldly gorgeous red of the setting sun fell on the brickyard and the villagers carried the fourth load of ruined bricks out, dismay piled up on people's faces like ashes. The villagers who had exhausted their funds to fire the kiln and build new houses wept as they carried the bricks, kicked the misshapen bricks, and hit the kiln that had ruined their bricks. Someone picked up a shovel and started digging up the kiln. The engineer who'd fired the kiln couldn't simply stand there: he squatted down and smacked his face time after time until pieces of his flesh fell off and blackish-red drops of blood splashed up and bounced in the air like beads of water and then fell to the ground. For a while, the brickyard, the kiln, and the road to the kiln were in an uproar, the weeping and shouting like a downpour.

Blood and saliva filled the air. The bitter smell of sulfur grew stronger. The engineer's keening remorse released the villagers from their inhibitions: their muddy tears and smoky anger were like the ruined bricks inside the kiln—expanding and twisting in various ugly ways.

Just then the old convict showed up. Stepping on the setting sun, he tottered over. He stood behind a pile of ruined bricks, greedily inhaling the purple smell of the kiln. His nostrils flared, and his breathing sounded gruff, like ironsmiths' bellows. His white-filmed eyes were staring hard at the ruined bricks, as though in the variegated bricks he was seeing tiny nuggets of gold and silver.

A long time passed. When the last echoes came from the sun setting in the west, he pushed over a pile of ruined bricks and took one out from the middle. He smashed it open and ate a fistful of powder from the center of the brick, and then ate another bite: it was as though he were chewing on freshly harvested wheat or corn. When he swallowed the brick powder, the villagers were startled by the *gudu* sound. They saw him eating the brick powder hungrily, as though it were delicious fried sesame seeds.

Someone said, "Ah."

The people all grew quiet and raised their eyes: their gazes knocked loudly at the old man's Adam's apple moving up and down. They all saw the red-brick powder drop from the corner of his mouth to the crow he held at his chest. Someone's eyes began burning such a bright red that the after-sunset brickyard glowed with light.

"Hey! What the fuck are you doing so sneakily over there?"

Startled, the old guy looked up. Seeping from his open mouth was a mud-red color.

"Answer me: what are you being so furtive about?"

The old guy bent his head, swallowed the brick powder, and said, "This kiln isn't set in the right direction. The next batch of bricks will be ruined, too."

The villagers' eyes all popped.

"The bricks from all four batches are warped on the edges and burned on the inside. Some taste bitter, some sour. This is all because the kiln isn't set up properly." The old guy lifted the crow up to his chest, and the crow grabbed his clothing with its one leg. It cawed sadly once; the old convict covered the sound with his hands. "When you build houses, you have to take *fengshui* into consideration. It's the same with firing bricks." He continued, "If this kiln isn't turned in another direction, it'll never fire a batch of good bricks."

A few villagers walked over to him.

He said, "When you fire bricks, there should be a sulfur smell on the first day, but it was three days before this kiln produced a sulfur smell."

The villagers stood right in front of his face.

"Bug off!" A villager said, "Bug off, you fucking evil mouth."

The old guy stared blankly.

"Also, the sulfur smelled normal enough on the third day, but it wasn't stinky enough."

The villager stood there. "Fuck you! You get the fuck out of here! Now! Before you came to Liujia Gully, our bricks were never ruined. Did you know that?"

The old convict turned around and left. After taking a few steps, he felt something hit his back: when he turned around, he saw a half-baked brick fall from his body. Then he saw a few children throwing bricks at him as if throwing corn. Like someone protecting a child, he shielded the crow with his chest. The crow felt smothered and hot from being covered up at the old man's chest: it let out a plangent caw that carried the old man's bloody grief. The caw drifted over to the kiln like a rising wind. Affected by the crow's cry, the adults shouted at the children to stop. All of a sudden, the sky darkened.

4

For three days, the villagers loaded the kiln.

They fired the kiln for eight days.

In the next three days, they doused the kiln with water.

After a fortnight, they opened the kiln. All the villagers were standing there. When the engineer pushed aside the seal at the kiln's opening, he saw bricks that were the usual tender blue color. The shipshape piles of blue bricks were emitting a sweet fragrance, like bread fresh from the oven. Like clouds, the fragrance slid to the gaunt faces of the villagers, who had been holding their breath for a fortnight. The engineer broke into tears. Kneeling in front of the kiln, he kowtowed three times and then turned away and prayed to heaven three times. The yellow-orange sunshine shone on the two streams of tears on his face. As if he were crazy, he ran around the brickyard shouting wildly, "I made it! I made it! This is the best batch I've ever fired in my whole life!" Then he ran shouting to the village streets, where his wild yelling shook the last autumn leaves whispering from the trees.

All of a sudden, in the midst of the engineer's wild shouting, the villagers woke from their trance. Like a tide, they shoved their way over to the kiln and started lifting the bricks out. When the first batch of blue bricks was carried out, the villagers stood in front of the stacks of ruined bricks. They didn't want to put the fresh blue bricks down, but kept gulping the hot scent of the fired bricks. Their joyful giggles, mixed with tears, fell onto the bricks and rolled to the ground. In no time, the ground was covered with tears. Someone feeling tired from the weight of the bricks he was carrying said, "Why are you crying? Why are you laughing? Hurry up and get the bricks out of the kiln. Even if we're exhausted, we can't let the kiln rest. We have to fire two more batches before winter so that each family can have its share of bricks." Everyone lined up—the head of the line at the kiln, the tail at the brickyard. Each time, four bricks were passed along the line; the bricks flowed like water from hand to hand. It took from sunrise to sunset to empty half the kiln. Suddenly, someone discovered that on the southeast wall of the kiln, which always used to be tightly sealed, holes the size of rolling pins opened at two-foot intervals. The villager counted twenty-seven holes. Wind blew in from each hole, sounding like the crow's sad caw. He discovered that though the holes were all the same size, the wind was different. Blowing from east to south, the wind changed from strong to light in the twenty-seven holes. As it moved from the top row of holes to the third and last row, the wind grew stronger.

The villagers stopped moving the bricks.

When they went over to the southeast part of the kiln, they immediately saw a straw mat hanging on the rise of the kiln's slope. Stuffed into it was a bundle of dry straw. In some places, it seemed that broken bricks had been placed at random. When they removed the straw mat, the kindling, and the bricks, light shone through the twenty-seven holes.

So, the holes where the wind had been strong were each covered lightly with a straw mat. The holes where the wind had been light were each covered with a cracked brick. The others were filled with either a large or small bundle of straw. The villagers couldn't figure this out. When they turned around, they saw that the engineer was dumbstruck. The copper-colored joy on his face that had been ringing out all day now faded away. His ashen face was like a cloud drifting behind the villagers.

The villagers recalled what the old convict had said about the kiln not being set up properly.

Someone slapped his thigh and said, "Fuck!"

Then the villagers headed toward Liu Bing's home.

Liu Bing's gate was locked, so they walked over to the hill across from the village and saw him hoeing wheat. His wheat was as vigorous as chives, the green leaves so dense that you couldn't see the earth under them. The people suddenly halted. In the center of the large green field, they saw a brand-new grave. The fresh earth's chilly brown smell assailed their noses and throats: for a moment they didn't know what had happened. Only when they heard the solitary call of the crow did they see the one-legged, broken-winged bird atop the new grave. It had been lying there quietly, but when it saw people coming, it was startled and spread one wing as if to fly. It collapsed on the ground and rolled down to the mound. Using its one wing as a crutch, it stood on the grave mound. It raised its walnut-sized head high and kept belting out half-black, half-purple cries—cries like the breaking of bricks. In the blink of an eye, it shook the air in the village and the mountain so much that the air began swelling and flowing like a raging fire.

Liu Bing turned around.

A villager called to him, "Did the old convict die? When did he die?"

Liu Bing didn't answer. His silence was as cold as the mountain in winter. He picked up his hoe, gathered up the crow, left the field, and headed home. He walked unhurriedly. The black cawing of the crow on his shoulder was like the *gugu gugu* of a pigeon, flowing gently like a river.

Translation by Karen Gernant and Chen Zeping

A Wandering Estonian

yesterday   I met   a wandering Estonian
he is not a Flying Dutchman
in your letter   Yan!   I understand your grandfather's days
unfurled the sails in a spacious garden   and I hear angels were
singing the song
   of the honeybees
I know nothing of   the old days of your grandfather's
grandfather's   grandfather   the boy who lost his father   when he
was a child
before he could remember   soon   will become
a wandering Estonian
no matter how hard he searched   and searched
there are only a hundred secrets   a thousand bits of evidence   about
his father
who had disappeared   been wiped out
"I   saw   your father   in the camp
when I worked with him   that man or
this man   father A   father B   father C
father D   the stories of those who happened to see your father
are all scattered tales"   so I think
now   if my father were to return to this world
I would never   live in a land like this again
I would   leave   here   be gone to a different continent
but   Yan!   a wandering modern Dutchman
an Estonian Dutchman
who is that professor   teaching
Polish on a ship in heaven with sails spread?   he has
wings on his back   but   there is a trace of frozen blood
on his chapped hands   and on his chest   don't cry
trees in what was your grandfather's garden!
birds that were singing there   insects   an infant boy!
you can hear the song, can't you   we   are the Flying Dutchmen
while we are alive   and when we are dead   Yan!   in your letter
your trees tremble

I can hear a poem   in Polish by the man who was your father
don't unfurl the sails   now is the time   that ship is
passing the garden   of your grandfather's days
when angels were singing the song of the honeybees

Translation by Samuel Grolmes and Yumiko Tsumura

The Return

We always received our first Christmas card of the year from my mother's Aunt Billie, sometimes as early as the middle of October—so that she could get it out of the way, Billie would explain to us if asked why the card had arrived so early.

Billie had many eccentric habits, such as turning her hearing aid off whenever she did not want to listen to what was being said to her, although she never informed those who were having a one-way conversation with her of this. She would simply nod her head up and down to simulate listening and reply "yeah, yeah, me too, me too" repeatedly, regardless of what had been said to her.

She also had peculiar dress sense, particularly in relation to the positioning of underwear. Billie would often turn up at the house on a Sunday afternoon wearing a motley fur coat that had been given to her by a bookie boyfriend many years earlier. We would sit at the table and wait in anticipation as she removed the coat, never entirely sure how she had arranged her clothing for the day, although we could be certain that she would be wearing her bra over the top of one of a variety of turtleneck sweaters that she favoured, regardless of the weather.

The rationale for the reverse order of Billie's clothing had not been questioned for many years. Her initial explanation—that it was "more comfortable and practical"—was a sufficient response, as far as Billie was concerned. She would become angry whenever the matter was pursued, so people stopped asking her, although none of us really got used to it.

After Billie's Christmas card arrived and had taken prime position on the mantle that would eventually overflow with cards, I would know that Christmas Day was not too far away.

And once we got into December, my grandmother would come and visit us and take Katie and me into town to look at the decorations in the Myer windows, along with thousands of other kids. It was during one of those early trips that I first spotted him. It was a day that I would not forget.

My grandmother had wheeled Katie into town in the pram. She tried to hurry me along as I daydreamed my way along the street in her wake.

Before we were taken to see the window decorations, we stopped at the Ladies' underground toilets outside the Post Office, on Elizabeth Street. One of my grandmother's closest friends, Jean Lambert, worked there cleaning the floors, toilets, and hand basins, while keeping up a ready supply of paper, clean towels, and soap.

Jean had her own small room in one corner. It contained a small fridge and electric jug, as well as a mantle-radio. She had decorated the walls with magazine posters of movie stars and racehorses. Whenever she got the chance for a break, she would sit in that room, drinking tea and listening to the races.

Nan and Jean chatted to each other while Katie's bottle was heated in the jug. Jean had raised six kids of her own, and even more grandchildren. And it showed. She managed to nurse Katie with one hand and smoke a cigarette and drink tea with the other, while listening to the race scratchings on the radio at the same time.

While Katie sucked ferociously at her bottle, the women talked together, picking up the threads of a conversation that they had left off several weeks before. As they spoke, I wandered out to the porcelain hand basins and started playing with the taps. I could both hear and feel the deep rumble of the trams in the street above me.

I adjusted the hot and cold taps until I had a steady stream of warm water running through my fingers. I looked over my shoulder, back towards Nan. The warm water reminded me of an occasion when Nan told me that her deepest wish in life was to spend a whole weekend in a beautiful deep bath, occasionally topping it up with hot water that never ran out. She would have nowhere else to go, and would rest in that big bath all day, playing with the taps. It did not seem like much of a wish at the time, but as I enjoyed the feeling of the warm water running against my skin and slipping between my fingertips, I understood what she meant.

I stood at the basin and looked into the large mirror in front of me. I pretended that I was studying my own face while actually looking at the women pursing their lips and combing their hair in the line of mirrors on either side of me.

These women had come seeking sanctuary from the bustling streets above. Some had their arms loaded up with shopping bags, and just wanted a toilet break. Others, particularly the younger women, went straight for the mirrors with their make-up cases, oblivious to my presence. I watched with fascination as they applied bright-red lipstick, rouged their cheeks, darkened their eyelashes, and brushed their hair.

They were beautiful, those women. They sounded beautiful. As they spoke to each other at the hand basins, their voices echoed off the tiled walls with a richness that I had not heard before—more a song than the spoken word.

After we had finished with Jean, Nan carried the pram up the stairs and into the sunlight. She propped Katie up in the pram so that Katie could take it all in. I walked on ahead of them. We turned into Bourke Street and towards the Myer windows. It appeared that half of Melbourne was pushing and shoving for a glimpse of Snow White and the Seven Dwarfs. The crowd overflowed from the footpath onto the roadway. Passing drivers were yelling and abusing people while slamming a hand down on a car horn. A couple of kids looked as if they were about to be run over for Christmas.

Nan took one look. "Jesus, it's a madhouse."

She tried to push the pram through the crowd, without success. She encouraged me to slip between the legs of the adults and get a closer look, but it was clear that this approach would only result in me getting trampled.

She peered over the shoulders of the crowd before deciding that we should retreat across the road. Nan had had enough of Christmas for one day, or maybe even for another year.

We walked up Bourke Street on the opposite footpath to Myer and headed for home. It was then that I saw him. Although the Woolworth's building stood seven storeys high, he managed to cover every inch of its height. His black boots rested comfortably above the ground-floor verandah. They ended between the first and second storeys. His red trousers were held up by a black belt, around the height of the fourth floor. A long white beard fell to meet the belt and stretched back up over a barrelled chest and wide shoulders. A strong and gentle face smiled down at me from the rooftop. His left hand rested at his side, while the index finger of his right hand beckoned to me.

I stood on the footpath watching that finger as it moved back and forth. I began walking towards him, hypnotised, all the way up Bourke Street, bumping into shoppers as I went.

Nan had not seen what I had.

"Michael! Michael! Where are you going?"

I did not hear her. She walked alongside me, pushing Katie in front of her. She tried grabbing me by the arm.

"Michael, what are you doing? Where do you think you're going?"

I pointed along the street to the Woolworth's building.

"I'm going to see Father Christmas."

Throughout that Christmas season of our first meeting, I continually pestered my grandmother to take me to the Woolworth's corner. Each time that I got there, I would stand on the adjacent corner, outside the Leviathan Building, watching as his finger coaxed children into the store.

My grandmother was reasonably patient with me, although following our third visit into town prior to Christmas, she'd had just about enough of me. "Michael, haven't you had enough of this? You've seen the show, now let's get going."

On the day that I went into town following the New Year, the giant Father Christmas had left. After visiting Jean at the Ladies' toilets again, we turned into Bourke Street. I looked towards his corner and lifted my head in anticipation, but he was gone. I stopped in the street and stared up at seven storeys of blank brick wall.

I raised my hand as I pointed upward. "He's gone. He's gone, Nan."

"Who's gone?" She looked around, all worried, with confusion on her face.

"The Father Christmas—he's gone?"

Nan could only laugh at me. "Yeah, I know he has, love, to the North Pole. You know the story. Don't think he'd hang around here all year. He'd get sick of the heat and noise. Don't worry. He'll be back next year. It's the only job he can get."

Nan thought that was funny and started to chuckle to herself, although I did not think there was anything to laugh about. But she was right. He did come back, the very next year, and for years after that. Once Billie's Christmas card had arrived, I would know that it was again time to lobby for a trip into town.

"Come on, Nan, let's go and see if he's back," I would plead with her.

She would curse Billie for being so early. When we got into town, there would be nothing to look at but a blank wall.

"Looks great," Nan would say.

But each year there would come the day when I would turn the corner at Elizabeth Street and he would be there, where he would stay until the end of the season. We never missed our visits to him, until we moved away and did not know how to get back there, to that street corner.

One day I was walking home from school to the house with Katie, and the next we were leaving the street for the final time, in the back of a furniture van, along with the few possessions that my mother had decided were in good-enough condition to take with us.

None of us dared look back—not me, not Katie, and not Mum, who stared blankly down at a box that she was nursing on her lap. The three-mile drive to the public-housing estate at Richmond might just as well have been three thousand. We knew nobody there, and nobody seemed to want to know us.

Each of us gradually went our separate ways in order to survive the move. The old man went to the pub, Katie retreated to her room, and my mum went to work the night shift in a local factory, baking crumpets, of all things. And I ventured downstairs and onto the basketball court in the middle of the estate. I did not play basketball, but then, nobody else around there did either. The basketball court was where most of the older kids hung out—and where most of the fights took place.

It was when our first Christmas on the estate approached that I fully realised that nothing would be as it had been before. My grandmother's house in Carlton seemed so far away from us now. It felt like we had not seen her in months. Aunt Billie had not visited, and if she had our address, she had not bothered to send a card, as yet.

Mum decided to decorate the Christmas tree early that first year, but it failed to lift us. I sulked around the flat most of the time. Katie was just as bored as I was and did little more than sit around on the new lounge, scuffing her shoes back and forth on the floor tiles. But at least she tried to motivate the two of us into doing something to somehow relocate ourselves.

"Michael, why don't we catch the tram into town, just the two of us, and go and see the Father Christmas? Do you think he'd be back yet?"

I was angry and wanted to take it out on somebody.

"Give up, Katie. Fuck Father Christmas. He's not fucken true. You know that. Jesus, grow up, we're not kids anymore. It's too early yet, anyway."

Katie turned and ran into her bedroom. I could hear her sobbing. I thought about saying sorry, but I couldn't do it. So I ran out of the flat, slamming the heavy steel door behind me. I ran downstairs and over to the basketball court, looking for somebody, anybody, to hang out with.

I found Charlie Noonan, a kid who lived in the block of flats opposite our place. His mother worked the same shift at the crumpet factory as my mum, so I sometimes stayed over at his place while he looked after his younger sister, Alice. She did not really need any looking after, though, seeing as she was not much more than a year younger than he was. They were close in age, but nothing else. They never so much as spoke a word to each other whenever I was over at their place, so I didn't speak to her either.

Charlie was hanging from the steel basketball ring, which along with the backboard was leaning precariously towards the court. It looked as if it was about to collapse on top of him.

He looked across at me. "What you doing?"

"Nothing. You?"

"Nothing. What you want to do?"

"Don't know. You?"

He jumped down from the ring, landing like a cat, on all fours. "You want to strip the roof at the rope works before they knock them down?"

"Yeah, why not."

I followed Charlie to his flat. He grabbed a Hessian bag and a crowbar from behind the kitchen sink.

The rope works were behind the estate. They were about to be bulldozed so that more flats could be built. Competition for the scrap lead and copper was as fierce as it had ever been, so it was important to get in early.

Charlie was quick. As soon as we got to the factory, he wedged the roller-door open with his crowbar, getting us into the factory yard. He then scaled the wall via a drainpipe and got onto the roof, where, after a quick site inspection, he began tearing the pipes away from the old sprinkler system and throwing the lengths of copper down to me.

When he had finished with the piping, he moved onto the skirts of lead around the chimney bases and the capping of the roof pitchers. I looked up for him while following the beat of his footsteps on the corrugated iron.

I heard the first rock smash into a window to the side of me, just seconds before another bounced off the concrete floor directly in front of me, sending out a flash of spark before ricocheting into the factory wall. I looked around.

The Lawrence brothers were standing on the other side of the factory. The three brothers were feared across the estate and beyond. And they never lost a fight, because they hunted together and fought together. And they were psychotic.

I did not know what to do, whether to run or stand. I hated stone fights, but they were hard to avoid. There was little point in running from a stone fight either; taking your chances by attempting to duck a missile was always more sensible than turning your back and getting hit.

A stone fight is not like a fistfight. There is not a lot of skill involved. By throwing rocks into a crowd of kids, somebody has to get hit, eventually. And it's *random*. You can never be sure whether you will be the one to cop it.

The Lawrence brothers looked as if they were about to commence hurling missiles at me. Each of them was holding a handful of broken bricks. The eldest of the three brothers, Arthur, pointed at me.

"You fucken little prick! This is our fucken factory! Fuck off! Leave the scrap on the ground and fuck off!"

The middle brother, Rex, hurled a rock in my general direction in order to give emphasis to Arthur's demand. I had to duck to be sure that it missed me. The rock shattered another pane of glass in the window behind me.

I looked around for Charlie, but I could no longer see or hear him. He may have seen them coming and escaped over the back of the roof. The only way out of the factory yard appeared to be the same roller-door where they were now standing sentry. Leaving the scrap for them wouldn't be enough. They'd give me a belting anyway, just to add to the enjoyment. The three of them began to walk across the yard towards me.

Arthur called to me again. "Are you fucken deaf, you little cunt? Leave the scrap and get the fuck out of here or take a kicking. It's up to you."

As they walked closer, I thought about trying to dodge around them and run out through the factory door. It was all that I could think to do, until I heard Charlie's voice coming from somewhere behind where I was standing.

"Michael! Michael!"

I turned around. I could just see Charlie in a darkened corner, holding an escape door open for me.

"Run, Michael, fucken run!"

I hesitated. My father always told me, "Never run, never run!"

The Lawrence brothers charged at me, hurling rocks and screaming at me as they did so.

Charlie was screaming as well. "Run, fucken run!"

I decided to take Charlie's advice over my father's. I turned and ran towards the narrow opening of the door. Rocks and stones were bouncing off the walls around me. And I could hear Arthur bearing down on me.

"You fucken little bastard! You're fucked, cunt! You're fucked!"

I felt the rock hit me in the back of the head, followed by the taste of vomit in my mouth and a ringing in my ears. I tumbled forward, scrambled on all fours, and then got to my feet again. I reached the doorway. Charlie grabbed hold of my arm and pulled me through, snapping a metal lever behind us.

I could feel the sensation of something warm oozing down the back of my neck. I put a hand to my head and then looked at it. It was blood. We ran across the factory floor and out through an open door on the other side. Charlie led me along a laneway that separated the rope works from the Victoria Street shopping strip. I had to stop. I leaned forward and vomited into the gutter. Charlie tried hurrying me along.

"Come on, Michael! It'll only take them a couple of minutes to catch up with us. If they get hold of us, they'll fucken kill us."

I could feel dampness against the neck of my T-shirt. It was soaked in blood. Charlie noticed it for the first time.

"Fuck! Look at you. You're bleeding."

My legs wobbled under me. Charlie knew that I would not be able to run too far. But he also understood that we could not stay where we were without suffering a lot more pain than I was now in.

He looked along the laneway. "We'll have to hide somewhere. We can't get back to the flats from here." He pointed a little further ahead of us. "Come on, we're going to hide in here."

We ran across the laneway and stopped at the back of the derelict Victory Theatre, which fronted Victoria Street.

"Come on! Come on! In here."

Charlie pushed me through a hole in a cyclone-wire fence. We climbed over piles of rubbish and made our way along a narrow path on the side of the building. The ground was littered with rusting canisters, spilling entrails of old film. Most of the windows into the theatre had been boarded up. Charlie moved along the path until he found a broken window high above us. He stopped.

"Michael, come on! I'll bunk you up. We can get in here. We can climb through the window. Come on. I can fucken hear them coming."

I was still feeling groggy and wanted to be sick again. I felt the back of my head, and the warm blood caked in my hair. I watched Charlie as he knelt forward against the side of the wall and created a stirrup by knitting his fingers together.

"Come on, Michael, let's go."

I put my foot into his hands and reached up for the window ledge at the same time that he lifted me. As I grabbed hold of the ledge, one of my hands was pierced by a piece of jagged glass. I would have stopped and given myself up to the Lawrence brothers there and then if it were not for Charlie's strength driving my body forward.

I poked my head through the window space, catching an immediate whiff of the musty breeze of the theatre. It was the familiar smell of damp plaster and rotting wood that I had grown up with. It was as if I had been transported back to our old place in Fitzroy. All of the seats in the theatre had been removed. A heavy red-velvet curtain remained draped across the stage, and the walls were decorated with old movie posters and signs advertising brands of ice cream and sweets. I could see that there was a chandelier hanging from the domed centre. Large drifting cobwebs also hung from the ceiling and downward to the floor. I could also see that there were cardboard boxes stacked against the walls.

A single large object dominated the floor of the old theatre. The light was poor, but I was immediately able to recognise the familiar figure resting on the ground in front of me. Although I could see him clearly, I had to shake my head a couple of times before I was satisfied that I was fully conscious.

I took another look, scanning him from head to toe.

"Wow. Fucken wow."

Charlie was still supporting my body.

"Come on, Michael. Hurry it up. What is it? What is it?"

I did not get out of the hospital until quite late that night. The doctor had to put twelve stitches in the back of my head and another five in my right hand. Mum waited with me in Casualty and took me home in a taxi.

While we were on our way home, she told me that we had received our Christmas card from Aunt Billie in that afternoon's mail. When we got out of the cab, I looked up to our flat high above the street. I was surprised to see that not only was Katie's bedroom light on, but that she was there at the window, smiling down at me and waving.

As soon as we got into the flat, I went to her room. I wanted her to know that I had found him. She had decorated her bed frame with different-coloured tinsels—red, green, and silver. Hanging over the bedpost was a drawing that she had done, of Father Christmas.

I pointed to the drawing. "Katie," I told her, "we can't go and see him yet. He's not back."

She looked at the drawing and then at me. She immediately understood who I was talking about but seemed puzzled as to how I knew that he was yet to reappear at the Woolworth's building.

"What do you mean, Michael? You haven't been into town today, have you? You've been getting in trouble, and you've been to hospital. Mum told me."

I sat down on her bed. "No, I haven't been into town. But I've seen him. He's still resting, getting ready for the season."

Katie thought that I was making fun of her, I'm sure.

"You seen him, Michael? Where? At the North Pole? Sure."

"No, not at the North Pole. Nan was wrong about that. I saw him at the Pictures. He was at the old picture theatre around in Victoria Street. That's where he goes after he's finished at Woolies for the year. He goes to the movies."

I reached over and brushed the hair from her face with my bandaged hand. "But he'll be back soon. It's the only work he can get. Remember that?" I stroked her forehead. "I'm sorry about what happened this morning, Katie. I hate it here. But I'm really sorry."

She did not say anything at first. She just smiled at me.

I stood up to leave.

"Michael, do you miss the old house?"

I did not have to think about her question.

"Yeah, I miss it a lot, all the time."

"I miss it too."

She moved down to the end of her bed and touched the face of her drawing.

"Can you take me on the tram to see Father Christmas? When he gets back there, that is?"

"Of course, Katie. He'd be lost without us. Looks for us every year, with that mad finger of his."

"And, Michael, can you take me down by our old house, and the old street? Show me where it all used to be, Michael? You think you'd remember? Even with all the places now gone? Can you remember?"

"Of course I can, Katie. That's what I'm here for. That's my job—to remember."

Eyes of the Heart _____

Cast of Characters
Thida San, a Cambodian woman, fifty.
Kim, a Cambodian man, forties.
Dr. Lynne Simpson, an American eye doctor, thirties.
Serey/Oun, a Cambodian woman, Americanized, eighteen. Oun is Thida's daughter, eighteen, seen in flashbacks.
Savath/K.R. Soldier/Sipha/Barber/Mugger, a Cambodian man, twenties.
Chhem, a Cambodian woman, traditional, fifties to sixties.

Notes on the Play
Scenes are played in different areas of the stage, locales are suggested. There are altars both in Kim's apartment and the Buddhist temple; a window in Kim's apartment by which Thida sits. Because Thida is blind, the play has a soundscape, which helps create the context of her world. The time is the late 1980s. The play takes place in Long Beach, California, and Cambodia.

We are sometimes in Thida's mind, and she uses a microphone to distinguish her internal thoughts from her dialogue. In the text, Thida's internal thoughts are italicized. Residents 1, 2, and 3 are heard as voiceovers. In one instance, Dr. Simpson also uses a microphone for internal thoughts.

Scene One _____

[*We hear a flight announcement mixed with airport sounds. The loud wail of a security alarm. Using a cane, Thida San is escorted in by Savath. Thida shrinks back from the assault of sounds. Kim rushes to her. He bows with palms together.*]

KIM   Thida! Sister, you are finally here! We've waited so long. I'm pleased to welcome you to my new home.

[*He embraces her.*]

Thida? It is me, your brother, Kim.

[*He looks at Thida.*]

SAVATH	She isn't speaking.
KIM	[*Confused.*] Isn't speaking? Why?
SAVATH	I'm not sure. They didn't mention it in the papers. She must be overwhelmed.
KIM	[*Maintaining cheerfulness.*] OK. [*Speaking louder.*] We are so happy to see you. It is a miracle you have finally arrived. How was your trip? Are you all right?
SAVATH	She can hear you. She's probably just not talking.
THIDA	*I asked to stay at the temple.*
	[*Kim quickly motions to Serey.*]
KIM	This is Serey, your niece.
	[*Serey lightly touches Thida's shoulder.*]
SEREY	Hello, Aunt.
THIDA	*Like Oun…*
KIM	You remember how she liked to visit you? In your house you had so many lovely things.
SEREY	Dad.
	[*Thida pats something under her shirt, near her heart.*]
THIDA	*Like Oun, in the photograph.*
	[*Kim introduces Savath.*]
KIM	And you met Savath Chin—he's the man who got you here! He never gave up. He flew to the Embassy in Phnom Penh. The paperwork sat there for ages.
SAVATH	Welcome to Los Angeles, Mrs. San.
THIDA	*Los Angeles?*
KIM	We're very relieved to see you. How was your trip? Comfortable?
	[*Kim touches a plastic bag Thida is clutching. Serey has moved away.*]
	[*Calling.*] Serey!…You have no baggage? Nothing?
	[*Thida pats something under her shirt.*]
THIDA	*It is all here.*
KIM	Just crackers from the plane?

[*Kim watches Thida.*]

SAVATH   The papers say she sat in the dark in the temple for years.

SEREY   She didn't want to come to America.

[*Thida pats her shirt, while Serey becomes the young woman Oun. Lights shift.*]

THIDA   *Miracle. A schoolgirl who eats, she breathes, she goes to school. When she comes home, everything is normal. Her father teases her, "Will she be a doctor?" One day my daughter says, "No, I will be a mid-wife." "Why not a doctor?" he asks her. His pride hurt, perhaps. She shrugs her shoulders. She walks away, to her room. To study. She is stubborn…Stop.*

[*Lights are restored to the airport.*]

KIM   Let's go home.

Scene Two

[*Dr. Lynne Simpson, wearing eyeglasses, shows slides while addressing her residents (the audience). Behind her, squiggly, abstract shapes float.*]

DR. SIMPSON   Everything is spectacularly ordered. [*Pointing to first slide on scrim.*] See, there's nothing on this retinal cell—it's clear. You wait for the oddity. It comes rarely. [*Showing second slide on scrim.*] There it is. In night blindness you know exactly what to expect. The retina has this white, murky surface, sometimes like a floating string. This is a floating world, a world where there is no speed, no weight. It's all here in front of us. Every day you wonder what you will discover.

[*Lights cross-fade to Kim leading Thida to an altar in his apartment as Cambodian music plays.*]

KIM   I've made a small offering at the altar for your well-being in America. Rest—we have prepared some food—fried shrimp, rice.

[*Chhem sets down dishes. Kim lights incense.*]

CHHEM   Welcome to Little Phnom Penh, Mrs. San.

THIDA   *Little Phnom Penh? They have renamed an American city?*

KIM   Chhem will be your guide. She is Savath's grandmother. She will take you to the temple.

THIDA   *You said I could live there.*

CHHEM	Yes, I will show you how to take the bus.
THIDA	*The bus?*
CHHEM	I've added some extra sauce. We must be generous. This is your first meal! [*Handing her a bowl.*] Don't be shy.
KIM	Please, take some food, Thida. I insist.
	[*Thida takes the bowl.*]
THIDA	*When I used to find food, I would cut off the smallest piece for me and give Oun the rest. This is for you.*
	[*Thida smells the food. Serey enters holding a book bag.*]
KIM	Come, Serey, sit—eat with us. Thida, you will have your own room with Serey. She has put clothing for you in her closet. [*To Serey.*] Come and talk to your aunt.
SEREY	She doesn't talk.
	[*Thida eats.*]
THIDA	*Delicious.*
SEREY	[*To Thida.*] I'm sorry, I have to go. I'm late.
KIM	Your aunt has just arrived.
SEREY	I know. She stole my room.
THIDA	[*Eating.*] *So flavorful.*
KIM	Stay. She has come from so far away.
	[*Kim goes to a window, lighting a cigarette. Serey puts on lipstick.*]
KIM	Who is that outside?
CHHEM	His name is Trouble.
THIDA	[*Smelling.*] *Smoking.*
SEREY	It's Lee Var, Father. He's helping me with an assignment.
CHHEM	Have you asked Savath for help? He's very intelligent.
KIM	[*Watching Serey; lowering voice.*] That lipstick is very red.
SEREY	"Karma-red"—for energy. I thought you'd like that, Dad. The "karma" thing.
KIM	No, I don't.
THIDA	*Karma lipstick? Is she this old? The age of Oun?*

[*Chhem inspects Serey. She speaks under her breath.*]

CHHEM   The short skirt.

SEREY   This is short?

KIM   Don't talk back to your elders.

SEREY   This is the eighties, Dad. I'll be right back.

[*Thida eats.*]

THIDA   *One more taste. So delicious.*

KIM   One hour. I'm watching the clock.

[*Serey exits.*]

THIDA   *Alone, in my rice world.*

CHHEM   [*To Kim.*] You know, the young do the "slow dance" with the bodies pressed so close together.

[*Chhem demonstrates the closeness with the palms of her hands.*]

I have seen it on TV. Skin-to-skin. The "slow dance."

THIDA   *"Slow dance?" Is that an English word?*

[*Thida stuffs more rice in her mouth as Chhem approaches and picks up her bowl. Thida is startled.*]

CHHEM   Come, look, Kim! Your sister is eating all the food.

THIDA   *The loud one!*

[*Kim goes to Thida, comfortingly.*]

KIM   When we first came, we were so tired we couldn't stop sleeping, couldn't stop eating. We'd look at the food in the grocery stores, and our stomachs would ache with longing. We wanted to eat, but then it would make us sick. We had to take it slow.

[*Kim leads Thida to the altar, where there are family photographs.*]

There is a green mango on the altar for you and a few flowers from my garden. I want to tell you—here, above, there are photographs. The few I was able to hide. They're on the wall. Even here our ancestors protect us.

[*Thida pats something under her shirt as Kim watches.*]

You're *home* now. I will take care of you. We'll bring you to an eye doctor, take you for a physical exam—we'll go to the herb market.

THIDA   *They said you promised I'd go to the temple.*

KIM	Sister, may I ask? I never knew…what happened to your daughter? What happened to Oun?…
THIDA	[*Patting under her shirt.*] *Still here? Are the photos still here?*
	[*Lights shift as Oun appears in front of Thida. She is weak and malnourished.*]
KIM	Why don't you talk? We've waited so long. *I* still have Serey. I wonder what happened…
	[*Oun works in a rice field.*]
THIDA	*She is hungry. The soup—or so they call it—is mostly water now, with only a few grains of rice floating on the surface. We see ourselves in the grains of rice, disappearing. We count them every day. One, two, three. They barely color the water anymore.*
	[*A young Khmer Rouge soldier appears, watching Oun.*]
	Stop. Swimming. On a beach, there were magnolia trees. Clear aqua water. [*Another memory intrudes.*] *Another magnolia tree. I want to die.*

Scene Three

	[*Thida stares off as Dr. Simpson studies a chart, speaking to Kim.*]
DR. SIMPSON	Before she came, they told you she was blind. It's true: she displays all the outward symptoms. But her exam reveals no physical problem. She has normal visual acuity. Her vision should improve to normal.
KIM	I don't understand.
DR. SIMPSON	Her eyes are sending signals to her brain.
	[*Kim motions to a printout in the chart.*]
KIM	May I see the results? Yes, it is very strange. Her eyes work, but she cannot see. She's not lying.
	[*Dr. Simpson makes a quick hand gesture in front of Thida's eyes. Thida doesn't react.*]
DR. SIMPSON	Can you explain how this might have happened?
KIM	No. There are many others like her.
	[*Dr. Simpson looks at Thida for a moment.*]
	She refuses to speak.

DR. SIMPSON	All the outward signs of blindness, but her eyes are healthy.
KIM	It defies all odds.
DR. SIMPSON	Let me try something else.

[*Dr. Simpson exits.*]

KIM	You're in America now, Sister. Perhaps you can explain to the doctor, and somebody can help. I've brought you to a specialist. If you could tell me when you lost your sight…What happened? You can trust me.

[*Thida pats under her shirt. Oun and the blue of ocean appear.*]

THIDA	*Swimming. We went only months before the schoolgirl photograph where all is normal. She was a fish. Standing at the shore, calling to her. "You are a fish! You are a fish!" And when she finally walked out of the sea at Kep, unconcerned, vain in her unawareness, simply… Oun…we would laugh. Sipha and I would laugh. We were so mad. It was late, we were hungry, and she would force us to stand on the shore calling to her, screaming for her. Her black head bobbing up and down in the waves, against the line of the horizon. But when she came, she was transformed. From so much time in the sea. And she would spray water through her teeth—a trick she learned—and we would laugh…We would laugh and walk under the magnolia trees…*

[*Dr. Simpson reenters and tapes electrodes to Thida's forehead.*]

Stop. All because there were also magnolias on the shore at Kep… Swimming, swimming…Anything to turn the clock back…Because the moments after—they are all accounted for, every detail, every movement. In my head I want it to stop.

DR. SIMPSON	Now I'm going to tip back your head and insert this contact lens in your eye…

[*Kim watches Dr. Simpson tip back Thida's head. Thida flinches.*]

KIM	I'm sorry—in Cambodia touching the head is considered very personal.
DR. SIMPSON	Perhaps it would be better if you put in the lens. It has an electrode on it.
KIM	Yes, I'll do it. Thank you.
DR. SIMPSON	You may want to tell her not to close her eye, or the lens will come out.
KIM	We know English, we were educated. She was a midwife, and I was a doctor. But she doesn't speak.

	[*Dr. Simpson studies Thida.*]
THIDA	*This doctor's quick—she has no time. Empty—without a soul. She drinks coffee, smokes. Sipha smoked.*
DR. SIMPSON	So she can't tell me what she sees?
	[*Thida stares off as colored lights flash in front of her. Dr. Simpson and Kim watch lines with jagged peaks dash across a screen.*]
KIM	Thida? If you see something, can you nod your head?
	[*Thida does not nod.*]
THIDA	*Darkness.*
DR. SIMPSON	If she can't talk, it makes it difficult to examine her.
THIDA	*Don't cry.*
DR. SIMPSON	Ask her if she sees the lights.
KIM	Sister, did you hear the doctor? Do you see the light?
THIDA	*I see nothing.*
	[*Dr. Simpson consults Thida's chart.*]
DR. SIMPSON	How did she lose her sight?
THIDA	*Don't cry.*
KIM	I don't know. It was during the Pol Pot regime. We were separated.
DR. SIMPSON	Did she have eye problems before that?
KIM	I know she wore glasses. For distances.
DR. SIMPSON	But with the glasses she could see.
KIM	Yes. The Khmer Rouge tried to eliminate all intellectuals. They killed people who wore glasses.
DR. SIMPSON	Does she have any other kinds of physical problems?
KIM	Not that a physical exam detects.
	[*As Dr. Simpson untapes the electrodes, the flashing lights fade.*]
DR. SIMPSON	Her eyes are sending signals to her brain.
KIM	Yes, I saw the ERG.
DR. SIMPSON	Your sister may be malingering, Mr. Lok. Is she applying for disability? Benefits for blindness are higher in California than anywhere else. I'd like to check something.

[*Dr. Simpson looks through charts as Kim touches Thida.*]

KIM Are you there? What would happen if you spoke? Would it be so bad? They've taken the time to see you, they want to help.

[*Thida keeps her head lowered.*]

DR. SIMPSON Does your sister know Bina Prak? She also lives in Long Beach.

KIM No, why do you ask?

DR. SIMPSON Well, she came in to be tested. She was applying for disability benefits too, and she had the same problem as your sister.

KIM Doctor, my sister just arrived from Cambodia. She's not applying for disability.

DR. SIMPSON Isn't it sort of strange—two women the same age, from the same country, living in the same city? It sounds suspicious.

KIM I said before, my sister would not lie. It's not strange. I've seen many other women like her. They are not making it up.

DR. SIMPSON How do you know?

KIM Because I've lived among them. Those of us who survived ended up in refugee camps in Thailand.

THIDA *Don't cry, don't cry, or they will kill you.*

DR. SIMPSON How did you get to Long Beach?

KIM My friend's grandson worked to bring us here.

DR. SIMPSON Have you seen the blind women here too?

KIM Yes.

DR. SIMPSON It's odd…Perhaps I could see more of them. Could you help?

KIM Why not? [*Looking at her, curious.*] If you are interested.

DR. SIMPSON Yes, yes, who knows? Clinically, it might prove useful.

[*Dr. Simpson looks at him, taking parking stickers from her doctor's coat. Cigarettes fall out.*]

I don't smoke.

KIM Me neither.

[*She nods, then scribbles.*]

DR. SIMPSON Make sure you give this validation to the parking guy, or he'll charge you an arm and a leg.

[*In Kim's apartment, Thida sits by an open window as light from a street lamp shines in. She unpins a plastic bag inside her shirt and takes out a photo. She passes her hand over it. Sipha, wearing a white doctor's coat, appears in the shadows.*]

THIDA   *He stands in the back of the truck. With other doctors in white coats.*

[*He mimes for her to be quiet.*]

He puts his finger to his mouth, telling me to be quiet.

[*She nods. He gestures.*]

He motions for me to take off my glasses.

[*She mimes.*]

I take them off. He gestures to get rid of them.

[*She mimes.*]

I throw them on the ground and I crush them with my foot. My sight is now blurred as I look at him. The man I love. He simply looks back. The truck starts to go. I look at him, but I cannot see him clearly. The truck begins to move away, a cloud of dust.

[*She extends her hand.*]

Sipha.

[*The sound of gunfire comes through the window. Thida holds the photo to her breast as Sipha disappears. A siren wails, and she crouches down. Kim and Serey enter.*]

KIM   Sister? What are you doing? What's happened to you?

SEREY   What's wrong with her? What's her problem?

[*Kim puts his arm around Thida as Serey takes books out of her bag.*]

KIM   Please don't be frightened. It is simply the police. I had to go outside and retrieve Serey from her own folly. You are safe.

SEREY   You're not actually that safe. There are gangs.

THIDA   *Are there boys with guns?…*

KIM   Serey, don't tell her that.

THIDA   *Smoking cigarettes, Brother?*

SEREY   They live in our building.

KIM	That was a police siren. You are fine inside. There is no problem.

[*Kim helps Thida to her seat by the window. Serey starts to go.*]

	Don't think I have forgotten what I saw.
SEREY	Forget it.
KIM	His car is enough.
THIDA	*His car?*
KIM	If your mother was alive, she would agree with me about Savath.
SEREY	You're the one in love with Savath.
KIM	That isn't funny. You liked him, you told me so. He's very respectable.
SEREY	Maybe too much. Have you seen how he dresses?
KIM	Is it because I like him, suddenly you don't? You've been out with him once—was it so bad?
SEREY	Yeah, I'm not ready. I need to have some fun.
KIM	One thing you won't have is fun with [*pointing outside*] the guy with the car, I can assure you.
SEREY	Oh, and you know this by telepathy?
KIM	I know you are very clever, but in this case you are not seeing clearly. You are too American. Try again with Savath. He was friends with your brother.

[*Kim lights a cigarette.*]

	My daughter has driven me to smoking.
THIDA	*You always smoked.*
KIM	Oh God, why won't you say anything?
THIDA	*You don't want to hear what I have to say.*

[*Kim exits as Serey gets some books.*]

SEREY	We yell all the time. Sorry I said that about the gangs. It's scary, but it's not that bad. Besides a few bullets coming in through the front door—just kidding. No, there were some once, but it's OK. He hardly ever mentions my mother. You really think she'd want me to marry Savath? Sometimes I pray to her. Savath is good looking, but who wants someone your dad picked out? My father was different when my mom was around. We used to have some fun. We'd catch fish together. Sing songs. We were just crazy. But that was before

Pol Pot. Now I'm supposed to marry Savath because he was friends with my brother? Everyone's dead. Good way to guilt people, huh? [*To herself.*] Asking *you?* What was I thinking?

[*Serey passes her hand in front of her aunt's expressionless eyes.*]

Can you see? He's wanted you to come so bad. You were supposed to save us from something.

[*Serey takes her mirrored sunglasses and puts them on Thida.*]

Hey, when you're around people, maybe you wanna wear these.

[*Thida feels them, surprised.*]

THIDA   *Are they eyeglasses?*

[*Serey looks at herself in the mirrored glasses.*]

SEREY   You can see yourself in them. They're sunglasses.

[*Thida stares out, wearing the sunglasses.*]

THIDA   *Words won't bring them back, Serey.*

[*Serey exits. Thida sits by the open window in Kim's apartment in darkness. Night slowly turns to day. She listens to the sound of construction vehicles, followed by the sound of a jackhammer. She takes out another photo from the plastic bag pinned to her shirt. She passes her hand over it.*]

A cloud of dust. Sipha disappears. I dress myself and my daughter as peasants. We work in the fields, pray to the spirits that the soldiers will not see us, that we will disappear. They find us—try to force Oun to marry.

[*Sunlight shines in Thida's eyes, and she shields them from the glare. Oun appears with a young Khmer Rouge soldier in the shadows.*]

SOLDIER   [*Commanding Thida.*] You, come here! You are the mother, you must watch!

THIDA   *Sun shines in my eyes—I leave my hut, walk towards the tree.* [*Stopping the memory.*] *Stop.*

SOLDIER   You must watch your daughter!

THIDA   *The people watch, expressionless. I search their eyes for clues. Stone faces.*

[*Communist propaganda music from loudspeakers becomes louder and louder.*]

Magnolia flowers fall. She is tied with rope. No!

[Lights are restored as Kim enters in gardening clothes.]

KIM   You never sleep? I want you to come outside to my garden for a little fresh air—*you must.*

THIDA   *Fresh? Where is this city where the smell is so bad?*

KIM   *[Giving her a lime.]* Here is a lime from California. Take it. I have avocados, too. They will soon be ripe. I never tasted avocado in Cambodia, did you? *[A new thought.]* Sister, do you remember that fruit we had in our garden when we were young? With the milky white flesh and the black seed? Teak dos ko? So delicious. It doesn't exist here. It has no name. But with time, it will come. Some Cambodian will learn to grow it. And then it will have a name, Americans will learn to love it, and they will mass-produce it. The fruit will become bigger and bigger, the colors more vibrant, and finally, it will lose all its flavor so that it tastes only like water.

[She drops the lime. He returns it and sees the photos on her lap.]

Can you see the photos, Thida?

[Thida finally responds by nodding.]

[Looking at her.] Ah, you made a sign. Finally. You said yes. You can see the photos. I don't understand.

THIDA   *I see Oun and Sipha.*

[He sees Thida put her hands together, praying.]

KIM   You want to pray. Yes, we will bring you to our new temple like I promised. *[Lying.]* It is much like the temples in Cambodia. Well, it is a haven for many, let us say.

THIDA   *I want to become a nun. I have nothing to hope for but the next life.*

[The construction sounds. She looks toward the sounds.]

KIM   Do you hear? They are repairing the road outside. It's a bulldozer. The other noise is a machine to break up the cement. All the soil they cover with cement here. Concrete. They want to seal away the earth.

Scene Five _____

[Sounds of busy traffic. Chhem looks up at a bus-stop sign as she guides Thida. Underneath the sign is another sign, which reads NO STANDING.]

CHHEM	The bus stops here, but we cannot wait here, Thida.
THIDA	*I would prefer to go home.*
CHHEM	Don't worry. We'll wait on the next corner. It's safe on the next corner.

[*Chhem leads Thida away from the bus stop.*]

THIDA	*The city's loud, always a hum like rushing water, an electric current. Is the city breathing?*
CHHEM	[*Stopping.*] Here, we will wait here. Your brother is very worried about you. Poor man, he must work during the day and cannot take you to the temple. You are safe with me. No problem, I'm a good guide. Serey, she is driving your brother to madness. The boyfriend, the car! The car is called a "Trans Am"! Very, very big. Very white! New: when the sun shines on it, it gleams like a jewel in her eyes.

[*Sound of a bus approaching.*]

The bus is coming, Thida! Now we must run!

[*Chhem tries to run and to pull Thida with her.*]

THIDA	*Why must we chase the bus?*
CHHEM	Hurry, Thida! Please!

[*Thida drops her cane. Chhem goes to pick it up. The sound of the bus pulling away.*]

[*Upset.*] Well, this is unfortunate. The monk is waiting at the temple, and now we'll be late. Don't worry, it is not your fault. Come.

[*Chhem leads Thida back to where they were waiting.*]

The sign says we cannot stand there. "NO STANDING"! There is an arrow that points in both directions!

[*Chhem points to something offstage near the bus stop.*]

Oh, I see a man is standing right next to the forbidding sign! Maybe we can stand behind him. This way if something happens, he will be punished first.

[*Chhem leads Thida as lights cross-fade to Kim with Dr. Simpson in a teashop, sampling tea and smoking.*]

DR. SIMPSON	I drink Lipton.
KIM	[*Horrified.*] In a teabag?
DR. SIMPSON	What else?

KIM	I'll buy you some tea on the way out so you can *enjoy* it.
DR. SIMPSON	What would I put it in?
KIM	A pot?
DR. SIMPSON	I drink coffee anyway.
KIM	You need to take a little time—go ahead, sip it slowly. Sustenance. Of course, the cigarette doesn't help. But we can't have everything.
DR. SIMPSON	No.
KIM	The temple is an old union hall on Willow Street. Some of the blind women pray there. Afternoons are best to find them.
DR. SIMPSON	They'll have to come to my office. When did you first see the blind women?
KIM	Among the refugees in the Thai camps.
DR. SIMPSON	It couldn't be malnutrition, or they would have regained their sight.
KIM	In our country, the head is considered the place where the soul resides. It's the window through which life enters and exits.
DR. SIMPSON	Would you consider bringing your sister by my office again? I want to start by looking for an organic basis in the women. What do they have in common?
KIM	That's what you have to find out. You know, doctors like myself, in Cambodia, are…were more experimental. My sister knew much about herbs, and I used many of her remedies. I used to love seeing the whole world.
DR. SIMPSON	What do you mean?
KIM	Before Pol Pot, I looked at everything. From my head to my feet. My heart, my brain. And outward. The infinite. Now it's the opposite. I see only limits. I walk on a tightrope. How will I survive?
	[*She looks at him a moment.*]
DR. SIMPSON	What is your answer?
KIM	My family. If I can save them, that's all that matters.
	[*He looks at her.*]
	What about your family?
	[*She does not answer the question.*]
DR. SIMPSON	If I can find the physical reason for the women's problem, I can help them. What would make them see again?

KIM	You didn't answer my question. [*Looking at her.*] You're right. What would make them see again? [*Asking about her.*] What would help?
	[*Chhem guides Thida into the darkness of a Buddhist temple. Above the altar is a faded sign:* OIL-CHEMICAL AND ATOMIC WORKERS UNION LOCAL 1-128. *Thida kneels as Chhem exits. Sipha appears in the shadows.*]
THIDA	*Sipha, you're here! I should never have forced her. I was always stubborn. Please say something. Say something to me. Come, sit.*
	[*He sits next to Thida.*]
	Tell me where you go.
	[*He stares straight ahead.*]
SIPHA	I travel through jungles where the forest's so thick I can barely squeeze by. Swim in rivers where you can catch the fish in thin air. At the seaside, the sand is mixed with the bones and teeth of farmers.
THIDA	*The temples—tell me about the temples!*
SIPHA	I dance with the celestial dancers—and there are thousands—on the walls of the ancient city.
THIDA	*Are you so popular?*
SIPHA	Yes, in the nighttime, serenaded by the soft rush of the wind, so seductive with their necklaces of jasmine falling on their breasts. The thieves in the night cut off the statues' heads. The heads reappear in foreign lands, chopped off, eyes gouged from their sockets.
THIDA	*The dancing!*
SIPHA	Vines grow through the rock, strangling, squeezing the stone, cracking the faces, erasing the shrines. Soon the temples of Angkor will vanish.
THIDA	*Dancing.*
SIPHA	In the distance you can hear the snap of land mines—another little boy running home, too careless.
THIDA	*Sipha.*
SIPHA	Near Siem Reap in an empty schoolhouse, there are rusted shackles from its days as a torture center. Bones piled high to the sky, mountains and mountains of bones. When the air is still, you can hear the skulls whispering to each other. [*He whispers menacingly.*] SSSsssssssss…snakes…

[*Thida speaks aloud for the first time.*]

THIDA   Stop!

[*Chhem reenters.*]

CHHEM   [*Shocked.*] Thida? You can talk? You are finally speaking.

[*Thida is silent.*]

Who are you talking to? Who is here?

[*Thida watches Sipha slip away.*]

THIDA   Sipha. He is not what I want him to be.

CHHEM   Sipha?

[*Thida stares at the place where Sipha was.*]

THIDA   [*To Chhem.*] I cannot speak about it. I am sorry. It is too difficult. I...

[*Chhem leads Thida out.*]

CHHEM   Come, you are haunted. You are speaking! At home I will coin you
             to make you feel better. Are you glad you came to the temple today?

[*Graffiti appears, and there are street sounds as Thida walks with
Chhem, who looks up.*]

The sign is usually right here, but it has disappeared. Perhaps the
wind blew it down in the storm.

THIDA   What storm?

CHHEM   All the buildings look the same. Ugly, so ugly. [*Panicking.*] No
             trees. Always the gangsters on the corners. One in my block has a
             tiger on his arm, a tattoo. Always smoking, just boys, painting the
             buildings all different colors like children!

[*Thida hears the construction sounds in the distance.*]

It is pitiful. We are lost, so lost.

[*Thida begins to speak aloud, soothingly.*]

THIDA   I believe I know the right direction, Chhem. I do hear the sound of
             the road construction. My brother told me they are repairing the
             road. Cement. [*With vigor.*] Yes, come now!

Scene Six

[*Chhem coins Thida as Kim stands near the altar.*]

CHHEM   And she told me to follow the bulldozer and got us home!

KIM	She spoke to you? Truly!
CHHEM	Yes.
THIDA	How else was I ever going to get home?
KIM	Thida!
CHHEM	She said *you* told her there was roadwork on the street—she heard it. And she was talking to ghosts at the temple. She's getting better.
KIM	I hope.
CHHEM	Your daughter, Serey, is getting older. She is very studious. [*Ominously.*] And very beautiful.
KIM	Thank you. You are kind.
CHHEM	[*Teasingly.*] You know, without my grandson your sister would still be in Cambodia.
KIM	We are very grateful.
THIDA	[*Muttering.*] No, we are not!
KIM	[*Looking at Thida.*] What, Sister?
CHHEM	Savath is at the agency from dawn to midnight, never stops. Meetings with bigwigs from government offices, visits to shelters, casinos. He goes because other people lose their shirts—not him! You know that he and Serey had a date…I did not hear that it was a failure. They did not run in opposite directions.
KIM	Perhaps we should adapt to the American way, encourage another date.
CHHEM	My grandson is old enough to be a monk.
KIM	Serey is younger. I worry…
CHHEM	In a blink of an eye, all this will change. [*Threateningly.*] In a car.
KIM	You don't need to tell me. But she is a good daughter. We have lost so much, I want to protect her.
CHHEM	Exactly! We're all that's left. Our families knew each other. Savath is the right choice, the best insurance a father could buy. He is Cambodian. A good man. College educated. We will bring two families together. I will consult the astrologer, and we can arrange a marriage.
KIM	Go ask him.

[*Kim exits with Chhem.*]

THIDA   *I am in between a tiger and a crocodile. Please let me out of here—I*
                 need to go home.

                 [*Dr. Simpson, alone, exhausted, drinking coffee, clicks through slides*
                 of healthy retinal cells. She shuts off the machine and gets up, search-
                 ing the darkness.]

DR. SIMPSON   Tom, are you there?

                 [*She lets down her guard to someone in the darkness.*]

                 Can you see me?

                 [*She searches a moment longer, then puts her armor back on.*]

                 I don't believe in ghosts.

                 [*Lights shift as Dr. Simpson clicks through slides of healthy retinal*
                 cells, addressing her residents (the audience).]

                 Sovandy Meng: her job was to carry bodies to mass graves. Fifty-
                 two years old. Blind in 1977. [*Referring to slide.*] Healthy retinal cell.
                 Chantha Li: last child died of starvation. Age sixty. Blind in 1978.
                 [*Showing slide.*] Healthy retinal cell. Ang Malay: saw a baby thrown
                 against a tree. Age fifty-four. 1976. [*Showing slide.*] Healthy retinal
                 cell. Navy Hun: saw her sister killed—because of her white skin? At
                 the beginning of the genocide. In her fifties. 1975. [*Showing slide.*]
                 Healthy retinal cell. Thida San: she won't talk about what happened
                 to her family…All of them should see.

Scene Seven _____

                 [*Thida listens to a siren as she sits at her usual seat by the window.*
                 At the altar, Kim smokes, showing Serey astrological charts.]

KIM   The stars say yes, Serey. Chhem has made a very substantial offer,
                 but more importantly I want to join Savath to our family. This will
                 please our ancestors and tie us to our lost country.

SEREY   I'm not in love with him, Father.

KIM   You will grow to love him, as I grew to love your mother.

SEREY   But that's not the way things are here. People date before they get
                 married—they fall in love!

KIM   We do, too. Simply in reverse. Since you were a little girl, you have
                 known that your mother and I would arrange your marriage. Now
                 that she is gone, it is up to me to make the right choice, to honor

her. It is the single most important way you can show her your respect.

SEREY   Everything has changed. We aren't in Cambodia.

KIM   We must honor our dead and preserve our traditions.

SEREY   But we live in a new country.

KIM   It is very important. Please don't contradict me, Serey. I am your father. You will thank me later.

SEREY   I can't start having babies now. What if I want to go to college?

KIM   Then you will go. You are no longer a girl. Savath is a sensitive soul, refined and ethical. He will make a good husband for you.

SEREY   I won't marry him.

[*Haunted, Thida hears Communist propaganda music. She addresses Kim.*]

THIDA   Yes, she will, she will. Give me a moment. Let me speak to her. Say yes, Oun—my girl. You must say yes.

[*Kim touches Thida.*]

KIM   Sister, what are you saying?

[*She pushes him away, continuing out loud.*]

THIDA   Rays of sunlight shine into my eyes. The loudspeakers are hanging in the tree. There are flowers on the tree. She is tied. Water drips from a tiny hole in a bucket, on her head. The drops of water mix with her tears. They tied Oun to a tree. A magnolia. They're forcing her to marry.

SEREY   [*To Kim, softly.*] Her daughter, Oun?

THIDA   The official, he unties her. He points to young soldier. "Will you marry him?" She shakes her head no. She is stubborn. *Will not accept.* The official takes out his blade. He grabs Oun by the hair. They cut off her head.

KIM   Sister…

THIDA   He looks at me. He holds her head. He throws it into a fire where a pile of corpses and body parts burn…Smoke got in my eye…Don't cry, don't cry, or they kill you. [*To Kim.*] Please. Let me die.

KIM   No, it is important to live.

[*Kim holds her. Lights black out.*]

[*Morning. Thida wears the mirrored sunglasses as rock music plays. A punk barber watches as she enters the barbershop with her cane.*]

THIDA There is very loud music in the barbershop, but it is cool. It smells of smoke and soap.

[*The barber spins around a chair for her.*]

BARBER Whoa, first customer. You're an early bird. Sit.

THIDA *He ties something around my neck.*

BARBER Hey, how'd you want it cut?

THIDA Shaved, please.

BARBER Sure you want it shaved?

THIDA Yes. Please. I am going to the temple. Now I must become a nun.

BARBER What's your name?

THIDA *This is not the practice in my country: to ask the name of the customer.* My name is Thida San. [*Politely.*] What is your name?

BARBER The Spider.

THIDA Hello, the Spider. *Am I wrong in remembering that the spider is an insect?*

[*The barber shaves her head, except for one spot. She stands with her cane and feels the spot with her fingertips. She realizes that it has her initials, TS.*]

Thank you.

[*Lights rise on Kim's apartment. He is near the altar and is frantic, waiting on the phone. Serey and Chhem stand nearby.*]

KIM You call the police, you get put on hold…I trusted you to watch her, Serey!

SEREY Dad, I stayed up until five A.M. with her. She was asleep.

KIM You promised me you'd stay awake. We said we'd take turns.

SEREY I dozed off!

KIM I can't trust you. [*On phone.*] What is taking so long?

SEREY It was terrible what she told us. What do you think she'll do, Dad? I'm scared.

CHHEM	[*Confused.*] Nowhere in the neighborhood. Perhaps she took the wrong bus.
SEREY	She kept on saying she wanted to be alone.
KIM	I can think of nothing scarier for her than to be alone outside in Long Beach. [*To Serey.*] How could you let this happen?
SEREY	It's not my fault. She hates it here—she can't rest. We yell too much.
KIM	She's been keeping Oun's death inside all this time. I didn't know what to say. I've tried so hard to forget. [*Listening on phone.*] Yes…I'll repeat it again. Thida San, Cambodian, blind…T-H-I-D-A, 245 Seventh, Little Phnom Penh…And please, I'll be right over. [*Hanging up.*] I'll go to the police station, then check back with the doctor.
CHHEM	We will find Thida. Thida knows more than she pretends. We will look everywhere. Savath always knows what to do.
KIM	Chhem, will you go back to the temple and check again? And go with Serey so you don't get lost, too!
	[*Lights shift to Thida, wearing the sunglasses and walking with her cane, as we hear street sounds.*]
THIDA	*I walk in a quiet place, the sun is so hot—hear only an occasional car. The wind blows sharply, as if through a tunnel.*
	[*Behind her a man appears.*]
MUGGER	Hey! Your money, man. Hey!
THIDA	*Grabs my arm so tight.*
	[*He spins her around, knocking her glasses to the ground.*]
MUGGER	Your money!
	[*He pulls a knife. Thida unpins the plastic bag pinned to her undershirt.*]
THIDA	My brother tells me to carry it always.
MUGGER	Whatever, lady.
	[*She pulls American bills from among her photos. Sound of a car approaching. The mugger grabs the plastic bag with photos and exits, crushing the sunglasses. Thida bends down and touches the ground.*]
THIDA	*Sipha. Oun.*
	[*Her fingers find the discarded plastic bag, the glasses.*]

I feel only crushed eyeglasses.

[*She stands, putting her hand to her breast where her photos just were. We hear the sound of cars speeding by. Against the blue, Thida bends down and feels the ground with her fingers.*]

I am now walking on earth, not on cement. In the distance I can hear the sound of strong wind in the trees…or perhaps it is the sound of waves.

[*The sound slowly becomes crashing waves. Lights shift to Savath, holding a map and hurrying to Serey and Chhem outside Kim's apartment.*]

CHHEM   What took you so long? We've searched every street…

SAVATH   Everyone's looking: my agency, the temple, the community center. I've broken up the area into sections on the map.

           [*Thida is walking.*]

THIDA   *Yes, I must be walking near the sea! Soon I will reach down and feel the sand. White. I say to Sipha as we walk, "Look at the sand, not the bones."*

SAVATH   [*To Chhem.*] I want you to go to every neighbor and ask what they saw. She could be hiding right around here—that can happen. [*To Serey.*] You go with her and page me on my beeper. What was she like last time you saw her?

SEREY   I think she probably wanted to kill herself.

SAVATH   You should've told me that on the phone.

SEREY   She told us something bad about her daughter.

SAVATH   That makes a big difference for the police.

           [*Thida continues to walk.*]

THIDA   *I'm going to the sea. Back to Cambodia.*

           [*Savath speaks to Serey.*]

SAVATH   Where would she go?

SEREY   Rushing traffic, the ocean? I don't know. It was a shock for her to let it out. I can't believe I let her run away.

SAVATH   It's OK, we'll report that, too. We've got about a hundred people looking—even the monks. Your father is out with the detective.

SEREY   What she told us…it makes me feel so empty. Like the worst part of the Thai camps.

SAVATH   I know…that's how I felt when I lost my sister.

               [*He looks at her, calm and optimistic.*]

               Hey, she survived the killing fields—she'll survive this.

               [*Thida sits cross-legged as the sun colors her face fiery orange. She lis-
               tens to the rhythmic sound of oil pumps.*]

THIDA   [*Lifting her head, sun on her face.*] Ah, sun. Was it waves I heard,
               lapping on the shore? No, I was tired, from walking. [*Listening.*] But
               what is that strange "Whir, whir, whir"? I don't recognize that. It
               comforts me…I'm floating. Below are the trees. And blue-green as
               far as I see. [*A beautiful vision.*] The beach at Kep!

               [*She meditates as lights fade to night and sits, listening to the oil
               pumps, as Savath, holding a flashlight, walks over to her and leans
               down, touching her gently so as not to frighten her.*]

SAVATH   Mrs. San? It's Savath. Your family is here now. We've been looking
               since yesterday. The police that found you said you didn't want to
               talk.

               [*Kim and Serey rush in, exclaiming relief.*]

KIM   Thida! Thida! [*Laughing from panic.*] I'm about to have a heart
               attack, and you're calmly meditating. You shaved your head?

THIDA   I tried to walk to the sea.

SEREY   You went in the wrong direction. If something had happened, I
               never would've forgiven myself.

KIM   You shouldn't have run away.

SAVATH   L.A.'s a dangerous place.

               [*Serey touches the initials on her scalp.*]

SEREY   Where did the letters on your head come from?

THIDA   The Spider.

KIM   I am more and more astonished.

               [*Serey touches Thida's ripped clothing.*]

SEREY   What happened to your shirt?

               [*Thida feels where the plastic bag was pinned to her shirt.*]

THIDA   They robbed me of the photographs of my family.

SAVATH   She got mugged.

THIDA	After that, I felt I must finally return.
KIM	Return where, Sister?
THIDA	To the beach at Kep. I am not alive.
KIM	Of course you are. We see you right here in front of us. Living, breathing.
THIDA	My soul left my body and traveled to Kep.
KIM	I was mistaken to leave you alone with Serey. Now I understand why you wanted to hide in the dark for so long in our country. I wish I could've been there to comfort you.
THIDA	You promised I could go to your temple to live. I have waited long enough!
KIM	You wouldn't be safe at the temple. It's with your family that you'll finally get better, surrounded by those who care for you.
SEREY	My dad's right. We want you to get better now, Auntie.
THIDA	Without my vision I am useless.
KIM	I sometimes feel that I can't live, but we go on for our ancestors. The doctor got money from the university to study your case. Here's someone who wants to solve the problem. Of course there's a scientific answer. And one day you'll see again. You will see Serey's children.
SEREY	I may not have children.
	[*Kim gives her a dirty look.*]
	But if I do, sure, you can see them. Or not. Whatever. We just want you to be happier. We meant no disrespect.
	[*Kim holds Thida to him.*]
KIM	We're the last survivors of our family. You have to trust me.
THIDA	I want to become a nun. That is final!
SEREY	The temple is a warehouse with peeling paint. You wouldn't want to live there.
THIDA	*He* said it was like the temples in Cambodia.
SEREY	He lies sometimes.
KIM	Serey.
SEREY	Sees things through rose-colored glasses. I'll take you to the temple more often, I promise.

[*Thida listens to the oil pumps.*]

THIDA   Where am I?

SAVATH   You're in an oil field.

Scene Nine

[*Thida taps her cane impatiently as Dr. Simpson shows Kim her research in her office.*]

DR. SIMPSON   There are about 150 survivors—a cluster of women in Long Beach who don't know each other. I can't find any anywhere else. We're testing blood pressure, heart rate, doing neurological tests. My colleagues are looking forward to meeting you, Thida.

THIDA   I am not here.

KIM   You need to stop saying that now. You are clearly here in front of us. [*To Dr. Simpson.*] She says her soul left her body and traveled to the beach at Kep. [*To Thida.*] A soul is a mysterious thing. It wanes like the moon, but it comes back to full, you'll see.

DR. SIMPSON   We'll do an ERG and an MRI so we can look at your brain.

THIDA   Do so at your own risk.

KIM   Stop that with your cane. They want to ask you some questions about your background.

THIDA   She doesn't listen.

DR. SIMPSON   What kind of suffering could be so great that it would blind someone? It's the grief that interests me and how that affects the eye.

THIDA   You do not understand.

KIM   What?

THIDA   I see the same things over and over in my head. At night I cannot sleep. My head pounds, as if a nail is being twisted into it.

DR. SIMPSON   We need to give you some medicine for your headache, Thida. That will help.

KIM   Of course. Why didn't you tell me this?

THIDA   [*To Dr. Simpson.*] I do not want the medicine. It's bad for you. [*To Kim.*] I want to go to the temple. Plan a ceremony for Sipha.

KIM   What are you talking about now?

THIDA	Release him.
DR. SIMPSON	Who is Sipha?
KIM	Her husband.
DR. SIMPSON	Medicine will help for your headache. [*To Kim.*] I'll need her to come with me to the resident presentation, and if she could come back for more tests, I have the women scheduled all week.
KIM	I'll be interested to see if you can find any organic basis for this.
DR. SIMPSON	Yes, the funders were generous with something that could easily be interpreted as psychosomatic. [*Joking.*] It also helps my reputation for not being a "people person."
KIM	I see. I loved doing research. Here, in this country, I'm a lab technician. This is more exciting than doing blood work.
DR. SIMPSON	I'm sure you were a good doctor. I'm grateful to you.
THIDA	I feel sick.
KIM	You must go with Dr. Simpson.
THIDA	[*Muttering to herself.*] The walking dead. [*To Dr. Simpson.*] Can you make yourself useful and take me to the temple, doctor?
KIM	Thida!
DR. SIMPSON	[*To Kim.*] I'll make sure someone gets her home, about five. Will someone be there?
KIM	Yes. Just don't lose her.
	[*Kim exits and lights shift as Dr. Simpson addresses her residents, who are in silhouette, examining Thida.*]
DR. SIMPSON	No country has lost such a sizable part of its population in such a short time and was stripped of an entire generation of people with education. [*Staring off.*] I'm sorry…The earth leaves me sometimes…Who had a question?
	[*We hear the residents interrogating Thida.*]
RESIDENT 1	[*v.o.*] You see nothing at all, Mrs. San?
THIDA	No.
RESIDENT 2	[*v.o.*] Did the insomnia and headaches come with the onset of the blindness, Mrs. San?
THIDA	I can't remember.

RESIDENT 3	[*v.o.*] Can you describe the nature of the forced labor, Mrs. San?
THIDA	Leave me alone.
RESIDENT 1	[*v.o.*] How long were the periods of starvation?
DR. SIMPSON	Trust in society was eroded; the perpetrators were often victims—many young boys were forced into the Khmer Rouge during the instability of the Viet Nam War bombings and the country's own civil war...
RESIDENT 2	[*v.o.*] Did you experience shell explosions, Mrs. San?
RESIDENT 3	[*v.o.*] Did you suffer injuries to the back of your head?
RESIDENT 1	[*v.o.*] Do you have a history of cataracts, glaucoma, Mrs. San?
RESIDENT 2	[*v.o.*] Can she speak?
RESIDENT 3	[*v.o.*] Were there remnants of Agent Orange in that area?
RESIDENT 2	[*v.o.*] Is this a symptom of PTSD?
RESIDENT 1	[*v.o.*] Does her culture somatize illness?
RESIDENT 3	[*v.o.*] Has she worn a halter monitor while she's been questioned about trauma?
RESIDENT 1	[*v.o.*] Have you repeated the MRI, Mrs. San?
RESIDENTS	[*v.o.*] Mrs. San?

Scene Ten

[Serey enters as Thida sits by the window.]

SEREY	You're really *pissed* at my dad. [*Explaining the word.*] Angry.
THIDA	Correct.
SEREY	He has that effect on people. When you ran away, it made me think of the camp. We lived in a hole, Aunt, before we got assigned a refugee number in Thailand. It was just he and I, and a jerrycan of water. He'd stay up at night, wouldn't let me stray anywhere. I found out later it was 'cause the Khmer Rouge from the next camp raped girls.
THIDA	On the day the Khmer Rouge came into Phnom Penh, a statue of the Buddha cried real tears.
SEREY	I'd ask him to show me my mother's photograph over and over. The only thing pretty. I'd ask, Where was she in the photo. At home?

Where would she go after the picture was taken? The color of the blouse? The little scarf? If I could just get back to where she was in the picture. He'd never say anything, just stare off. He'd put the photo back in the plastic bag, fold it in a square, and pin it back to the inside of his undershirt. I miss her so much, but I didn't even really know her.

[*Serey is filled with grief for what she can't have and won't ever know.*]

THIDA   Serey? The photo as you describe it would not be taken in her house. She would be in the studio at a photographer's: a room with a red-velvet drape. After the picture was taken, she would accompany your father for tea at an outdoor café with white tablecloths and silver. They would hold hands and watch the sun setting, the villas changing color. There would be a soft wind. They would have sandals, which they would slip off under the table. Their feet would touch. Her blouse is pink, I'm certain, and the scarf blue.

SEREY   I'm sorry about Oun.

THIDA   You are a stubborn one, like her. She was a fighter.

SEREY   Did you choose your own husband?

THIDA   No, it is my parents who chose him.

SEREY   Did you love him?

THIDA   He saved my life, warning me to take off my glasses. Our last moment together, I understood what love was.

[*Serey kisses her aunt and exits.*]

I stand in the blue-green water, feel my baby kick. Hear the sound of waves breaking, smell the salt air. At Kep, I waded in the aqua water, lay on the white sand beach. Sipha would rub my shoulders...

Scene Eleven

[*Serey and Savath are sipping espresso after dinner in a restaurant. The room is turning.*]

SEREY   I like the way this restaurant spins. So you can see different parts of the city all the time. Not that the smog makes it possible. I'd like to live in a house that spins.

SAVATH   Why?

SEREY   So you could see the world from all different sides. It's boring to look out a window and see the same thing. In my case, a trash dumpster, thank you. But think if you saw a waterfall, a volcano, a cabana, and a child playing. If it was always changing.

SAVATH   A cabana?

SEREY   Like in Hawaii. I really want to go there. I want to scuba dive.

SAVATH   So do I. Think of how good you'd feel if you breathed underwater. Like a fish. Want to go to Hawaii?

SEREY   Isn't that the big "honeymoon" place?

SAVATH   [*Noticing.*] Are you hyped on coffee?

SEREY   My head's spinning a little. It feels good. I thought you were the big Buddhist-of-the-year. You drink double espressos?

SAVATH   Of course. With my job I need all the help I can get. Living in court-rooms, the DMV? Writing petitions so Khmer people don't get arrested for child abuse when they coin their kids? Plus, this espresso is good.

SEREY   We should go dancing. Except not that corny Khmer stuff. We should go to a club. Get all sweaty. It makes you forget.

SAVATH   I love the Khmer stuff. Sin Sisamouth.

SEREY   He died at Tuol Sleng, you know. It's like if America sent Elvis to a concentration camp. Why would anyone do that?

SAVATH   You're right. I don't know why anyone would do that.

SEREY   OK. [*She gulps her espresso.*] So we've been on their "second date." I like this place. I like the tablecloths and the silverware.

SAVATH   I'm glad you like it so much.

SEREY   My aunt would like it. She's classy. I used to lust after her makeup when I was little. I wished I could steal her lipstick.

SAVATH   You look very classy in that silk.

SEREY   My dad's never seen this.

              [*She shows a tiny tattoo on her skin above her breast.*]

SAVATH   A lotus. It's sexy.

SEREY   You found my aunt. You know everyone. It's good the way you never get freaked.

              [*He touches her hand.*]

              So. I have an idea. It's bold. These two weirdos are breathing down our necks. [*Quoting them.*] "We want to adapt to the American

	ways. Go on a date." They think they're trying to be so smart. So we one-up them.
SAVATH	I think I may know what you're talking about. But I may just be dreaming.
SEREY	I mean, I hate to say this, it sounds, I don't know, but doesn't it always come down to?… I mean if *that* doesn't work, if that part's not happening, then it's a kind of a big commitment to make for an entire lifetime.
SAVATH	[*Teasing her.*] I like that you're bold. I really like that.
SEREY	I thought…

[*He leans over and kisses her.*]

I think you're really good looking. Sometimes I worry you're too serious. |
SAVATH	I am serious.
SEREY	[*Making up her mind.*] OK. Let's check into the spinning hotel.
SAVATH	Get the biggest, most expensive room, with a tape player. Make it beautiful. I have my credit card.
SEREY	You know the hotel part doesn't spin.
SAVATH	We might be able to make it spin. I'm not as square as you think.

[*She looks at him.*] |
| SEREY | It's my first time. |
| SAVATH | Me too. [*Protectively.*] It will be our secret. |

Scene Twelve _____

	[*Dr. Simpson talks to Kim near the altar as Thida sits by the window.*]
DR. SIMPSON	Has she spoken since the residents' presentation?
KIM	No.
DR. SIMPSON	They were asking her questions and she stopped suddenly. She wouldn't say anything.
KIM	Sister, Lynne needs you to answer when people ask questions. If you see, then perhaps it will stop the memories in your head. They will be replaced by new ones.
THIDA	She knows nothing.

KIM	Thida!
DR. SIMPSON	I had to reschedule. We'll see if she can do it next week. It's hard to get all the doctors in the same room.
KIM	Yes, she'll be better next week.
DR. SIMPSON	And she refused to have another MRI so we could look at her brain.
KIM	Perhaps she got overly tired. How did the MRI research turn out?
DR. SIMPSON	They do have similar problems—high blood pressure, heart palpitations—but it's still somewhat of a mystery. I should go.
KIM	May I ask…do you eat, doctor? You look thin.
DR. SIMPSON	I drink too much coffee and smoke. [*Ironic.*] In some ways, it really functions almost better than food.
KIM	Did I tell you? I'm quitting.
DR. SIMPSON	Really?
KIM	Soon, very soon.
DR. SIMPSON	Just about the time I do.
KIM	Perhaps stay for dinner? Any good doctor knows one must eat. Shrimp with lemongrass and pepper, squash soup. Chicken in coconut milk and lime, with Chinese broccoli?
DR. SIMPSON	I better run. I'll check in with you tomorrow and see how she's doing.
KIM	We received good news. My daughter just got into college.
DR. SIMPSON	Congratulations.
KIM	But I ask myself over and over: what can happen in four years?
DR. SIMPSON	I think by then we'll find a cure for your sister.
KIM	Yes. I always cook too much food, and my sister eats none of it. Serey's always at the library. Can I put some food in a container for you? I hope you don't stay up all night with that research. You need to *sleep,* too.
DR. SIMPSON	It's a fantastic project. There has to be something—I just know it.
KIM	Sit and have tea, while you wait for the food. Take a breath. Enjoy yourself. You're so lucky.
DR. SIMPSON	Lucky?
KIM	You have everything.

DR. SIMPSON	Everything?
KIM	I miss my work. I miss a lot of things.
DR. SIMPSON	I'll stay and eat. It smells good.
	[*He touches her hand.*]
KIM	Just sit, I'll serve you. Don't worry about anything.
	[*Kim starts to exit and runs into Serey. Kim and Serey try to keep their voices down as Thida sits in her chair by the window and Dr. Simpson waits.*]
KIM	Chhem has already rented an entire restaurant!
SEREY	So what?! I'm not doing it. I told you that already. We both told you.
KIM	I wish your mother was here. [*Putting his hands together.*] I wish to Buddha and all the gods in the sky and all the gods in the Long Beach cement that she was here.
SEREY	What's gotten into you?
KIM	[*To himself.*] Why do *I* have to be the one to do this? Why?!
SEREY	Do what? Cool out. Take a breath.
KIM	Cool out?
DR. SIMPSON	[*Starting to leave.*] I'll go.
SEREY	[*To Dr. Simpson.*] Sorry he's acting so strange.
KIM	Forgive us, this is poor timing. Please come back for dinner.
DR. SIMPSON	Yes.
	[*Dr. Simpson exits.*]
SEREY	Savath's grandmother is having a bad influence on you, Dad.
KIM	[*Trying to gather his courage.*] OK, OK, OK.
SEREY	Jesus.
KIM	Don't swear.
SEREY	"Jesus" isn't swearing; plus, we're not Christian.
KIM	So why do you talk about Jesus? We're off the subject. If you do what the Americans do...You know...the...[*Trying to explain sex, partly using the palms-pressed-together-slow dance analogy Chhem used.*] You know...I can't say it.
SEREY	Dad, you are so goofy.

KIM	Don't call me goofy! Have you had conjugal relations with a man?!
SEREY	Look…it's different here.
KIM	What are you saying?
SEREY	I had to "check it out"…
KIM	"Check it out"?
SEREY	…I've had sex with Savath.
KIM	Oh no, god! [*An aside.*] Do you think your aunt can hear?
THIDA	Every word.
SEREY	I don't want a marriage where in ten years we hate each other.
KIM	Serey? You are a fallen woman! Why did you do this? What is wrong with you?!
SEREY	It's fine.
KIM	No, it's not fine!
SEREY	It was good…
KIM	You've ruined my life. [*Repeating; deadpan.*] "It was good." [*To Thida.*] America has turned her into nothing!
SEREY	I can't help who I am…He's a lot different than I thought.
KIM	Oh. [*Deadpan.*] Wonderful. [*Freaking about what they are discussing; to Thida.*] Why me, Sister? [*To Serey.*] You are worthless! What will people say?!
SEREY	It's none of their business.
KIM	It's everyone's business! You'll see! You have to get married right now, Serey.
SEREY	Thanks for trusting me.
KIM	I don't. And now I don't trust Savath.
SEREY	He loves that I'm going to college first; he wouldn't care if I went to graduate school.
KIM	Graduate school? No! What am I saying? Yes, go to graduate school, get your Ph.D. [*To Thida.*] I don't care what she does anymore.
THIDA	[*To Kim.*] Maybe you picked the right man for her after all.
	[*He takes a pen from his pocket.*]

KIM	You want me to undo all the plans with Chhem? Cancel everything? Pay her back for what she has bought?
SEREY	You're not listening. You never do.
KIM	I *did* listen, and it was a disaster.
SEREY	Well, too bad my mother isn't here. Too bad there isn't anyone here who *gets it*. It's hard. You think I like being the only child left? We're supposed to look to the future—that's what you say—but all you do is live in the past. I'm going to college and maybe I'll transfer. Transfer right out of here.
KIM	Fine, transfer. Be like all the other American families, *separated* and alone.

[*Serey looks at the pen he is holding.*]

| SEREY | Why do you steal pens, Dad? You take them from everywhere—banks, gas stations, stores? |

[*Serey takes another pen out of his pocket.*]

| THIDA | The officials killed us because we could read and write, then they kept pens in their pockets to show us their power. |
| KIM | I guess I can't help myself. |

Scene Thirteen

[*Chhem is in Kim's garden, calling to Thida, who sits inside. Savath enters.*]

CHHEM	[*To Thida.*] What were you thinking, to get those initials on your head?
SAVATH	Grandma?
CHHEM	His sister is slowly going crazy. Kim is so patient, but we have to watch her every minute.

[*Chhem has gathered some fruit.*]

My mother used to give me a hook and let me climb the ladder to gather the ripe ones. How I loved to see the trees from above.

| SAVATH | Grandma, I need to talk to you. Don't bug Serey anymore. [*Taking out a letter.*] Listen, and try not to talk. |
| CHHEM | I should go inside and attend to Thida. |

SAVATH	This is Serey's college acceptance letter. She showed it to me…on our "date." She's very proud.
CHHEM	But the wedding will be next month. We have already purchased the bedroom set.
SAVATH	Look, it's generous to get the bedroom set, but that's not really what we need.
CHHEM	She will have children! When your mother died, I prayed that you would stay with me and promised in return I would do good.
SAVATH	You're seeing all this in your head, but it's not going to happen that way. She'll go to college for four years. Then, if we want, maybe we'll get married.
CHHEM	Four years? Who will cook your food?
SAVATH	I eat out.
CHHEM	Who will do your laundry? Clean your house? You will wait for four years to be "together"? To have children?
SAVATH	It's a whole different thing here, Grandma…
CHHEM	No engagement? No party? No announcement? No invitations? No prayers? I want to give back to the monks.
SAVATH	None of that. We'll date, maybe take a trip to Hawaii at her break, go out dancing.
CHHEM	Slow dancing?
SAVATH	I think she likes rock.
CHHEM	[Hearing "rock."] I will go buy her a ring tomorrow!
SAVATH	I already bought one. [Taking out a box with a ring.] You want to see it?
CHHEM	Ah, why did you not let me pick it out?
SAVATH	I think our tastes are at opposite ends of the planet.
CHHEM	I want to pay for it. The rock is too small, the band too thin.
SAVATH	She likes it.
CHHEM	No! She cannot see it before the wedding!
SAVATH	I showed it to her in a window. I didn't say it was for her. It's a double thing: college, engagement. And actually, something else…love.
CHHEM	Love? You must get married now, Savath. I have already made the invitations and reserved the temple.

SAVATH	Well, unreserve it! Tear them up.
CHHEM	You are disrespectful.
SAVATH	*I* need to respect Serey.
CHHEM	All the evil we saw—we must preserve our customs. The astrologer is very optimistic.
SAVATH	We're not getting married because of the stars!
CHHEM	Think: the gold I hid in the soles of my shoes, the chains in my clothing's seams. *They* did not find it. It is for you and your new family. She is "easy," she'll sleep with anyone.
SAVATH	I won't listen to that!
CHHEM	You will make me lose face with Serey's father.
SAVATH	It's not about *you.* [*Vulnerable.*] Look, it may not work out, OK? We don't know. It's a risk I have to take.
CHHEM	You'll see that everything good about our country will disappear!

Scene Fourteen _____

[*Dr. Simpson and Kim smoke in Kim's garden. Sirens are heard in the distance.*]

KIM	Now the three women in my life aren't talking to me. My sister is angry at me, my daughter hates me, and my daughter's fiancé's grandmother has taken out a contract on me by now.
DR. SIMPSON	You're very funny.
KIM	Why?
DR. SIMPSON	I don't know. You just are.
KIM	My daughter says "goofy." Thida refuses to see you. I wonder what happened. Ever since the meeting with the residents, she seems worse.
DR. SIMPSON	Let me talk to her.
KIM	Anything new on the research?
DR. SIMPSON	There are no links. The women have some of the same symptoms—that's the best conclusion. I won't be able to get the second part of the funding if I can't prove more. There may have been something I missed. The other women are reacting like your sister:

they're withdrawing, don't want to be tested, don't want to be seen. It's hard to do a study when the subjects don't want to get better.

KIM   Why not visit the temple on Willow Street? Take a look.

DR. SIMPSON   I ask myself this question. You saw trauma. Why didn't you go blind?

KIM   Have you ever had a moment when medical science doesn't help?

DR. SIMPSON   …Yes.

KIM   We discovered recently that Thida's daughter refused to marry a Khmer Rouge soldier and was killed in front of her. We did not know this before. Her daughter was beheaded. Thida saw her burn.

DR. SIMPSON   You can't reverse that.

KIM   I promised my wife I'd take care of our children. As a doctor, I was a marked man. I pretended I was a farmer, rubbed my hands in the dirt until they had calluses. [*Looking at his cigarette.*] You know, the Khmer Rouge rolled their cigarettes with pages from books and plays. Serey is all I have left. You're lucky your eyes have not seen such horror.

DR. SIMPSON   This is a beautiful garden.

KIM   Thank you. Sometimes, solutions are found outside? Prayer, food, family? Growing beans, a nap?

DR. SIMPSON   A nap would be good.

KIM   Sitting around and doing nothing at all.

DR. SIMPSON   Laughing a lot.

KIM   Who knows?

DR. SIMPSON   I don't.

KIM   Go talk to Thida. Let me get some food for you to bring home.

           [*Lights up on Thida, who sits as Dr. Simpson approaches.*]

DR. SIMPSON   In this country, we get so carried away with the diagnostic procedures, we lose sight of the patient.

THIDA   You smoke too much.

DR. SIMPSON   I'm sorry.

THIDA   I will never again have a test.

DR. SIMPSON   Were they uncomfortable?

THIDA	Everything is uncomfortable. I am a prisoner.
DR. SIMPSON	Let me ask you this. You said your soul left your body and traveled to the beach at Kep. How does a soul leave a body?
THIDA	How does it, doctor?
DR. SIMPSON	Yes, that's what I asked.
THIDA	What do you think?
DR. SIMPSON	Well, perhaps because the pain is too great?
THIDA	Yes. What do you do with your day?
DR. SIMPSON	Work.
THIDA	Do you ever go to sleep?
DR. SIMPSON	Not much. What was at the beach at Kep?
THIDA	Such beauty. Do you have a family? Are you married?
DR. SIMPSON	Yes. My husband, Tom, is dead.
THIDA	How did Tom die?

[*Dr. Simpson sees Thida is waiting.*]

DR. SIMPSON	He had an illness.
THIDA	What type?
DR. SIMPSON	I can't talk about it.
THIDA	I know.
DR. SIMPSON	A disease of the nervous system. It was like a bomb that went off in his body. And in mine.
THIDA	Where did your soul go?
DR. SIMPSON	Nowhere beautiful.

[*Dr. Simpson takes a photo from her wallet. She takes Thida's hand and passes it over the photo.*]

We were everything to each other. I lost my only family. It happened fast…I don't know.

[*Dr. Simpson breaks down.*]

I couldn't bear it. That kind of illness can't be explained—it's too cruel.

THIDA	You see, telling the story is very difficult. Almost like being strangled.

[*Kim enters with a food container. Dr. Simpson puts away the photo. She takes the food container and leaves.*]

KIM   What happened to the doctor?

THIDA   She lost her husband sometime ago.

KIM   She wears the ring. Why did you talk *to her* if you are so unwilling to talk?

THIDA   I must find you and her some herbs. Margosa, coconut milk… Release of stress for you, sleep for her.

KIM   [*Puzzled.*] Why did the doctor make you feel better?

THIDA   I felt useful. She did not know something, and *I* knew.

KIM   *I* need your help too, Sister. You're useful to me. I need you to live.

THIDA   Why not take me to your garden? I'm sorry I've always refused your invitations.

KIM   Really you'd like to come?

[*He starts to take her to his garden. Lights shift to Dr. Simpson slowly entering the temple. She speaks to herself, with a microphone.*]

DR. SIMPSON   *I add my shoes to the mountain of shoes. The temple is crowded with bright silk, an American flag, a stray skeleton from Halloween. Monks in orange robes sit cross-legged on dainty satin pillows eating from an array of bowls. People kneel, talking. The altar is filled with baskets of tea, money, cigarettes, Oreos. A statue of Buddha is cloaked in the same robe as the monks. Blind women, shoulders slumped, eyes staring off, expressionless, holding canes. Life whirs around them, but they aren't there. Where? How can they come back?* [*A realization.*] *You almost have to die first before you live again.*

Scene Fifteen

[*Kim takes a photo of Serey and Savath as Dr. Simpson sits in Kim's living room with Thida. Chhem serves dessert.*]

CHHEM   [*To Dr. Simpson.*] After this engagement party, I have four years to wait for my grandson's marriage. I have taken up embroidery, doctor. A very long project. I hope I don't die before the wedding.

DR. SIMPSON   I'm sure it will be OK.

CHHEM   OK? The tradition is ruined.

[*Kim, Serey, and Savath join the others as Dr. Simpson gives Thida a box, which she opens. Outside we hear sirens.*]

THIDA   I would like to preserve the wrapping. [*Showing a skirt.*] It is a sampot.

DR. SIMPSON   Red and yellow. Serey told me about the shop.

SEREY   The lady gets the silk from a co-op in Takeo. It's pretty…

CHHEM   And I helped pick it out.

THIDA   [*To Dr. Simpson.*] You must take it. I will never again have the occasion.

DR. SIMPSON   It's for you. I wanted to thank you. The tea helped me sleep. I started thinking.

THIDA   About what?

DR. SIMPSON   Memories.

THIDA   You've changed. You seem lighter.

               [*Thida feels the fabric.*]

               You have good taste. Why do you not try it on? It would give me so much pleasure to see you dressed in something different for once.

DR. SIMPSON   You can't see me.

THIDA   I do know what you wear. I asked my brother to tell me.

KIM   I said you dressed very well. [*To Thida.*] Why don't you try it on?

THIDA   [*To Dr. Simpson.*] I do not feel like changing.

DR. SIMPSON   Serey says you were a city lady. I'm sure you were very elegant.

THIDA   I adored clothes. It was another life…I cannot imagine. It would give me pleasure if you would try it on…just to see.

               [*Thida holds out the long skirt.*]

               Take it.

               [*Dr. Simpson takes the skirt and tries it on.*]

               It is from my country. Let me feel.

               [*Thida feels and adjusts it. Dr. Simpson stands in the skirt.*]

               You have given me something very beautiful.

DR. SIMPSON   What?

THIDA	A way to imagine something different. I always admired doctors. And now there's you.
SEREY	It's nice. [*To Savath.*] You should buy me one!

[*Savath puts his arm around Serey.*]

CHHEM	They show the world. They are a mystery to me.

[*Thida touches Serey, speaking softly.*]

THIDA	You know, I was a midwife. I will be able to help you someday.

[*Kim listens to sirens.*]

KIM	Why don't these gangs stop? War follows us everywhere.
THIDA	It's always that way. A little girl drops a grain of rice on the floor, and a lizard grabs it. A cat sees the lizard and pounces, which brings the dog. The cat's owner starts to beat the dog, and this angers the dog's owner. The two men start to fight, and the families, neighbors join in until everyone is fighting. Word reaches Angkor that a fight is raging. The king thinks it's an attack by foreign enemy and rushes out with ten thousand men and elephants. The king of Siam thinks the Khmers are mobilizing to attack him and rushes out with his men and elephants. All because a careless little girl drops a grain of rice, a war breaks out. I never thought war could touch a place like Kep, but we've always had fighting. Siam. Viet Nam. The u.s. We are a small country.
KIM	I'm so happy you told us that story. My sister was always an excellent storyteller.
SEREY	You know, Aunt, maybe only big countries survive? A simple law of size.

[*Savath puts on some Willie Nelson music.*]

CHHEM	Ah, now is the time! Would you like some more to eat?

[*Thida listens to the music.*]

THIDA	Sipha loved him.
KIM	Who?
THIDA	Willie Nelson.
DR. SIMPSON	Your husband loved Willie Nelson?

[*Savath puts the ring on Serey's finger.*]

CHHEM	Finally, the ring.

[*Serey looks at the ring.*]

SEREY OK, we've made a commitment to each other. We think we want to have children, but I really need to go to college. We'll probably have a traditional wedding, but we also want to help plan it. [*Taking something out.*] I have a ring.

CHHEM Another?

[*Serey puts it on Savath's finger.*]

SEREY [*To Kim.*] I want to honor you. And my mother. I know we can never forget what happened, Dad. [*To Thida.*] You know, maybe big countries like this survive because of the stuff from the little countries? We're family. We have to stay together, and we have to grow up.

KIM I don't know. Fate has put part of you here and part of you there.

[*Kim looks anxiously at Serey. Thida turns in Kim's direction.*]

THIDA She's intelligent. A fighter. You must trust her.

KIM Yes.

Scene Sixteen

[*We see the blue of ocean and hear waves. Thida sits with Dr. Simpson, who looks out to sea.*]

DR. SIMPSON Do you see colors?

THIDA Yellow powder spread on a woman's body after giving birth. Green lemon leaves steamed for the new mother to bathe in. Brown Star of Anise with its delicate flower. Cook it in a curry and take her to the sea. Let her play until she gets hungry, then feed her the dish. When she is finished, tell her your stories, take her to the top of the mountain, and show her how beautiful when the sun goes down. [*She points out.*] Look…[*Turning to Dr. Simpson.*] Thank you for bringing me here. What is the color of the water?

DR. SIMPSON It's blue-gray, darker in the parts where there's seaweed. The shore is flat all the way to the sea. The sand is brown. The waves, you hear them?

THIDA Yes.

DR. SIMPSON They break in one place, then ripple in a straight, white line.

[*Thida hears the sound of a wave breaking. She wades into the water, holding up her dress.*]

THIDA   Colder than Kep.

DR. SIMPSON   Blindness. That's how you survived.

THIDA   There was once a lady who poured all her misfortunes to the Buddha. He told her these miseries would go away if she obtained a seed from a house that had never known sorrow. When the Buddha asked the woman if she had found the Seed of Happiness, she replied, No. I went to every house seeking it and found no house that had not known sorrow.

               [*The two women stand in the water.*]

THIDA   In my country, we believe your husband's spirit will always protect you.

               [*Thida faces far out.*]

               Lynne?

DR. SIMPSON   Yes?

THIDA   I still see her head bobbing up and down against the line of the horizon. I still hear Sipha and myself calling her name. She said no to them.

               [*Oun appears against the blue. She slowly walks out of the sea. Lights fade. End of play.*]

               [*A projection reads:* "At least 150 Cambodian women living in Southern California have functional blindness, a psychosomatic vision loss linked to what they saw in the years of Khmer Rouge rule." *The New York Times,* August 8, 1989.]

Two Poems

A CHOREOGRAPHY OF CORPSES

Something wants to come near,
a choreography of corpses.
Landmines, tattoos
and boys cooking rice
in the alley behind the jail.

Girls so young you could snap
them between two fingers.
Why did you join the rebels?
Nothing. Nobody. Because
the world is hard and undisturbed

by hacked roots, shallow graves wrenched from frost.
Thin flies listen for transition.
Your laughter sparks its own friends.
Something wants to come near, in boots,
with exposed wounds, brute opposites.

I know you can graph this violence,
indigestible myth, the heavy price of freedom,
fragmented families, bones, halfway sunrise to democracy.
Civilization of suffering, genius of wounding,
doubled padlocks on doubled gates.

Graph the equation: 385 prisoners in a jail
built for 125. Nails stand up through boards
to shred hijacked bus tires.
Exhausted kingdoms return to stories.
Thus the colossal waste of time.

Whiskey reveals the moon in plaster,
glittering afternoons circle disappearing jobs.
Warmth and bad fog come nearer and nearer.
There is a graph; there is a bridge
which inevitably washes away.

VARIATIONS ON THE HEART SUTRA, NEPAL 2006

Listen, Shariputra, listen.
I was kept blindfolded in a ball court for thirteen months.
I memorized the names of fifty prisoners thinking
I would be released the next day and could tell their families they
were alive.
I lost track of the days after I was hung upside down
by my feet and plunged headfirst, naked, into a tub of cold water.
Awaken to perfect enlightenment. I lost track after the electric shock.

Listen, Shariputra.
Three days on a concrete floor in the snow, no shoes.
Four whacks to go to the bathroom, four whacks to come back.
No old age and no death. Listen.
No man who beats you thirty times with the plastic pipe
and also no ending of the man who beats you thirty times
with the plastic pipe.

No names of those who lay there in silence.
No names of those who were hauled away.
No names of those who were transferred to the jail,
and no ending of names of those who died,
of those who were released and arrested again.
How old was this one? What did that one do for a living?
Fled to India? Went underground?

We give thanks to those who gave us milk to drink
when we were hungry. All those women long since gone.
I've been swept up in a tide beyond my control, Shariputra.
It is bearing me towards the fields of battle, Shariputra,
fields of cartridges, caps, candy wrappers, and flowers.
Children throwing rocks at unexploded bombs.
All living beings great beings. The heart of perfect wisdom.

Bombs dropping all around.
Just a little bit, just a little bit of mercy.
The house of a baby born two hours before the attack
burnt to the ground, a child spirited away under fire,
born into a world without shoes on its feet, without bread to eat.
May you some way, some way be healed.
Kuan Yin, find us on that dark and broken cement.

We give thanks to the fire of a heart in snow, the gate of sleep,
to those who held us in their arms when we cried.
May they cross on over. Cross the bridge, nicknames
family names caste names, cross on over. Cross the bridge.
Walk through all the gates. Don't stop: the gate of the Capital,
the gate of razor wire, the gate of the prison,
the gate the gate the gate.

*Note: Shariputra is the student to whom the Heart Sutra, spoken by
Avalokitesvara, is addressed.*

Wandering Souls _____

Family and friends wondered why we were so angry. "What are you crying about?" they would ask…Our fathers and grandfathers had gone off to war, done their duty, come home and got on with it. What made our generation so different? As it turns out, nothing. No difference at all. When old soldiers from "good" wars are dragged from behind the curtain of myth and sentiment and brought into the light, they too seem to smolder with choler and alienation…So we were angry. Our anger was old, atavistic. We were angry as all civilized men who have ever been sent to make murder in the name of virtue were angry.

Michael Norman, *These Good Men: Friendship Forged from War*

On 18 March 1969, Homer Steedly, a young American infantry lieutenant, turned a bend in a trail in Kontum Province and came face to face with a North Vietnamese soldier, his weapon slung over his shoulder. The soldier, whom Steedly first took for an enemy officer, was Hoang Ngoc Dam, a twenty-four-year-old medic from the village of Thai Giang, near Hai Phong—a fact the lieutenant would not discover for another thirty years. There was no time then for more than a quick glimpse. As soon as Dam saw Homer, he snatched his weapon off his shoulder and brought it around. "I shouted the phrase to surrender," Homer wrote in his journal, "but he continued to draw down on me. I fired just before he got his rifle on me. If I had not been so scared, I might have had the presence of mind to just wound him, but in my adrenaline-rush panic, I killed him with one shot through the heart."

Dazed, he stared at the body for a while. The man he'd killed was young, his pith helmet clean, his uniform starched, and the SKS rifle clutched in his hands new, the greasy cosmoline used as an anti-rust still gooped on its bayonet hinge. Someone new to the war, Homer concluded. He bent down and went through the dead man's pockets, drawing out a notebook with a colorful picture of a man and woman in what he took to be traditional or ancient Vietnamese dress on the front cover, a daily and monthly calendar grid labeled in English SCHEDULE on the back, a smaller black notebook, and a number of loose papers—letters, I.D. cards, certificates of some sort. The spine and corners of the larger notebook had been neatly reinforced with black tape.

Thirty-five years later, as I handed that notebook to Dam's brother, I was again struck by the care Dam had taken in binding it. He was a soldier in an army where nothing could be thrown away, nothing wasted, and I thought, not for the first time, of what the appearance of that book must have meant to Homer as he looked through it on that dark trail. Raised on a small, hardscrabble farm, Homer knew the preciousness of things that could not be replaced, knew how to shepherd them. The way he had shot Dam was unusual: a gunfighter duel in a war in which the enemy often remained faceless to Americans—known only as sudden flashes of fire from the jungle, targets to be annihilated. That invisibility was frustrating to the G.I.s, but at least it allowed them to dehumanize the enemy, making him into ghost, demon, target. Seeing not only the face of the man he'd killed, but also the carefully rebound covers and the force of will that the meticulous writing and drawings inside the book revealed, Homer had been confronted with a mirrored and valuable humanity. He'd tried not to think about it. There was scarcely the time anyway, and later that day, he'd have one more encounter with a soldier who wanted to shoot him—this time, an American whom the war had broken, who had already shot and killed another soldier. Homer was able to talk that man into laying down his weapon, and so that day he had taken a life and saved a life. He couldn't dwell on the former. It was, in any case, a killing justified by custom and law, by survival.

Homer sent the documents to the rear area, where he knew they'd be assessed and then burnt. But later that evening, he changed his mind, contacted a friend in S-2, intelligence, and asked him to bring everything back. He couldn't bear to have the documents, the last evidence of the life he'd taken, destroyed. "I kept his personal documents and will send them home," he wrote to his mother. "Someday, perhaps, I will be able to contact his relatives." By refusing to let go of the notebooks he'd taken from Dam's body, Homer somehow understood, though he could not put it into words or coherent thoughts until years later, that he was hanging onto a grief that was the price of remaining human.

The shy son of a South Carolina sharecropper and his German war bride, Homer considered himself an unlikely officer. He had grown up poor in the rural South. Unable to afford more than a year of college, he enlisted in the army in order to get training and save money for his education. But the army saw leadership potential in him, and in 1967, he was sent to Officer Candidate School, graduating as a second lieutenant. One of his classmates was William J. Calley, who, one year and two days before Homer would shoot Dam, led and participated in the massacre of over five hundred women, old men, and children—all civilians—in the village Americans called My Lai, far from the arena where Homer fought his war.

"It's a strange thing to say, because combat was so much heavier where we were in the highlands, fighting the regular NVA," Homer said. "But for me it was a blessing not to be in those areas where you couldn't tell the VC from civilians." He was spared from having to make the moral choice facing the soldiers at My Lai. His enemy was the highly trained, well-armed regular forces of the People's Army of Viet Nam. Homer's unit, the First Battalion of the Eighth Infantry Regiment, Fourth Infantry Division, was not engaged in the guerilla war of rice paddies and hamlets, in which most casualties came from mine and booby traps and Americans couldn't tell enemy from civilian. Instead, Homer and his men had humped ninety-pound loads in ninety-plus-degree heat and humidity and were locked for months in savage jungle fighting, in rugged mountain country where the triple-canopy trees made it dark at midday.

It was as clear-cut as a war could be. He and his men killed, as he had killed Dam on that mountain trail, in order to stay alive. He came to see that goal as his main job; by 1969, it was obvious to all of them that the war was only a holding action. Homer did his best, even extending his own time in the field—army officers were only required to serve six months in combat—unwilling to let his company be led by an inexperienced commander. And then he had come home. There was nothing he needed to feel guilty about. He had committed no atrocities, was no baby killer. He had been promoted and decorated. He had participated in the defining history of his time. He had experienced the close camaraderie of combat soldiers, had fought bravely and led competently, and had come back relatively intact. There were men who would and did take such experiences as the high-water marks of their lives. There were others who were foolish enough to envy them.

"When I came back," Homer said, "I tried to talk to people. But I could see they changed towards me, so I just shut up, threw myself into work." He threw himself into a bottle as well, and at the same time began engaging in solitary and dangerous sports—cave and sky diving, small-plane piloting, motorcycle racing—activities in which a careless or irresponsible move could get him killed. "The deaths and injuries [that] occurred under my leadership still haunt my memories," he would write. "I expect they will be among the memories that flash before my eyes when I lie on my deathbed. Somehow I feel guilty for having come back alive."

He had sent the documents he'd taken from the body of the man he'd killed to his mother. She had lived through a war and its aftermath herself, and she understood his need to preserve what he had taken. She carefully stored the documents in a box, which she placed in the attic. They remained there for almost three decades, locked away in a space of contained darkness, a physical anamnesis of the memories of the war that Homer locked away inside his own mind. He had seen and done things that he knew the people around him did not want to know about or would not believe. His ears rang continuously—the result of a 105-mm shell that had landed in his fighting position and splattered him with the blood of the two sergeants with him—a thin, constant scream in the center of his mind that has never gone away. There were certain images burned into his brain, certain smells seared into his nostrils, certain tastes still on his tongue, and he felt they composed a wall between himself and those who had not seen, felt, smelled, heard what he had. He was afraid that difference made him monstrous. He was afraid that he would turn anyone with whom he truly shared those tastes, those sounds, those sights into himself, and because there were some people he loved and wanted to protect, he remained silent.

Besides, he knew that nobody would believe him.

He might tell people, for example, of the time when one of his men out in the jungle on a listening post had been seized by a tiger, felt without any warning the terrible clamp of the animal's jaws on his skull, its hot breath and slobber encasing his face. As he was being dragged off into the trees, the soldier had had the presence of mind to bring the barrel of his M-16 up to the animal's flank and fire. The tiger, wounded, dropped him and disappeared. The G.I. was left with its mark: a perfect indentation on each side of his forehead. Homer could tell the story, but people would stare at him, say nothing, or, worse, say, sure, they'd seen that, and think he was making it up. They had the illusion, in their safe lives, that there were no beasts. They didn't understand that the tiger had come into him, Homer, into all of them eventually, and had left its mark on them, in them, and in him. Once, on a jungle trail, he had been the tiger.

He could tell how from 21 March, three days after he'd shot Dam, to 30 March, he—a twenty-two-year-old country boy, a sharecropper's kid—had commanded an under-strength company that held a hill against an overwhelming enemy force. His men—with little and then no water, food, or ammunition—were shelled constantly, sometimes hundreds of rounds of 105-mm howitzer fire, as well as uncounted mortar rounds, landing inside their fifty-meter perimeter. He could tell of how the North Vietnamese tried to swarm the hill, of their insane bravery as they were chopped to pieces in the American cross-fire, of the insane bravery of his own men fighting them off. His own insane bravery—he could never use that noun without that adjective. He could tell of the true insanity of a battalion commander who countermanded his urgent request for ammunition, food, and water, and instead risked helicopters to bring them rations they couldn't even use without the water they didn't have and so desperately needed. In spite of that, his men fought on for days in that heat, their throats swollen and parched, one man going berserk and trying to drink from a canister of diesel fuel. He could tell how a door gunner had vomited when he saw a corpse's eyes come alive with maggots when the helicopters finally were able to take out the wounded and dead, and how on the final day of the siege, after he had made sure all his men were evacuated in the helicopters, there were so many enemy soldiers pouring into the perimeter that he thought he and the last three men with him would have to make a run for the jungle. An equally insane and brave helicopter crew disobeyed orders and extracted them in a hail of gunfire, and he looked down from the door of the helicopter to see the North Vietnamese covering the hill "like angry ants" and then saw his rifle's handguard and magazine guide scarred by gunfire, bullet holes in his rucksack, through his radio—saw the crease a round left in his helmet.

Sure, people would say; they'd seen that movie too. So he kept his mouth shut. Sealed his lips. Swallowed it. Once, he had lain in the saw and elephant grass when his company had been ambushed, the boy next to him—who had pushed him down when the firing started and had saved his life—with the top of his head blown off, and he stared into the empty pink skull-cup, the sheltering grass being mowed down as if by a giant scythe. He knew he would die then, and then he went away, the smell of the bullet-mulched grass suddenly evocative of peaceful summer lawns, the sun warm and gentle on his face, the noise fading, and then suddenly back again, deafening, and then again fading away. Inches away from his eyes, he saw a line of ants carrying bits of insect corpses and pieces of a strange pink fungus to their nest, their normality, their indifferent life comforting and amazing him. He slowly felt his body, the pieces of his own physicality; he could even taste, feel with his tongue a large chunk of the C-ration ham and eggs he'd had for breakfast still lodged in his cheek. He idly chewed it, and swallowed, detached from the sounds of mortars, grenades, and AK-47 rounds cracking over his head. He focused again on the ants, so busy, and he glimpsed again the empty skull of the boy who had gone down near him, and it came to him in a wave of bilious nausea what the strange pink chunks carried in those mandibles were, and what that glob of breakfast meat and eggs he'd felt in his cheek and swallowed really was, and he screamed, ignoring the bullets, getting on his hands and knees and vomiting. He didn't tell that story. Even years later, when he wrote it, he put it in italics and red font and warned people not to read it if they didn't want to be changed. It was the kind of story you sealed behind your lips. How could you kiss anyone again, ever, seal your mouth to the mouth of someone you loved; how could you not be afraid to let her taste what you had tasted? It all stayed inside of him, like the box in the attic, not to be opened until he opened.

Trauma, according to Judith Herman, M.D., in her seminal book *Trauma and Recovery*, occurs when a horrible event or set of events causes a break in your life narrative. On the other side of that break, you can no longer see yourself in the same way. Recovery from trauma starts to occur when you are able to tell your story, in sensory detail, to people willing to listen without judgment and willing to be changed by what they hear—in other words, when you can be taken back into a community that is willing to be wounded itself, willing to break through a protective shell of comforting myths and learn what you have learned. If you can't do that—or if they can't do that—you remain forever alienated, forever outside your community. You are what the Vietnamese call a wandering soul.

That is what Hoang Ngoc Dam became to his family. In the Vietnamese belief, the spirits of those killed far from home, through violence, accident, or war, wander the earth aimlessly, far from the family altar. There were one hundred and ninety-eight such from Dam's home village of Thai Giang, one of them his older brother, Hoang Ngoc Chi. They'd gone South, disappeared into the war as if they had stepped off the earth. Dam's family was able to learn more than most through a hometown friend of Dam's, Pham Quang Huy, who had fought in the same area of operations in the Central Highlands.

Although the two were not in the same regiment, they tried to see each other periodically to exchange news and pass on letters. A month after it occurred, Huy found out about Dam's death from a nurse named Sinh. Dam had been in a unit that had been trying to overrun an American outpost (probably what the Americans called Fire Support Base 20—Homer's base). When they failed, Dam was attached to a small reconnaissance group whose mission was to scout out alternative attack routes. They were engaged in that when they fell into the ambush Homer's company had set up; it was in the pursuit that followed that Homer had come across Dam. Later, Huy asked others in the unit what had happened to Dam's body and was told that it had been buried by local guerillas. After the war, his body and three others were excavated and reburied at the A Giun Pa military cemetery, in Gia Lai Province. But the excavators had not properly identified any of them, and Dam's remains lay among the other unidentified bodies in the cemetery. Huy and Dam's brother-in-law, Hoang Ngoc Dieu, visited the cemetery in 2002, hoping to find the body and bring it home to be placed among the family tombs. But all they could do was grieve for the many anonymous dead in that place. No remains, no objects could be put on the family altar to draw Dam's soul back to the family hearth.

He had become one of the 300,000 wandering souls—the missing in action from the war—that still haunt Viet Nam. Without their remains being brought home and the proper ceremonies being followed—without, that is, commemoration, a physical knitting back into the community— they cannot find peace. *Strangers have buried you in careless haste,* writes the poet and war veteran Nguyen Du of all the missing, *no loved ones near, no friend, no proper rites…and under the wan moon, no kindly smoke of incense wreathes for you.*

What were left, of course, were memories and family mythologies. Dam had been, they remembered, a bright, studious, and very neat boy who, at seventeen, had taken seriously the role of eldest brother. They remembered the tenderness with which he had bathed the youngest, most beloved girl of the family, Tuoi. For the first years of her life, she had suffered from a skin condition, probably eczema, that marred her and caused her to be teased cruelly by the other children; adults, though they would pretend to be indifferent to the ugly lesions, would often hesitate to touch her, hold her, pick her up. It was only Dam, his clothing always meticulously pressed and neat, his hands and face always scrubbed, who would hug her without hesitation, pick her up, kiss her, wash her, dress her. It was that same neatness that would later haunt Homer, who, looking at Dam's clean, well-kept uniform, assumed he must have been an officer or a new guy. "We were very poor," his brother Cat said, "so I never understood how Dam got a white suit, but he wore it whenever he went out. And he studied very hard. We did not have paper, so we would take used paper and soak it in lime water and use it again as scrap paper. Dam always kept his books in order, and he was very careful; he was neat from his hair to his way of walking to his clothes. We did not have many clothes, but his clothes always looked pressed, even though we did not have an iron."

And then one day Dam disappeared beyond the village gate, as all the other young men had, and his sister was left only with an emptiness and an ache, as was his wife, Pham Thi Minh. They'd only been married ten days before he'd gone South to the war. She never saw him again. A month before he'd left, he had written to her to come visit him at his training base. Other women from the village were coming to be with their husbands for a few days; it was a last chance, everyone understood, to leave behind a child. But she was too shy, and only seventeen, to go there, to have everyone know she was going for that reason, and instead Dam stood guard for the other couples as they made love. It is something she regrets to this day. "I wish I could have had a daughter with him; I would have never married again. My current husband was also a soldier, wounded in the war, but he is an alcoholic, and I'm miserable. I keep thinking, If only I had a daughter with Dam, then my life would not be this miserable."

What would Dam have been if he'd returned? What had been lost? When he died, he became what each of the 300,000 was: a lingering question. A question that his mother, Hoang Thi Thuy, tried to answer by going to a fortuneteller.

Dam and his brother had left behind their parents—their father, Hoang Dinh Luc, was a farmer, like Homer's father—two younger brothers, Luong and Cat, and three sisters, Thi Dam, Tham, and Tuoi. The family worried constantly about its safety; its hometown was only nominally a rear area, a haven. The town's closeness to the port of Hai Phong made it a target of American bombs; at one point, an errant bomb fell on the schoolhouse, killing thirty-six children. Most of the young men went off to the war; some hung back. A postscript in one of the letters Dam was carrying speaks archly of a young man who used his influence to stay out of the army. "When I think of him, I get embarrassed for myself and the neighborhood," the writer says. Loyalty, accepting one's military duty unquestioningly, fighting when the country called—these were as expected of young people in Thai Binh Province as in Homer's South Carolina. The families of soldiers who were "war martyrs" were compensated with stipends, job advantages, and, mainly, honor.

What the fortuneteller told Dam's parents was disturbing. Their eldest boy, Chi, was indeed dead, and lay somewhere under the ocean. When they finally got official notification of death, they learned how accurate the fortuneteller had been. Chi had been taken prisoner of war and had died in an island prison, his body flung into the sea. That accuracy stabbed like a knife when they later heard the second fortune: Dam was in America—a fate they found impossible to explain. Had he somehow survived and gone over to the enemy? Or was his soul there, waiting to be commemorated and reborn? The consultation was supposedly only between his mother and the fortuneteller, but soon malicious people in the town were whispering rumors about betrayal, spurring an outraged Huy and Dieu to go South and try to find Dam's body.

It was an issue Dam's parents did not live to see resolved. Both passed away before we were able to return his documents and allow the family and the rest of the village to finally understand what the fortuneteller had seen.

For a number of years, I've been involved in projects with Vietnamese writers and filmmakers, returning at least once a year to that place where, as a marine, I had spent my own youth. Early in 2005, I met another writer and veteran, Tom Lacombe, who asked me to use my contacts in Viet Nam to help a man who was trying to return the documents he had taken from the body of an NVA soldier he'd killed.

Over the decade leading up to 2005, Homer's life had changed to the point where he was ready to confront his past. In the late seventies, as he worked towards a master's degree in sociology, he had become fascinated by the then new field of computers and had made himself an expert in the early days of information technology, securing a position as assistant director of the computer lab at the University of South Carolina's college of liberal arts. It was an occupation challenging enough to fill his time and his thoughts, and it kept him from dwelling too much on the past. It was also one that allowed him to be alone, to become a workaholic, until the day he met Tibby Dozier, a coworker who consulted him about some problems with her computer. He fixed it, and they fell in love and got married in 1995. Tibby, the soft-spoken granddaughter of a World War II general and Medal of Honor recipient, understood the nightmares and secrets of soldiers. With her encouragement, Homer began to open up and find a measure of peace in his life. He stopped drinking, then reached the point, with Tibby's urging, where he needed and wanted to examine the war that in so many ways had formed him as a human being; he needed, in Herman's model, to tell his story in a way that would make his community listen and allow it to change.

It is a need that has long preexisted the psychological terms invented to describe it. Phil Caputo, in his Viet Nam memoir, writes of the tradition of the battle singer, whose role was "to wring order and meaning out of the chaotic clash of arms, to keep the tribe human by providing it with models of virtuous behavior—heroes who reflected the tribe's loftiest aspirations—and with examples of impious behavior that reflected its worst failings." Homer became what his name called him to be—a battle singer—but he did so in his own terms: by creating a website that provided photographs and detailed accounts of his time in the war. Then, ready to retire, assessing his past, he had come across Dam's documents, forgotten in his mother's attic.

Although the face-to-face encounter that had taken Dam's life was rare in that war, Homer's impulse to hang on to the documents was not. Nearly all North Vietnamese soldiers and Southern National Liberation Front fighters—whom the Americans called Viet Cong—kept journals or diaries in which they copied and recorded poetry, their thoughts, the events of their days, and it was common practice for American G.I.s to take and keep these, or to give them to military intelligence. In fact, so many personal documents were collected that thousands were eventually put on microfiche and stored in the National Archives. No one knows how many thousands more were brought home by G.I.s and stored away, locked up. The lag between locking the documents away and bringing them into the light again—acting on the need, decades later, to not only confront and tell the unfinished past, but also to redeem it through concrete acts—was a common reaction. Over the last ten years, many veterans have made the effort Homer vowed to make back in 1969: to find the families of the men or women whose documents and diaries they kept and to return these personal belongings. To this date, over nine thousand have been returned to Vietnamese veterans' organizations through the Vietnam Veterans of America Initiative Program.

Homer had spent hours scanning those documents for his website, and when I wrote via email to some friends in Viet Nam—Phan Thanh Hao, a journalist and director of a social agency, and the writer Ho Anh Thai—I sent along the scans as attachments. My friends told me that the best solution was to bring the documents in May 2005, when I was planning to return to Viet Nam, and hand them over to the Vietnamese Veterans' Association. But a week later, I received an email message from Hao: she had written an article that was published, along with photos of the documents, in the newspaper. Ho Anh Thai had also gotten an article published in a major paper. The Hoang family had read the articles on the anniversary of their mother's death and had immediately called Hao. They were very excited. They wanted to get the documents back, and they wanted Homer himself "to place them on the family altar." They felt no bitterness or anger towards him, they said. It was war, and they understood war. All they felt now was gratitude.

On 22 April 2005, Homer emailed the following letter, through Hao, to the brother of the man he'd killed:

Dear Mr. Hoang Dang Cat,

I would love to have given the documents back personally, but I can't possibly afford a trip to Vietnam. I am retired, on a fixed income and with recent health problems, just don't have the money. Even if I did, I am afraid I am far too shy to meet with strangers, whose language I do not even speak. I was raised on a small farm and have always been very shy. I still do not know how I managed to be a Platoon Leader and Company Commander in the Army.

I am very touched that you have an altar that keeps Dam's memory alive. It makes me feel good to know that his brave soul is still honored in such a wonderful manner. It hurts to think of the hundreds of thousands on both sides of that tragic war, who still mourn the loss of their loved ones.

Sometimes the guilt of surviving can be overwhelming. What will I say, when I enter into eternity? Is there a little known footnote to the commandment "Thou Shalt Not Kill," that forgives killing in combat? Look what I did in the ignorance and folly of my youth. I thought I was a true patriot. So why doesn't that give me comfort at age 59?

Dam and I met by chance on a trail. He and I saw each other and both of us attempted to shoot the other. I lived. He died instantly. For over a quarter century I have carried the image of his young body lying there lifeless. It was my first kill. I wish I could say it was my last. Why did a medic die and I live? I don't know.

Maybe someday humanity will gain the wisdom to settle conflicts without sending its youth to kill strangers. Know that my website www.swampfox.info is an attempt to educate those who have not lived the horrors of war. People should know what our leaders are doing when they resort to armed conflict to solve political problems.

In my dying moment, Dam and many of his comrades will surely call to me. I am not afraid...only saddened. Perhaps we will meet again as friends.

Respectfully yours,
Homer

"I just can't do it," Homer told me. He asked if I would take the documents. A day later, they arrived at my house by express mail. He had let them go.

I hesitated a long time before I opened the padded envelope. The Vietnamese believe a male contains seven souls, a female nine, and I knew that for the Hoang family what I had was truly a piece of Dam's soul. For a moment, I felt a kind of resentment, fueled by an atavistic fear. What was I releasing into my home? I had not killed this man. As soon as the thought came to me, I tried to struggle against it. One of my Vietnamese friends had written me, when I told her that Homer might come over, that she would not want to meet the man, was not sure she could look into his face. Homer could have been me, I replied to her; he could have been any of us.

I opened the envelope and drew out the notebooks and papers, the smell of very old, very dry paper wafting to my nostrils. Everything had been kept in pristine condition. I looked through the documents as carefully as if I were an archaeologist examining an ancient and precious text. On one of the title pages, Dam had drawn an elaborate red and green orchid and printed his full name under the date 1-1-1966, using the kind of ornate lettering teenagers use to inscribe their school notebooks; another page was decorated with a drawing of a pair of surgical scissors. The book was divided into sections, each about the treatment for a different type of wound, though surprisingly the first section was about midwifery. Page after page was illustrated with painstakingly done medical drawings—head and neck arteries, bones of the leg, the hip, and so on—as if Dam had copied an entire medical textbook. The work is beautiful, and it is astonishing to think of Dam doing it in jungles, tunnels, and caves, under bom-

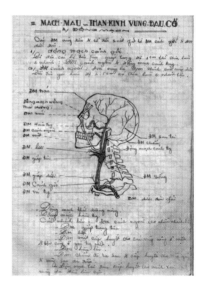

bardment and artillery fire. On the last page was the only drawing that did not seem neat: scrawled grids, five squares per line. I wondered if they were tactical positions, battle plans. When I showed them to a Vietnamese friend, he grinned and told me they were Vietnamese tic-tac-toe diagrams; he had played the same game when he was a kid.

Seeing and touching Dam's neat, precise handwriting, the letters tiny and taking as little space as possible, the exquisitely done anatomical drawings, I thought of Homer's anguished cry in his letter to Cat: *why did a medic die and I live?* What would Dam have become? What would he have accomplished? Who else had been taken from us? The book raised the questions war always raised, that war should always raise, the questions that should always be asked before a war and never are. But what pierced me deeply was the hope those meticulous drawings and notes revealed: the book was an amulet bound and filled by a young man trying his hardest to give himself the illusion of a future.

The notebook was not the only document. Inside it were four "Certificates of Commendation" that Dam had received. The earliest one, dated 20 October 1965, cited his "model" performance in serving the wounded soldiers of an unnamed artillery unit. He was elected (named) "outstanding individual" for the year 1965. The second, dated 22 December 1966, commended him for having "contributed to the building of a good unit during the first 6 months of 1966." The third citation was issued on 1 September 1967 for "accomplishments in the first 6 months of 1967," and the fourth commended him for his accomplishment "during the general offensive and uprising of 1968," that is, the Tet Offensive. It was dated 10 February 1969, a little more than a month before he would be killed.

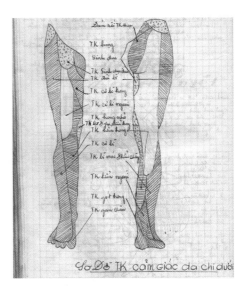

All of the other documents belonged to another man, an army truck driver named Nguyen Van Hai. The first was his license, affixed with his photo. Hai was a very handsome young man, and indeed one of the other papers seemed to be a love letter and poem to him from a girl he left behind:

When you left, I was speechless; I couldn't find the words to say. In every step you take away from here, I carry with me the feeling that I have...Our feelings for each other are as wide as the ocean. What is in your heart is also in my heart. Your image has faded away beyond the bamboo hedge, but you brought me to life. I was so moved when you told me to wait and do my duty, so touched that I didn't know how to reply to your words...Now you have left to fight the Americans and I must stay here to build the country. But I will see you again one day.

As long as there is still Heaven
As long as there is still earth
As long as there are still clouds
You and I will meet again.

When you left, I didn't know who to talk to, to be with. You left behind your spirit, which inspires me to keep strong. Now that you are on your way, I wish you good health and success in the fight against the Americans to save the country, so that we can be reunited one day. I promise to fulfill my duties as a younger sister should while you are away, and when you sit down to your meals, remember that there is still a younger sister who waits for you.

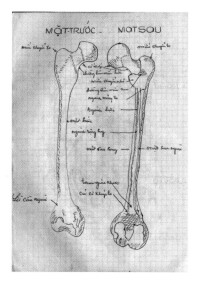
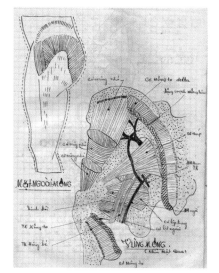

Had Nguyen Van Hai been a patient of Dam's who had died? We hadn't found out anything about him, though I would also give his documents to Dam's family. In the packet there were other letters to him, a black notebook filled with math problems, and copies of poems by Ho Chi Minh, in tiny handwriting. A friend wrote:

> I miss you like a son misses his father. I bought some cloth, and will buy some for your family if they need it. On August 26-28 the hamlet was bombed and children and old people had to be evacuated. Remember to write to me.

On the bottom of the letter is a note from Nguyen Van Hai's mother:

> Your departure had made me miss you so much; I will never forget you, Son. I feel sick from missing you so much.

We left for Dam's village of Thai Giang, in Thai Binh Province, at six in the morning on Saturday, 28 May, two days after I flew into Ha Noi. Phan Thanh Hao, who had written the article that the Hoang family read, had made and received hundreds of telephone calls arranging the visit. The village is located deep in the countryside south of Hai Phong, and we rode out in a small van, past the new textile and clothing factories lining the Ha Noi–Hai Phong highway, their products destined for Wal-Marts and Targets all over the territory of the old enemy. These businesses were the concrete forms reconciliation took when it occurred between nations, and they were raising the standard of living in Viet Nam, we are told, but there was something bitter and mocking about them to me, about the unanswered

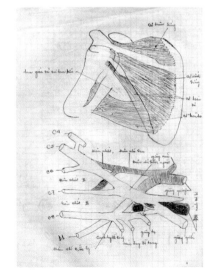

question they raised: what had all that killing been about? The reconciliation our small group was engaged in was modest in scale, more personal; it was the only kind that could bring about a true peace. We rode deep into the Vietnamese countryside, away from the new factories and into an older time.

With me were Hao, the novelist Y Ban, who is the editor-in-chief of Hao's paper, and George Evans and Daisy Zamora, two poets who were on that trip to help interview Vietnamese writers for another project we were doing. George is also a Viet Nam veteran and had also been a medic. He had arrived in the country in March 1969, the month Dam was killed and a year after his best friend, also a medic, had been killed. It was George's first time back in Viet Nam since the war. His wife, Daisy, is also a war veteran: in her youth, she had been a Sandinista guerilla.

It took us more than three hours to get to Thai Giang even though it is only, as the crow flies, about forty or fifty kilometers from Ha Noi. There were no direct roads, and on the way, we made a stop that also seemed to take us back into the war. Y Ban's father had died the month before, and we stopped at her family's house to pay respects and to light incense at the family altar. When I asked Y Ban how he had died, she hesitated and then said he had suffered from the effects of Agent Orange since the war; now, it had finally taken him.

Some of the members of Dam's family had arranged to meet us at a bridge near the main road, where they would lead us to the village. We stopped the van at the top of the bridge and waited. After a few moments, another car slowly drove past us and then pulled in front of us and stopped. Dam's brother and sisters were wearing the white headbands that signify mourning in Viet Nam. They were all weeping. They clutched my hand, the depth of their grief surprising me: it was as if Dam had died yesterday instead of many years ago. They asked us to follow them and for me to hold on to the documents rather than turn them over at that time. As we drove through the lush green countryside surrounded by rice fields, they would from time to time throw pieces of green and orange paper from their windows: Buddhist symbolic currency. They were leading Dam's soul back to his village.

I had come to Viet Nam with a small NPR crew to interview Vietnamese writers. I had asked that the crew not come out with us to Dam's village because I expected there to be a small ceremony just for the family. But as we came into the village, I was stunned to see that the street was lined with people, hundreds of them, the entire village, most of whom were wearing white headbands and many of whom were weeping and keening. I got out of the car and walked alone for a time, into the gauntlet, the rest of the party hesitant to get out of the car. I was there for Homer, as his surrogate, as his brother, and I was walking into the village of the man he had killed, holding the documents in front of me like an offering. I felt the naked vulnerability of a man walking point, as if I was offering my body to something, as if I was a surrogate for more than Homer.

The others in our party emerged from the van and caught up to me. George looked dazed. It was the first time he had returned to Viet Nam, and he'd only been there two days. Other relatives of Dam's gathered around us: an extended family of aunts, uncles, nephews, nieces, cousins. His sisters, Thi Dam, Tuoi, and Tham, and his brothers, Cat and Luong, were all weeping, touching the notebook—as was a woman I found out later was his widow, Phan Thi Minh. "I know war," Phan Thi Minh would say afterward. "It was horrible—all the young people had to go. My biggest memory of that time was of ceremonies to see young people off to the front. Families and everybody would come see them off, and we all cried, even the officials. We did not have much hope that they would come back, and so it was as if we were parting, forever parting. The war ended more than thirty years ago, but I don't know when its consequences will end. The war still lingers, like blood trickling in our hearts."

Surrounded by a small sea of grieving people, we walked in procession to the community center, its veranda ten deep with people. They crowded around us, needing to touch us, the women petting Daisy. On a stage inside, an altar had been set up; it held incense, flowers, and a large photo of Dam and was flanked by two Vietnamese veterans in dress-white uniforms standing at rigid attention. The small, hot hall was packed with men, women, and children.

A series of village and district notables mounted the stage and made speeches. Finally, Dam's brother Cat rose. His voice breaking, he thanked Homer for allowing the family this release. He bowed towards me as he spoke, and when he was finished, I climbed on the stage and presented the documents, wrapped in the national flag, to him. He placed them on the altar. Many in the crowd were wailing, crying out; Dam, folded back into his village now, was himself a surrogate, a point man, for the two hundred that had been taken from this small place.

When the ceremonies were finished, we rose and walked through a soft rain to the Hoang family's compound. Thi Dam, the second youngest sister, had been weeping continuously, her face so suffused with pain that I couldn't look at her. Daisy, unable to bear it any longer, put her arm around her shoulder, and the two collapsed against each other. She had been drawn back, Daisy told me later, into the griefs of her own war.

At the house, dozens of people crowded inside, and more were on a kind of patio area under some fruit trees outside, where tables and chairs had been set up for a huge feast. The family altar was against the wall; on it were photos of Dam, his other brother, killed in the prisoner-of-war camp, and their parents. People kept filing in to see and touch the documents, and children stared at us, softly pulling the hair on my arms and George's—the way I remembered Vietnamese kids doing during the war, amazed at our monkey hairiness. I sat next to Cat and to Pham Quang Huy, who had been Dam's friend and who would give me the details of Dam's death and burial. I had brought the papers of Nguyen Van Hai, the truck driver, along with Dam's, and I asked Huy what could be done with them. He looked at me in surprise, blinking. Hadn't anyone told me? Hai was alive and would come to the village soon to collect his things.

We ate with the family for about an hour and spoke about simple things: our families, our homes, and the losses of war, the price of hatred. I was told many times that the family wished Homer could be there. They would always welcome him, they said; the village had even offered to purchase a plane ticket for him. He was now a part of them.

After I returned from the village, it was a few days before I could get myself to sit down and write to Homer. A day later, I received two email messages in return. One was from him:

> I have a huge lump in my throat. I am sure I would have been a basket case, if I had been there. I am still trying to comprehend the totality of your email…I know it must have been difficult. Knowing that the family has the documents gives me great peace of mind…will get back in touch later, after I stop sobbing.

The other came from his wife, Tibby:

> When I asked Homer how he felt after reading your email tonight, he said, "Complete."

Two months later, sitting in the Steedlys' living room in western North Carolina, an area in some ways not unlike Viet Nam's Central Highlands, I again told Homer how eager the Hoang family was to have him visit them. The Steedlys' dog, Dottie, pushed her forehead against my side, and I scratched her ears. Moments before, Tibby had told me the story of how the small black dog had come into the family. Homer had noticed her cowering under a low bridge, starved and, judging from her reaction to his advances, apparently abused. He had sat with her for five hours, talking softly, and had finally stuck his hand out. When she sank her teeth into his thumb, he had not reacted, just let her grip him until she understood he would not harm her. And then she had come out and become their dog. It was something, Tibby said, that she wanted to tell me.

I'll go there, Homer said to me. He was ready now.

'Onipa'a

KE ALOHA O KA HAKU	THE QUEEN'S PRAYER
Mai nānā 'ino'ino	Behold not with
Nā hewa o kānaka,	Malevolence the sins of man
Akā, e huikala	But forgive
A ma'ema'e nō.	And cleanse
. . .	. . .
Ko mākou maluhia	And let peace be our portion
A mau loa aku nō.	Now and forever more.

The verses composed by Queen Lili'uokalani while imprisoned, as well as her motto, 'Onipa'a—be steadfast, firm, resolute—continue to wield profound influence over the Kānaka Maoli in their struggle for sovereignty and self-determination, in their strivings for justice.

In 1993, the people of Hawai'i came together to commemorate the centennial of the overthrow of the Hawaiian monarchy. The following passage is from *'Onipa'a: Five Days in the History of the Hawaiian Nation,* published by the Office of Hawaiian Affairs:

> For five days in January, 1993, thousands of kānaka maoli, Native Hawaiians, traveled from throughout the Hawaiian islands to gather at 'Iolani Palace for one of the most extraordinary events to have taken place in modern Hawaiian history. Although they came from all walks of life and backgrounds, the descendants of the ancient civilization that once thrived in these Pacific islands united to express their love for the memory of their Queen Lili'uokalani, to mourn the overthrow of the Hawaiian Kingdom on January 17, 1893, and to call out to the world that the right of self-determination must be restored to their sovereign nation. After 100 years of dishonor, neglect and shame, the Hawaiian people were renewed in their efforts to seek justice for historic wrongs....
>
> In the words and drama which were conveyed through the many 'Onipa'a ceremonies, vigils and theatrical re-creations of history, one understands the unresolved pain of past injustices and the vision for reconciliation and restitution for a healed Hawaiian nation.

*One hundred years after
Queen Liliʻuokalani
surrendered to the illegal
occupation by U.S.
government troops, her
statue stands above the
commemoration events
that echoed her plea
for justice.*

Photograph by
Franco Salmoiraghi, 1993

*The statue of Queen
Lili'uokalani stands
between 'Iolani Palace and
the Hawai'i State Capitol.
The Queen is an icon for
generations of Native
Hawaiians who have
rallied for sovereignty.*

Photograph by
Franco Salmoiraghi, 1993

My recollection of ʻOnipaʻa is at once overwhelmed by the thousands who gathered, of the many good friends who have since passed away—their expressions of exultation, their tears, their voices, mournful chants before sunrise in front of Washington Place, Queen Liliʻuokalani's last residence; their rousing oratory; the torchlight ceremonies, torchlight marches, vigils, hoʻokupu ceremonies, ʻawa ceremonies; the sight of many thousands, representing each of the islands, small communities, families, all marching together for love of the Queen—all believing in the future restoration of their nation—all welcomed with protocol ceremonies and chants at the gates of ʻIolani Palace; the Papakōlea kūpuna and keiki with whom I marched down the slopes of Pūowaina, Punchbowl Crater, to the Palace; the stirring speeches by sovereignty leaders; joining with throngs, bearing witness to the historical re-enactments, the sixteen-act "street drama" scripted by acclaimed playwright Victoria Nālani Kneubuhl, directed by the late Dallas Mossman Vogeler, acted out by ordinary citizens, activists and the extraordinary Glenn Grant—joining with a vast and wonderful audience picnic-style on the grass in a surround of trees to express displeasure with annexationists and to cheer Kānaka Maoli patriots; circulating petitions to express support for the governor's decision to allow only one flag—the Hawaiian flag—to be flown at ʻIolani Palace during ʻOnipaʻa—these and many other memories are fondly recalled.

I was also deeply affected by a personal experience that occurred when a young haole soldier began marching about the Palace grounds, proudly carrying a very large American flag. There was great concern that his actions would provoke confrontation, a most unwelcome possibility, as the organizers had, up to that point, succeeded in keeping the event peaceful.

I was asked to speak to the young man, and I did, accompanying him stride for stride about the grounds and around the entire block. As I am fairly well known in the Hawaiian community, my gesture protected him, disarmed those who might have been riled by his actions. We had a very good exchange—I found him well spoken, well mannered, and very polite. He expressed love for and pride in America; I explained that we meant no disrespect, but also wished to demonstrate love for our country.

Our conversation took place in less than an hour, I in a formal Hawaiian holomuʻu, he outfitted in civilian clothes, side by side. When we said goodbye, I hoped we could be friends, for he reminded me of my son, who is also fair skinned and blond and has hazel eyes. I invited the soldier to return the following day; he smiled politely and suggested he might take me up on the offer, but we never saw each other again.—Māhealani Perez-Wendt

A contemporary gathering for an historic observance. Opposite: Kūahu Kihe Ka Mauli Ola—The Breath of Life—was built January 16, 1993, on the grounds of ʻIolani Palace as a lasting reminder of the centennial observance of the armed usurpation of the sovereign government of Hawaiʻi by U.S. naval forces. The memorial was built with pōhaku brought by ʻohana from throughout the islands of Hawaiʻi as a symbol of commitment, strength, and unity for the revitalization and rebuilding of the Kānaka Maoli nation. It was dedicated the following day by Parley Kanakaʻole. Reverend Paul Sherry offered the first hoʻokupu: the apology of the United Church of Christ for the complicit role of its missionaries with agents of the U.S. government in the overthrow of the Hawaiian monarchy on January 17, 1893.

Photographs by
Franco Salmoiraghi, 1993

Night vigil: Kū ka lau lama i kukui hoʻokahi! *Many torches stand together to give one light! Opposite: Light reflects off the windows of the room where Queen Liliʻuokalani was imprisoned for eight months by the Republic of Hawaiʻi in retaliation for her role in the royalist restoration of January 7, 1895.*

Photographs by
Franco Salmoiraghi, 1993

*Kūpuna, mākua and
keiki who marched
from Papakōlea enter
the grounds of ʻIolani
Palace with hoʻokupu,
signs, and aloha.*

Photograph by
Franco Salmoiraghi, 1993

*Leaders of the Royal
Order of Kamehameha
honored the Kamehameha
and Kalākaua aliʻi at their
sovereign resting place
at Mauna Ala.*

Photograph by
Franco Salmoiraghi, 1993

The Queen's love of her
ancestors, people, land,
and nation lives on in
her songs, her genealogy
chant, and the Constitu-
tion of 1893, as displayed
on her statue. The
people's love for her
has been passed down
through the generations
to our time.

Photographs by
Franco Salmoiraghi, 1993

Letters of Farewell

8

Dear Y,

We never met. And yet I feel as if I knew you because, as you wrote, "Everything that lives and endures/for more than a day after we die/is eternal"—lines that live and breathe as surely as the mourning dove cooing from the eaves of a dormitory in Prague, which used to house the secret police. Ironic, no? Here in a tiny room, in which dissidents may once have been interrogated, I wonder what you would make of the wall they have built in your holy city of Jerusalem to separate the Israelis from the Palestinians.

This afternoon, to escape the heat of high summer and the crowd of tourists at the castle, I went to a café on Petrin Hill and, brushing away the bees that circled the bottle of black currant juice I had drained after my hike up from the river, read Kafka's "Jackals and Arabs"—a prescient work, it seems to me, about the situation in your homeland. You will recall how the jackals descend upon the carcass of a donkey, tearing its flesh to pieces even as the Arab leader of the caravan beats them with his whip. The narrator, who is from the north and presumably open to the jackals' arguments about the despicable Arabs (the mere sight of whom is enough to send the pack running off into the desert in search of purer air), finally catches hold of the leader's arm to stop the beating.

This brought to mind the story of a woman with a view of the castle from her flat. She went to her cottage in the country just before the Velvet Revolution, and although she heard something about a disturbance in the capital, she was not prepared, upon her return, to open her curtains to the banner hanging from the ramparts: HAVEL TO THE CASTLE. She wondered if she had lost her mind, for when she had left town, it was forbidden even to mention the playwright's name in public. Now he was being summoned to the castle, like Kafka's surveyor "gazing upward into the seeming emptiness," and like the pair of identical twins rising from the next table: two elderly women dressed in the same khaki suit, with the same graying hairdo. I took this as my signal to call for the check.

The walk from the elevator to my room is two hundred paces, down one corridor after another, all painted white—to disorient the prisoners; and when the surly desk clerk gave me the wrong key again, it took a half hour to reach my room, by which time I was in no mood to plot out a route to the Jewish Cemetery, where Kafka was buried. That I will not visit his grave—I have an early flight tomorrow—grieves me to no end.

After the Great War, when his lungs were ravaged and his hopes for love all but extinguished, Kafka dreamed of immigrating to Palestine. In the desert's dry air, freed from the tyranny of his father, the office, and the Jew-baiting gangs roaming the streets, he might have recovered from consumption and lived into old age. Then of an evening he would meet you and the other young writers in a café to read aloud his latest parable. It is comforting to imagine such a scenario: this is how peace is won or lost, no?

Yours sincerely,

9

Dear E,

The seminar on leadership was canceled at the last minute, and so the caterers and waiters joined the generals in the tent to hear a lecture on the connection between *The Old Man and the Sea* and the Book of Job. No doubt you would have scorned the scholar, not for his effeminate ways but for his bloodless discussion of religion. Even the generals snickered at his definition of suffering, which revealed his vast ignorance of a subject you understood better than any of your literary colleagues—and many soldiers.

Smoke was on the wind from the wildfire at Galena Pass. But the smoke-jumpers refused to work until they received their back pay, the air tankers were grounded while inspectors tested the spare parts supplied by a foreign manufacturer, and there was more heat lightning in the forecast. Alas, the National Guard was deployed overseas, building prisons for a conflict that you would have derided, in the sparest prose, filing dispatches from beyond the confines of the protected areas dear to modern journalists. Nor could we tell if the governor's proposal to have convicted felons dig firebreaks was made in jest. So much uncertainty in the new dispensation, and ashes falling everywhere.

After the lecture, the caterers spread on the tables at the back of the tent the hors d'oeuvres they had prepared for the seminar, which the waiters devoured during the question-and-answer period. It was unfortunate that the scholar's refusal to define the role of pleasure and pain in the distribution of gifts in the final days turned the affair into a free-for-all, in which, of course, the generals came out on top.

Poor horse, said the child whose father had not returned from a pack trip into the mountains. His mother stood on the roof, hosing down the cedar shakes and staring at the horizon to gauge the progress of the fire. It was time to decide whether to stay or flee, and she didn't trust herself to do the right thing, not after the debacle of her last performance at the community theater. What to do? She was in love with a man whose foolishness had rubbed off on her, and for all she knew he had accidentally set off the fire sweeping toward their house. The child gazed up at her. *Poor horse,* he began to sing.

Sincerely,

13

Dear E,

I recognize the inherent contradiction in addressing you directly. But I hope that you will forgive my impertinence: we are, as you know, returning to our origins, using letters from the Greek alphabet to name the hurricanes gathering force in the Caribbean, and since time seems to be running out, with glaciers in Greenland advancing on the sea or retreating into the interior, it occurs to me that a petition to you might be in order. For I take no pleasure in the prospect of London disappearing underwater, despite what some of my detractors have intimated in the press. Such are the hazards of public life.

The exhibit on the lost city of Pompeii sparked little interest among the delegates to the conference on eschatology, and with the nets on the tennis courts rolled up for the season, there was nothing to distract them from devising a rubric for a warming climate. Nevertheless, a proposal to market the ancient air bubbles retrieved from ice-core samples taken in Antarctica was not dismissed out of hand but tabled for later discussion, which may suggest the depth of my colleagues' aversion to change.

But this is no time for the faint of heart. We have been summoned to consider a range of measures to replace the old liturgies and declarations, treaties and protocols—in short, the conventional wisdom that has brought us to this impasse. Creative thinking is demanded, if we hope to avert catastrophe. Hence we must invent new forms of address, new litanies to chant by day and night: the grandest version of call and response, in which we will be the bondsmen and you will be every woman.

For it is a calling, is it not, to heed the signs by which you reveal your various selves—flora and fauna, wind and weather, elements and law: every color, every gesture. Thus we praise the patience of a woman who sat in the desert sun for four hours to watch a swallow build its nest under a bridge. And the lost notes of a man who tracked monarch butterflies through the mountains. And the slow accumulation of details, gathered on a nun's daily walk around the peninsula, about the action of the tides on the salt marsh, which she will pass on to the novices before their final vows. From such lore may emerge rites and ceremonies suitable for the age—that is, elastic and enduring.

Alpha, beta, gamma. It is time to learn the language in which your wisdom was vouchsafed to us. To harness the force of the winds sweeping over the sea. To weigh the evidence contained in the air bubbles. No doubt your verdict will be just.

Respectfully,

19

Dear S,

When I heard the scholar lecture on human rights, describing to a crowded theater the seven elements of reconciliation, I recalled the story of a secretary who worked in an office above the headquarters of the Quisling government, writing messages to her fellow members of the Resistance, in invisible ink, between the lines of the Nazi propaganda she was typing, and then I wondered what had become of you.

The story of your father's wartime escape, on skis, over the mountains to Sweden was what convinced me that he would put his own interests ahead of family and country. Nor was I impressed by his success in the New World, though I knew what it meant to you: our affair was doomed as soon as I declared that business acumen and poetry could not be reconciled—a belief that might have been dispelled by reading a biography of Wallace Stevens. What did I know? It was not a surprise that our last phone conversation ended abruptly, when the connection failed. *Damn*, you muttered. Then—silence.

That was ten years ago. But this morning, when the scholar began to list some of the landscapes of violence around the world, historical and figurative, I remembered the time that we broke into your parents' house to make love, and then, when your mother came home early from the club, quickly hid in your closet. She must have known that we were there, for she stood by the unmade bed, calling to you in the singsong voice she used to coax the cat down from the tree. We huddled together in the dark, under your dresses and slips—naked, frightened, and slick with sweat. It was thrilling.

The pain in my fingertips and toes I owe to a foolish decision dating from our last winter together. We had spent Christmas apart, and when you missed your flight back to Vermont so that you could see where things stood with your friend from the old country, I drank myself into a stupor. The temperature dropped to thirty below that night; in the morning, when I left for the airport hung-over and unshaven, the car jerked slowly down the hill, as if I was learning how to use the stick shift. The emergency brake had frozen, said the mechanic who thawed it out in his garage, while I hitchhiked to Burlington to meet you, without socks or gloves. It took me three hours to get there, by which time my hands and feet ached and you had made your decision about our future.

A thief made an imprint of my credit card in the kitchen of a restaurant in Oslo, where I had drunk a glass of aquavit in honor of the life we did not share, and sold it to someone in Milan who used it to buy a pair of gravestones—a crime that haunts me with its strangeness, its intimacy. I wonder if the buyer was arrested and imprisoned—and if he is still alive. Were the gravestones for his wife and himself? For his mistress? His parents? Sometimes I even imagine that our names are engraved on them.

Yeats said that whenever he turned to politics as a subject, he ended up writing a love poem. Just so, I had imagined this letter to be a farewell to the possibility of peace in our time, our adventure in the Middle East having provoked yet more bloodshed. But it became instead an excursion into love—ending, inevitably, with you. We had long since parted when out of the blue you invited me to spend a week in your flat near the Presidio; and though I knew this was your way of saying goodbye I prayed—*prayed*—for a change of heart. Foghorns sounded every morning, and in the afternoon we ran in the park, past boarded-up barracks and eucalyptus trees. I was trying to write a haiku sequence titled "Autumn in San Francisco"—which was, of course, just apprentice work. Still it pleased me to think that I was recording, if not redeeming, some portion of our time together. I doubt if you ever saw the finished poem, which closes with these lines:

> *The mallards on the pond*
> *By the Palace of Fine Arts*
> *Will never leave.*

Lucky sevens: sins, sacraments, and virtues. The Seven Seas, seven wonders of the ancient world, seven hills of Rome, seven churches of Asia, seven days, Seven Sisters, Seven Years' War. *The House of the Seven Gables.* Sabbaticals, and the seventh son, and the seven-year itch. The seven arts and sciences, seven orders of architecture, seven dwarves. The seven elements of reconciliation, of which I remember only the need to let go of bitterness. Why in the name of God did you betray me?

1

Dear X,

We will not meet again—that much is clear from my last conversation with your family—and since this letter may not reach you in time or, if it does, may not coax you from the depths you are exploring with the single-mindedness of the scholar who refuses to share the fruits of his discovery, I write in the belief that words matter, even if they are never articulated in the presence of the living. This much we learned on our journey through Persia, when everything changed between us.

We should have stopped. True, it was too dark to see beyond what the lights of our borrowed car revealed, and our fear of the bandits hiding in the mountains led us to drive too fast for safety. Through the open windows we heard the howling of wild dogs or jackals, a gunshot, a muffled sound we could not name. There was no time to swerve when a face suddenly appeared before us—just the thud of the car striking a figure in the dark. Was it a bandit? Somebody in need of help? Neither of us said a word. And when you pressed down on the accelerator, I nodded, though you couldn't see me.

The rest of the journey was eventless. When we returned the car, the owner said nothing about the dented bumper, accepting our extravagant tip with a benign smile. We took his advice to leave the country directly— the student demonstrations were gathering momentum—and soon after, our government broke off diplomatic relations, leaving us in the clear. Nor did we ever discuss what happened that night.

The cooling of our friendship was no doubt inevitable. Years passed; and if on the occasions that brought us together we seemed outwardly devoted to each other, trading jokes and gossip, we understood our bond for what it was: an essay in erasure. We wanted to believe that we had driven through the night in a strange land about to fissure, where we were granted an intimation of what was coming.

But in fact we saw nothing more than a face, which sometimes rises up before my eyes, when I am dropping off to sleep or drunk on wine, to tell me in a strangled voice that we are not absolved. I suspect you reached the same conclusion. Hence your refusal to return my phone calls once it became clear that time was running out.

I wish I knew her name. Perhaps you know it now.

Yours,

3

Dear Z,

We had to rebuild the wooden staircase in the dunes three times before the entire walkway was swept into the sea. I tell you this not because I imagine you will understand why we drifted apart, but because sometimes I think the tidal surge that led us to sell the house, which had been in my family for generations, might have saved us.

Renewal was our theme, and so we were obsessed with endings: leaves swirling in a cracked fountain, the ruins of a stone wall deep in the woods, exhibits of endangered and extinct animals—a dodo's skeleton pieced together from bones scattered on the island of Mauritius, a stuffed passenger pigeon, wax figurines of the white rhinoceros and the wild yak, the jawbone of a gray whale. Our collection of tin soldiers grew. Likewise the number of copies of Revelation distributed to the sailors we enlisted for our journey to the ends of the earth. We promised them everything. And they believed us.

Or so we told ourselves. This was the source of our break—not, as some imagine, because of the difficulties encountered on our voyage: the gun battle with pirates in the Straits of Malacca, the outbreak of cholera in an Indian backwater, the month in a prison in Oman due to a mistake in our logbook. Indeed we grew to like our jailors: turbaned men who took an ironic view of our situation. They were passionate about chess, women, and theology, and when they tired of interrogating you, they would challenge me to a match. This was their chance to speculate on the nature of God and women, which for them seemed to be one and the same—at least when you were out of earshot. Alas, they didn't appreciate my sense of humor, for which I beg your forgiveness.

Not that I expect absolution, now or in the hereafter. But I believe that what we discovered during our internment will guide us on our separate journeys: the importance of discerning the difference between truth and self-regard; the way that faith resembles an underground river, which occasionally emerges underfoot to carve a new bed in the earth; how difficult it is to sleep when you are falling in or out of love.

I will always love you.

Yours,

5

Dear K,

The scientist who germinated a palm seed excavated from Masada nicknamed it Methuselah—a date palm from the time of the Crucifixion, the razing of Jerusalem, and the mass suicide of the Zealots, who refused to surrender to the Roman garrison besieging their cliff fortress. The seed lay in a drawer for thirty years before the scientist roused it from dormancy, soaking it first in hot water, then in acid, and then in a broth of seaweed before she planted it in a pot. And now a palm from the shore of the Dead Sea is growing in her laboratory in California, with the breath of the defenders of Masada circulating among the other seedlings, like rumors of war.

I write this, though you can no longer read, because resurrection was your theme. True, you disdained religion—the bloodshed visited upon your land in its name defined our friendship—and yet you took a sacred view of the texts in your keeping, especially the Haggadah vouchsafed to you during the siege. And when I consider the unlikely settings in which we met (a hotel in Barcelona, a townhouse in Boston) to discuss the mystery of survival—of books, culture, civilization—I think we were really celebrating an order of values dear to the Psalmist: *The righteous shall flourish like the palm tree. They shall bring forth fruit in old age. They shall be fat and flourishing.*

Just as a library can be partially reconstructed from the records assembled over the centuries—even if the illuminated manuscripts and codices, literary correspondence, and handwritten accounts of heresies and political feuds destroyed in the conflagration cannot be replaced—so the past remains alive in our gestures, like dormant seeds. Hence the story of the lending library you set up in your neighborhood, with the books spared from the fires kindled for cooking and heating, must prepare us for the next loss.

The area of the brain excised in surgery, for example, or burned away by radiation therapy, taking away your sense of smell, pitch, colors, memory, grammar, words.

The righteous? They occupied the high ground around the city, took aim at young and old alike, and emptied the streets with their shells. They flourished for a while before fleeing into the hills, where they remain, protected by their followers. And perhaps they will escape justice, living into old age, grown fat on their legendary deeds.

In Genesis we read that Methuselah lived for 969 years, and then he died. In my ledger of war casualties, I will record that there are oranges, dates, figs, and everything you could wish for in the market, where once there was only blood.

Yours,

The Homecoming of an Old Beijing Man

Just ten years, and the city is gone. Old square yards with elms and wisterias, gone; narrow lanes patrolled by sharp-eyed, tiny-footed ladies from the neighborhood committee, gone. Skyscrapers shoot up into the sky like bamboo shoots. Highways, streets, alleys, and sidewalks are covered with cars spitting fumes into air. No more blue sky. No more dirt or weeds. Everything is smoothed over with concrete. My shoes never get muddy; my collar stays clean for a whole week, quite unlike the old dusty days. Restaurants line up along the street like sparrows on wires, and beautiful girls lean on doors, their sweet voices snatching souls, their painted eyes making knees tremble. What choice do I have but to enter and sit down at a table? I've never eaten out so much. Four times a week at least: roast duck, lamb fondue, pig's feet, donkey's ass, and fish that cost eighty-six yuan a pound, half of my monthly salary before I retired. I eat and drink till my stomach is about to explode, and then stroll into a hotel for a whole body massage to digest the meat and wine. If I'm not too tired after that, I go to a karaoke bar with my son for more drinks and fun. Six months in Beijing, I just eat, drink, and sing, going to places in my son's 2004 Mercedes or my daughter's Audi. I put on thirty pounds. What a lucky old man I am!

I didn't mean to stay this long. I had promised my youngest daughter I'd return to Minnesota in a month, as soon as I finished this monkey business with my son-in-law in Beijing. "Ba, your home is in Minnesota," my youngest daughter reminds me almost every day on the phone. True, for ten years I've lived in Minnesota with her and her kids and my old wife. Three years ago, I became a naturalized alien. That's what the paper says. I guess I'm a natural American citizen now, head to toe, inside and out. And I have a really nice home in Minnesota—a big house on a crystal-clear lake full of fish and five acres of rich land. The property is worth at least a million now. My daughter is a great business woman. The first thing she did when she came to America was go to school at Hamline University. She had to study harder than her classmates because her English was bad. I don't quite get it. Her English was good enough to get her a job as an interpreter for foreign tourists in Beijing, and to get herself a great husband. Anyway, she got her MBA and now stays home managing the stocks her husband left behind. Still, she needs me: her kids still young, and her mother, my old wife, still wanders outside and gets lost all the time. For almost ten years, I've been the only man in her household. I don't speak English or drive, yet, but I'm a man, the pillar of the house. I promised her I'd go home after the Mid-autumn Festival, as soon as I had a chance to eat the Muslim-style moon cakes. How can any filial daughter deny an old man such a simple request?

But my son and daughter in Beijing come up with all sorts of ways to get me to stay one more week, then another. Soon one month becomes two, and two turns into three. Then it's Thanksgiving, and my daughter starts marinating three fat chickens with garlic, soy sauce, and tea leaves for roasting, so what else can I do but stay another two weeks? In the blink of an eye, Christmas arrives. My son insists I should experience how Chinese celebrate Christmas nowadays. It has become a big deal, almost bigger than the Spring Festival. He takes me to a church on Christmas Eve. Nice music, short service, and a big feast. I've never seen so much food in my life. We eat and drink till dawn. By then, everyone is singing and dancing and making merry. I'm sure Lord Jesus himself is smiling happily from the sky. That's the way to celebrate his Lord's birthday, anyone's birthday.

When life is good, time flies.

Beijing seems to have become a paradise for the rich. They dress well, eat well, and travel to Paris, London, New York, and other nice places for vacations. They are loaded with money. Just look at my son's apartment in the heart of the city: six bedrooms, 250 square meters, all for himself, and his rotating girlfriends. Do you know how much a place like that costs? Ten thousand yuan a square meter. Go figure. I worked my ass off my entire life. All I got was a crummy apartment with less than twenty square meters, no kitchen, no bathroom, no water. A rat hole, as my son called it. In that rat hole, I raised my three kids plus my adopted son, who later became my son-in-law. And you know what? I was much more content than my rich playboy son, who constantly complains about his place being too small and out of fashion and is looking to put two million yuan down on a mountain villa at the foot of the Great Wall.

Same thing with my daughter. She has an apartment just as big as her brother's place for her family of three: herself, her son, and her husband (before she kicked him out after his affair with a seventeen-year-old). What a sin! I often wonder how she feels when she drives by the slums where migrant workers and unemployed people congregate. She used to be such a conscientious girl, giving and generous, hardworking like her husband. When she turned eighteen, she joined the Party, a young, promising member and an ideal companion to her husband, the most hardworking and honest man I've ever seen. I knew what I was doing when I did the matchmaking.

But ten years later, both she and my son-in-law joined my son's camp of ruthless greed. Now she's buying another apartment in my name, just because she can. She hates to see her money rotting in the bank. An apartment in the city will triple its value within a year. Why in my name? Not because I'm moving back to Beijing. No. She doesn't want her husband to get it if they get a divorce. You see the kind of brain she has?

I try not to ask how on earth she got that kind of money. As far as I know, she's still a good daughter, filial and capable. When I left for America ten years ago, she was working as a government employee making sixty-five yuan a month, not enough for a cup of tea these days in Beijing. And my good-for-nothing son didn't even have a job. You may ask why I didn't find a job for my only son. I did, a dozen at least, in my own department, in my friends' departments. All office jobs, no manual labor, unthinkable for someone who didn't even have a high-school diploma. But my boy couldn't hold anything longer than a week, couldn't stand being shut in a cubbyhole from nine to five every day, six days a week. Just couldn't. I thought he'd end up on the street as a beggar. Instead, he became a millionaire, richer than his sister.

I don't know how they made their fortunes. I don't want to know. They're grown-ups. I taught them what's good, what's bad. They surely work hard, but not the way I worked for the Party. For forty-six years, I never arrived late or left early a single time, never stole a fen, never had an affair. You bet I had opportunities. Too many. I was the secretary to the minister of hydraulic power. All the dams we built for the new China. Big responsibilities, big money deals, and always surrounded by beautiful girls. But the idea of pocketing a penny never entered my mind, let alone glancing at a girl who was not my wife. That's how we were, the pure, dyed-in-the-wool communists. Our only dream was to build a paradise where everything was just and everyone was equal and happy. Most of my buddies are dead now. Those still alive have quit the Party. They're sick to death over what's going on. Everyone steals. The big shots steal big bucks, and the small potatoes steal pennies and nickels. Those who refuse to steal can't hold their jobs for more than a month, because they make the thieves look bad, and the bad guys get rid of the good guys in order to steal with ease. Sure, the government tries to intervene. Every year they catch a few and kill them to send a message. Last year two lieutenant governors and the vice chairman of the People's Congress were shot—the biggest chickens ever killed—to scare the monkeys. Have the monkeys gotten the message? You bet your ass they have. They started stealing more and faster. Grab as much as possible while you can, before you get caught, that's the mantra. And what's the chance of getting caught anyway? Less than a plane crash a year, less than being hit by lightning. Besides, there's always the escape route to America or Canada or Europe. With the millions of dollars they've stashed away in Swiss banks, they can live anywhere like kings and queens.

Would I be corrupt like them if I had stayed in China? I don't think so. I'm old-fashioned, a die-hard communist. I would have quit the Party, too, like my buddies. I miss Mao, miss our good old days. Sure we had only one pair of pants and a jacket in those days, had meat to eat once a week at most, and a one-room apartment to raise kids. But we were clean, our souls full of fire for a better society. Now we live in big apartments and go around in nice cars and eat out every day, but my conscience is ill. The rich are so rich they don't even know how to squander. The other night in a karaoke bar, I saw a guy throw out two stacks of hundred-yuan notes for his waitress. I asked my server if it happens often that a client leaves a ten-thousand-yuan tip and she said, "Grandpa, that's not a ten. That's a twenty-thousand-yuan tip, and it's the norm in this bar."

How I wish I could have smacked that smirk off her fox face!

Instead, I fled. Twenty thousand yuan to a hooker bitch? No way!

When a worker is laid off, he gets two hundred yuan from the government, if he's lucky. That tip could feed two hundred poor workers and their families for a whole month.

Let me tell you how the poor live in Beijing. One morning I couldn't sleep, so I went for a walk. In the dim light, I saw a man picking food from a garbage can. "Rotten Egg's son, what the hell are you doing here?" I shouted. Of course I knew exactly what he was doing and why, from his hollowed cheeks and patched clothes, from the stale cabbage leaves clutched in one hand, and the plastic bag with empty Coke bottles in the other. He looked up. For a split second, I thought I had the wrong man. Rotten Egg's son was the same age as my oldest daughter, forty-two, and this man looked older than me. But the old man answered in a choking voice.

"Uncle Wu, Uncle Wu, I can't believe you're still alive! I can't believe you still remember me!"

I started weeping myself. Of course I remembered him. His father, Rotten Egg, had shared the same office with me for twenty-five years. We were drinking buddies. We played cards every weekend. I called him Rotten Egg because he was the biggest cheater I'd ever met, and his hands reeked with the odor of bad luck. Whenever we lost, I'd yell, "Rotten Egg, you need to move your ancestors' tombs to a better spot so you can get some luck for once in your life."

Indeed, Rotten Egg was an incarnation of ill stars. His parents died when he was seven. At thirteen, he ran away from his uncle to join Mao's army. With his long years in the army and the Party, he should have been a minister at least, if not a governor. Yet he had never gone beyond being the vice minister's secretary. And his only son inherited the same luck: sent at seventeen to Mongolia, where he herded cows and sheep for ten years, he didn't return to the city until his father retired. I used my back-door connections to get him a job in the dam construction company associated with the Hydraulic Power Ministry. It was manual labor in the open air all year round, but the pay was good, and the job was secure, considering the kid had no degree or skill or brains. Before I left for America, I found him a nice spinster. Not a young beauty for sure, but a virgin all right. Time for Rotten Egg to hold a grandson in his arms.

On the eve of my departure, Rotten Egg got drunk. "Brother Wu, Brother Wu," he wept. "Who's going to play with me when you're gone? Who's going to take care of my son when I'm gone?"

"Shut up!" I yelled. "Can't you say something auspicious before my flight? You and I will live at least twenty or thirty more years. And I'll be back in no time, brother, and we'll play cards again. I promise."

Had I only known it would take me ten years to come back! Had I only known Rotten Egg would be crushed by a car while crossing the street, and his son would end up a scavenger in the garbage!

What could I have done? What could I have done to make things better?

"I'd like to invite you to my place, Uncle Wu," Rotten Egg's son murmured. He sounded exactly like his father, the same nasal whine, same twitching eyes that indicated bad luck. "But I have no chair for you to sit on, no water or electricity to make you a cup of tea."

So we chatted on the street. He had been squatting in his father's apartment after he lost his job. The company was privatized four years ago, and he was dismissed with a two-thousand-yuan retirement package. Couldn't find another job, not even as a temp. No one would hire a forty-year-old man when the city was swarmed with hordes of young peasants willing to do anything for almost nothing. The housing department had been trying to get him out, cutting off water, electricity, and other services.

"Still, I'm better off than most of my ex-coworkers," he chuckled. "At least I still have an apartment. Luckily I don't have a family to support. My wife left when I lost my job. Don't fret, Uncle Wu. It's fate. I want her to live on. No need to hang two people on one tree."

I slipped two hundred yuan into his pocket. "Buy some bread for yourself, son," I said and walked away fast. I couldn't say a word. I'm sure Chairman Mao couldn't say a word either from his grave.

I heard there are millions of unemployed workers like Rotten Egg's son: those who lost jobs and apartments and had nowhere to go, and those who lost their land and poured into cities for a meager living. We're sitting on a volcano.

I said to my daughter one day, "I'm not questioning how you've made your money. I just want to say this: Don't be greedy. Stop when you've made enough for a comfortable life."

"Yes, Father," she said.

Can she quit? Will she? I doubt it. She manages the designer-clothes section at Saite, the biggest department store in Beijing. Her floor has over two hundred workers, making huge profits every month, though every other floor loses money. She tried to quit twice so she could spend more time with her son and keep a better eye on her husband, but the company wouldn't let her. They bribed her with a limo, two personal assistants, big bonuses, power. Every morning a handsome young man drives her to an air-conditioned office, her secretary brings her Blue Mountain espresso and the *People's Daily* on a silver tray. She sips her morning elixir, reads the paper, and gives instructions for the day's plan, then takes off, doing whatever she wants. Her days are swamped with lunch and dinner invitations from designers and wholesalers. Their fortune depends on her, and they'll do anything to keep their products on her floor. Should I name some of the gifts piled in her closets? Chanel perfumes, Lancôme cosmetics, Gucci bags, Armani dresses…oh, there's her son's college fund, half a million under his name, and the boy is only seven. Unbelievable! But this is nothing compared to what the big shots get: cars, apartments, mansions in Canada and America…You ask me why such elaborate gifts? Go figure.

I'm afraid. So is she. We all know we are sitting on a volcano. Our butts feel the heat and quiver. She wants to quit, but can't. She's already on the pirate ship. Around her, nothing but the vast sea. To quit is to lose everything. Without things, she's worthless, better off dead than alive, especially for a woman her age—forty and up. She's lost her youth, her face wrinkled, waist round and puffy. Neither makeup nor cosmetic surgery will ever make her young again. If her husband takes on a few mistresses, what can she do but weep and swallow her tears in silence?

Let me tell you something about Chinese men these days. As soon as they get a few extra yuan in their hands, they run out and find themselves some girls: hookers, mistresses, concubines. Doesn't matter if he is a high-ranking official or pulls a rickshaw. Every man is a rotten egg, including my own son, including my son-in-law, that son of a rabbit. When I took him home to Beijing from Tang Shan twenty-eight years ago, he was nothing but a scrawny country bumpkin. I gave him a home, sent him to school, got him a job in my department, introduced him to the Party, promoted him to the head of the department, and then gave him my oldest daughter. I thought I had an eye for a good man. He had been good, exceptionally good. My kids, at least my daughters, had regarded him as a big brother and role model. And he was the best worker, the straightest person I'd ever encountered. When I was interrogated for corruption, my wife went mad and wandered around the streets for days and weeks without returning home. He came to see me every day in jail, every day for a whole year, bringing me food and clothes and kind words. He was the only one who believed in my innocence, the only one who wrote hundreds of letters to higher authorities to expose the crooks who had put me in jail because I had refused to cooperate in their corruption schemes.

When he married my daughter at thirty-three, he was still a virgin. How did I know? Because my daughter asked for a divorce a year after their marriage. I asked her why. She started crying and said the husband I'd chosen for her was a eunuch. No way, I said. I'd seen his body as we walked those two hundred miles from Tang Shan to Beijing. He had a perfect body, nothing missing or deformed. So I questioned him. He blushed hard, this thirty-four-year-old man, and mumbled that he didn't know much about sex and he'd been hoping I'd give him some advice. So I did, and two years later, their son was born.

My heart broke when I heard he took his secretary, a seventeen-year-old girl, for his concubine.

What turned an old virgin into a playboy?

Perhaps I shouldn't be too hard on him. After all, who doesn't like the tender flesh of a seventeen-year-old? But eating tender meat is one thing; beating your wife is another. A man can have as many concubines as he wants, but he must respect his wife, put her first, no matter how old and ugly, how unpleasantly shrewd. A wife is a wife, just as a concubine is a concubine. There's an order in things, a place for everyone. You break that order, society will turn upside down. You'd think that son of a rabbit would know better. But no, he beat up his own dear wife, his son's mother, in front of his little whore. How pathetic! How is she going to live again? How is she going to show her face in public, let alone run a big company?

Before that happened, I'd been telling my oldest to swallow it, just swallow it, for the sake of her son, her own happiness in the long run. She had never been much of a looker when she was young. Now she's past forty. If divorced, how on earth would she find another man? Even if she finds one, there's no guarantee that a new husband wouldn't pick up a concubine. It's the trend of the nation, as old and mysterious as human desires. Old Confucius was absolutely right: when the body is clothed and stomach fed, lust comes racing.

She had called at five o'clock in the morning Minnesota time, weeping like a little girl. Her husband hit her in front of the little bitch concubine. She was going to kill herself because she had lost her face.

"He brought her home?" I gasped.

"No, I followed them to a restaurant. They sat together like real lovers, holding hands even while they ate. I couldn't stand it. He never treated me like this. Never! For the first year, he was nothing but a eunuch, then he was a cold fish. All these years, I slept next to him feeling dry and old and worthless."

"You have your charm and you definitely have a brain," I said, trying to console her. Unlike my youngest daughter, who has fair skin and watery big eyes, my eldest is endowed with a thick torso, short limbs, high cheekbones, small eyes, and a dry, flaky complexion. She's lucky she has a husband at all.

"I couldn't stand watching them chat and neck like lovebirds. So I burst in and scratched the bitch's face and pulled her hair. I pushed her to the floor and kicked her in the stomach. And the bastard slapped me."

"Tell him to sleep in his office for a week," I said. "That'll teach the son of a rabbit a lesson."

"I already changed the lock and dumped all his suits into a trash can. He's not coming back."

That was when I decided to go home, after ten years in America, to take care of the monkey business my son-in-law and my daughter had created.

My youngest daughter said, "Ba, you vowed never to go back again. Have you forgotten the year you spent in jail, your high blood pressure? Since you came to Minnesota, you've never been so happy, so peaceful. You can double the size of your vegetable garden if you want, go fishing as long as you want, and I promise I won't say a word about your fatty pork, your grandson won't laugh at your pig-feet casserole again. I promise. But don't go back. You'll lose your temper, you'll have a stroke, and—"

"Your big sister needs me, and your brother, too."

She cried, "What about me, Ba?"

I sighed. At the hospital, her husband wouldn't let go of my hand. He couldn't speak, couldn't close his eyes until I said I'd stay till my grandchildren grew up. Poor Jimmy, so kind, so intelligent, so loving! You can't find such a gentleman among Chinese anymore. Why did he have to be diabetic? Why did he have to die at fifty-seven? My poor daughter, widowed in her twenties, with two young kids and the ferocious relatives of her late husband who called her a vixen and tried all sorts of tricks to strip her rights. Of course I stayed. I'm her father, for heaven's sake, grandfather of a lovely girl and a smart boy. I know my daughter, my pigheaded child. She'll never marry again. After a husband like this, she can't look at another man again. It was love at first sight. He went to Beijing for a conference, and she was assigned to him as an interpreter. She was twenty-two, a flower ready to bloom. He had just turned fifty, had three grown-up kids from his first marriage. But no matter. Before his trip was over, they were engaged. Their love was the kind you hear only in fairy tales or see in movies. How she suffered during the year waiting for her immigration papers! And how he traveled to Beijing every other month to comfort her! I still remember the tears in her eyes when she boarded the plane to America. It was her decision to have a kid to keep their love going. She knew he would die ahead of her, way ahead. So she persuaded him to let her get pregnant. The first one was a girl. He was thrilled, having wanted a girl all his life. But no, she wanted a son, a son to carry on his name, his spirit, his intelligence, his face. Jimmy wrote to me, begging me to come over. He was about to have his legs amputated, and his wife was pregnant with their second child. The man knew he didn't have too much time. So I came. It was good timing. China had started the reforms, and things were changing fast. The new government was dumping old Party loyalists to clear the path. After I got out of jail, I returned to my old job, but nothing was the same. I was losing my temper every day, throwing things, yelling at my wife, quarreling with my boss, my friends. My blood pressure shot up to two-fifty.

Is America as heavenly as my daughter described? Well, everyone has his own heaven. For my daughter, it was her husband. For my son, it's his Mercedes. For me, it's a good meal over a bottle of Er Guo Tou liquor and a chat with old friends. During my first year in Minnesota, I had no one to talk to. There were only a handful of Chinese in the Twin Cities in those days, and most of them were restaurant workers who spoke only Cantonese and were too busy to chat with a customer. The streets were nice and clean, so clean that I stopped my spitting habit. No one forced me to. No police or old ladies with red armbands scolded me or gave me tickets like in Beijing. If I wouldn't spit on the carpet in my own house, I wouldn't spit on a street that seemed cleaner than my floor. But the streets were worse than a maze, no garbage can or a store or a person to mark my way home. After I got lost a dozen times, after my daughter drove around searching for me in dark streets and parks, she begged me to stick to Summit Avenue. "Don't go off on other streets, please," she said with tears in her eyes. But I'm a human, not an inmate or a dog to be let out for relief. If I see something interesting, I like to cross the street and take a look. Not that there is much to see anyway, except for trees that don't talk. It took me ten years to like their silence. My daughter and her husband were living in a big condo on Summit Avenue at that time, ten times bigger than my apartment in Beijing, but I was dying from loneliness. My American son-in-law was a cultured man, having held many important jobs in his life, directing museums in big cities. He tried to entertain me with his funny Chinese, and I shouted back with my pidgin English, and we just ended up laughing. He did teach me how to enjoy football and turned me into a Vikings fan. He found a church near the University campus, which had a few dozen Chinese followers. The first time my daughter took me there, I talked two hours nonstop with some men, before I got to know their names and where they came from. It turned out they barely spoke Mandarin, but they listened as if they were listening to a sermon. Such good Christian lambs! Since then we've been going there every Sunday. We're not converted. Not yet. I tell my Chinese pastor I am still thinking, just so he won't shut his door on me. I have no interest in the Bible stories or Jesus' deeds. The food there is terrible, but it is free, and I get my salvation: to speak Chinese for a whole afternoon.

After his amputation, my son-in-law bought a house on the lake, a house equipped for wheelchairs, surrounded by five acres of trees. Every day I dig and fish. The water calmed me down, and the garden, too. Since we moved there, we've never bought a single fish or vegetable. Everything comes from the lake and garden. Morning and evening, I play with my grandchildren. Smart, smart kids, just like their daddy, and so good looking, like most of the mixed bloods. When they go to school, I move rocks, fix the fence, plant vegetables and trees, weed, fertilize, feed chickens and goats…Yes, I have two goats, one black, one white. Great milk, tasty meat. I would have raised pigs if my neighbors let me.

My daughter said, "Ba, you're a Minnesotan, a true Minnesota farmer."

I nodded and smiled. I was born in a peasant family of many generations. I grew up digging in the fields until I joined Mao's army to fight Japanese devils, then the evil Nationalists and greedy landlords, until we finally threw out those bloodsucking imperialist colonizers from the West and established a new China. My Yellow Plateau and its hard clay soil! How my parents and grandparents would have cried with joy if they had seen the Minnesota land, so rich you can squeeze oil from it! Fate is a big laughing mouth. Sixty years ago, I ran away from home to fight the landlords and American imperialists. Now I have become an American citizen, own five acres of the richest land on the cleanest lake, a landlord a hundred times bigger and richer than those country bumpkins I had helped to execute.

China had become a memory, far away and long ago. And Beijing, my beloved city, came to me only in my dreams, as fragrances of duck feet, cow tongues, pig elbows, and dumplings with pork and white cabbage.

"Ba," my daughter said, "I've never seen you so calm, never seen you get along with Ma so well. America has made you healthy again, and happy."

"Happy, yes, happy," I said.

In Beijing, I eat like a pig, all the fatty stuff cooked with soy sauce my Americanized daughter didn't allow me to touch for ten years, all the delicious things my American grandson scoffed at. Ba is making up for his lost dreams, my Chinese daughter said, laughing. She bought me the largest pig head she could find. I gnawed on its crunchy ears, its chewy nose and tongue, its tender cheeks. For ten years in Minnesota, I had to beg like a child to buy meat other than steak or chicken breast, the most boring kind, like white bread. No flavor, no personality, no fat to oil my joints or smooth my intestines. I still can't believe how Americans throw away feet, head, and intestines, liver and heart, and grind them to feed chickens and cows, cats and dogs. My daughter claims it is the American way. O.K., but is it also the American way to cook food either boiled or broiled only, with no salt, sugar, oil, or soy sauce? Only Tartars from two thousand years ago cooked this way.

"It's to prevent diabetes and high blood pressure, Ba," said my Americanized daughter. Well, I'm not diabetic, nor am I a barbaric. I'm sick of cooking my meat in the fireplace in the middle of the night, when my daughter and grandchildren are sound asleep, sick of not being allowed to use the stove. Chinese cooking ruins the house, she said, all the frying and smoke and grease. Well, she might as well seal up my mouth and give me an I.V. The clean way, the American way.

So I open my belly and stuff myself like a pig. Not just to fulfill my carnal desires, but also to fool that good-for-nothing son-in-law of mine. He called the day I got home, offering to drive me around the city and visit my old friends in his car, offering to take me out to a stand that sells smoked donkey.

"The only one left in Beijing, and the best one, Ba," he said.

Son of a rabbit, the nerve he has to call me "Ba." How could he face me again after he broke my heart like this? When I took him to Beijing in 1976,

I treated him like a son, an eldest son. Whatever I gave to my children, he had a share: food, clothes, books, education…except for whipping. I never raised my voice to him, never lifted my belt over his head. He owes everything to me: his job, his Party membership, his rank, his home, his wife and son. And what did he give me in return? A slap in my face! As far as I'm concerned, boxing my daughter's ear in public is equivalent to boxing my ear in public. If I had my way, I'd punch his face till he got his senses back. A real Chinese man never shows disrespect to his wife in public, no matter how many concubines he takes in.

I'd also ask him how he changed from a communist into a beast.

But I just *mmmhed* and *aahaaed* with him over the phone. I guess I have been re-educated in America, tamed and cultivated by "Minnesota nice." Not really. I just wanted to find out the truth before taking action. I'd only heard my daughter's side of the story. The girl has a tendency toward imagination and exaggeration, a womanly tendency, if you know what I mean. Finding truth takes patience and strategy. You beat around the bush till you find the path. You never confront, never say, "Hey, son, I heard you've taken in a concubine. Is it true?" Of course he'll say, "No, sir, that's not the truth." Of course he'll hide his woman while waiting to weather the storm. So I just eat all day and play with my grandson, who is seven years old and smart as an elf. The boy spends weekends with my son-in-law after my daughter kicked him out.

My son gets more and more impatient. He assumes the only reason I came back was to help him beat the shit out of that ungrateful beast, and he's been pumping his muscles lifting weights and doing sit-ups to prepare for the fight. The moment I took my Tang Shan orphan home, my son disliked him. The boy who twice saved my life dwarfed him in every respect. When I left for America, I made my son-in-law the trustee. He drew money from my monthly retirement pay and gave my son a weekly allowance. It was humiliating, but what else could I do? My son could not be trusted with money. He would have spent his monthly allowance in five minutes.

"What are you waiting for, Ba?" he growls. "His little whore's belly is getting big. If we don't teach him a lesson now, we'll have endless trouble. The bastard is desperate. He wants half of my sister's money. Half! Do you hear?"

That's news to me, serious news. When the baby is born, when the rice is cooked, my daughter will lose her husband, and I'll lose my eldest son, forever.

I approach my grandson.

"What a game, what a brain, sonny boy." I praise the boy bending over the little square machine. That's all he does now: play Game Boy and watch TV. No more talking with his mother or grandpa or anyone else. "Who taught you this complicated game: your dad or your aunt?"

"Aunt Li," he said without looking up.

"Is she as pretty and young as your other aunt?" I pointed to my American daughter's wedding photo of ten years ago.

"Not as pretty, but she's fun and laughs a lot. She plays with me like the big sister I've always wanted."

Tender meat, that bastard loves tender meat.

"Is your daddy's new place as big as your mom's?"

The boy shook his head. "Grandpa," he said, stopping his Game Boy and looking at me with his dark bright eyes, "can Daddy come back home? He said he was sorry he hit Mommy, but he is entitled to the apartment. He wants to move back with Mommy."

Over my dead body! I shouted to myself.

"Don't you worry about a thing." I stroked the boy's soft hair. "Grandpa will take care of it."

"Let's teach that son of a rabbit a real lesson," I said to my son.

"Finally!" He beamed, his cheeks flushed like a monkey butt. "The old fox has sent his little whore to her parents in the countryside, and he himself has been hiding in his company compound. If we show up there, he'll start screaming for help, and the security will come right away. So we have to get him on the street. He goes back to his apartment to do laundry Sunday afternoons, after he drops off his son at my sister's place. I just talked to my ex-girlfriend, who lives next door. He's home eating duck feet."

"What are we waiting for? Let's go."

His red Mercedes shoots forward like an arrow—much faster than the cherry-colored Ford van my Minnesota daughter drives.

"Good detective work, son," I murmured.

"I learned it on the job. Never thought it would come in handy in this kind of business," he laughed, his nose scarlet from excitement. He'd been bored to death idling at home since the government closed his real-estate agency. He didn't tell me why it was shut down, and I didn't ask. My daughter hinted that he had made millions within two years, and I believed it. Just look at his brand-new car. I don't know how much it cost, how much his gigantic apartment with the view of Tiananmen Square cost, or his mansion in the suburbs with live-in servants, his Rolex studded with diamonds, his Armani suits in the overflowing walk-in closet. Don't want to know. Something is not right if a young man without any skill or a college degree can make so much in two years. I'm just worried. How deep is his connection with Zhong Nan Hai, the center of all power? Maybe he does know a few big shots there. How else would he have made this kind of money? Maybe they closed his agency to protect him and themselves. When the storm is over, they'll let him out. But what if they can't weather the storm? What if the big tree topples? He can go to jail, just like that, get executed without a trial. I suggested that I could get him a green card. He might have to wait ten, twelve years, but he would get it eventually, since I'm a citizen now. A cunning rabbit needs three holes. But he curled his lips.

"I'd rather die a tiger than live in a hole as a rabbit."

True, in China he is a tiger, though he's been crouching for the past six months. He can have ten girls a day if he wants, goes to the best restaurants, lives in the best apartment, drives the best car, goes to the best gym, and travels to the best places. All these require money. He has money. But he doesn't speak a word of English, and his talent for smooching will go kaput in America. The boy has been a lazybones since the day he was born. Didn't like to work or study or learn any skills. His brain is like a sieve. Nothing holds. But boy, he's a charmer! When he opens his mouth, the dead stand up and start dancing for him. People say he looks like David from the Bible, with his six-foot height and broad shoulders, his big eyes and high nose, his deep, silky voice and olive skin, all the features rare for a Chinese that make him a star in Beijing. But in Minnesota he'd be nothing. Everyone there looks like David—to me at least—taller and bigger-nosed. His good looks wouldn't earn him a bowl of rice there.

His phone rang. He pulled it open and started talking. If a cop saw us, we could be fined two hundred yuan, plus a warning. Six warnings a year, and you lose your license. But my son drove as if he owned the city. He must have connections with the cops, too, who are getting rich from fines and bribes.

"Hurry, the old fox is leaving his hole." He accelerated.

The traffic was awful. Before I left China, the streets were crowded, but you could still walk or bike through, at least for the strong ones like me who knew how to push elbows and legs. But what can you do with cars? The way my son drives, he would lose his license on day one in America. No one here follows rules, no one waits for pedestrians. It's the law of the jungle: the fit get their way, the weak get crushed. I see accidents every day. You have to be an Olympic athlete to dodge the flying cars. The government just passed a bill: in any accident that involves a car and pedestrian, the driver takes the full responsibility. There's uproar among fancy-car drivers. Go figure! They never slow down, even if you are crossing on the white pedestrian line. The only things they recognize are cars fancier and bigger than theirs. Why? Because they don't want to be crushed.

"Trust me, Ba, I've never had an accident!" A hurt look came over his face when I grabbed the door handle to steady myself.

Never say never, I muttered to myself.

He wove through the traffic as smoothly as he seduces people. He'd been waiting for this moment since my return. His knuckles turned white from gripping the wheel. Suddenly, I began to worry.

"Sonny, we just want to teach that son of a gun a lesson. That's all. No blood or bruises, hear me? You're already in the mud, and we don't want to go deeper."

"Don't worry, Ba, everything will be fine, just fine."

He sped through another red light and turned onto Wood-chopping Lane. I used to come here every Sunday to drink and eat smoked pig's elbows with my son-in-law. The little restaurant that had the best smoked meat had vanished, together with the gray tile-roofed square compounds. We drove by shiny apartment buildings with orange glazed tiles. A two-bedroom unit in those buildings costs at least half a million. My son-in-law wasn't doing too bad if he could afford living in this area.

The car made a few more turns, and suddenly we were in a different world: worn, crowded compounds lined an old gray street dotted with shabby Muslim eateries where old men and women squatted, smoking pipes and playing with bare-bottom kids next to a tall stove. On top, a giant steamer was puffing white clouds, and in the clouds crouched the loveliest, puffiest, whitest mutton buns wafting the most delicious fragrance.

I closed my eyes and inhaled. *This is my home, my old Beijing.* I wanted to get out and buy a dozen buns to share with the old folks and kids. Perhaps I could give my son-in-law a call and invite him here. We could drink Er Guo Tou and talk things over. Perhaps he'd come to his senses, give up his concubine, and go back to his wife and boy.

My son slammed on the brakes. "There he is, the old fox!"

A gray Honda was passing us. The driver braked at the screech and looked in our direction. When our eyes met, his face went ashy and I started shaking. My adopted son, my son-in-law. How he had aged: those deep wrinkles that cut into the corners of his eyes and mouth! And the abandoned look on his face, as if he had nothing to live for. The fire had died in his eyes—the fire that had lit the pitch-dark night when he appeared out of nowhere and dug me out of the rubble the night 240,000 people perished in their sleep in the Great Tang Shan Earthquake July 28, 1976.

How many times did I awaken to the same scene? The earth rumbled as it opened its belly and ate us alive. Within sixteen seconds, a quarter-million people died and the entire city was leveled. Many never had a chance to wake up, thank heavens, and many died slowly under the debris. The irony was I had been sent to Tang Shan to meet the leaders there to warn them about the quake. But no one paid much attention, including myself. Tang Shan had never had an earthquake. It was not supposed to. We were in deep mourning: our beloved Premier Zhou had just died, and Chairman Mao was dying in Zhong Nan Hai. Maybe the heavens wanted to bury us alive along with these great leaders as a sacrifice? Only fate knows—just as fate sent this skinny boy to me that deadly morning as I gazed up at the dust mushroom in the sky and prepared for a slow death. In the darkness, I couldn't make out his face, only his eyes burning like twin stars. Without a word, he knelt in front of me and started digging. He used a thick tree branch first, then used his hands so that I wouldn't get hurt. A beam fell on his head and knocked him down. I reached for his hand. There was no pulse. *Don't die, buddy,* I prayed. *If we survive this, I'll take you and your family to Beijing, and I'll make sure you have a bright future.* And he must have heard my prayer. Within minutes, he opened his eyes, jumped up, and started digging again with his bleeding fingers.

And I came out of the rubble without a broken bone. We waited for two days in the eerie silence. Most people had died. Those who got out alive just stared into space in a daze. No one came except for a few planes that dropped some water and bread. Finally I said, "Let's get out of here," and we started walking toward home, toward Beijing. The entire city of Tang Shan had been flattened. There was nothing but rubble reeking with rotting bodies trapped under collapsed buildings. We walked by mass makeshift graves. Heavy rains had washed away the mud, and the bodies were exposed, some gnawed on by hungry dogs. We walked along the road, joined by those who could still move. We were hungry and thirsty. We had given our water and food to the sick, the wounded, and the kids. The loud-speakers on the roadside blasted the Party's slogan: "Resist the earthquake, rescue ourselves." We heard rumors that this earthquake presaged Chairman Mao's death, that there was a fierce power struggle in Zhong Nan Hai. To show that everything was still normal and under control, the Party had rejected offers of international aid. I held the boy's hand and kept walking. From then on, I was his father. In fact, he looked more and more like my son, my first son who had died before he reached a year old.

On the day he married my daughter, I asked how he found me that morning. I wasn't even supposed to be in that building, the building where my uncle and his family lived. I was visiting them the night before, and had meant to tell my uncle about the earthquake warning as a joke. But a few cups of wine opened my chatterbox, and we talked into the early hours. I was so tired I just crashed on the bunk bed with my clothes on. Two hours later, everyone in the building died except for me and my future son-in-law, who was staying up late reading *The Count of Monte Cristo*.

"Did you know you were digging out the wrong person?"

He looked me in the eyes. "You were the right person. Still are."

"Did you ever realize I was not your father?" I insisted.

He hesitated a moment. "Yes, when you held my hand and prayed for me. My own father never touched me. He only whipped me with his belt."

The gray Honda fled, and we gave chase. We snaked through narrow, winding lanes, sending kids and old people scrambling for their lives. Finally, we nailed him at the end of a dead lane. My son jumped out, shattered the Honda's window with one kick, plucked the hunched man from the wheel, and threw him on the ground.

"*What are you waiting for, Ba?!*" my son roared as he punched and kicked.

I lifted my steel-clad boot. Since I arrived in Beijing, I'd been wearing my work boots every day for this moment. But I couldn't stamp down. Not on the soft body that offered no resistance. Curled into a fetal position, it looked like a giant meatball fallen in the mud. Both were my sons, both my flesh and spirit, the palm and back of my hand. Why did we have to do this? Why?

"Can we talk it over somewhere else?" I pleaded.

"*No!* How can you talk to a filthy pig who sleeps with teenage girls, beats up your daughter, and schemes to steal her apartment? He's not your son. *Never!* I am your son, your only son."

I looked into my son's bloodshot eyes. As he was growing up, I whipped him constantly to make him behave like his adopted brother. I had sown hatred in his young heart.

A big crowd gathered around us. A young boy shouted in a thrilled voice, "*Come quickly!* Come watch Mercedes beating up Honda! Watch the rich guys beating up a poor bastard!"

Blood rushed to my head.

"*This is not some poor bastard!*" I shouted, pointing to the muddy meatball. "This is my son. He's taken a wrong path, and I'm here to get him back."

And I started kicking. I kicked at his thighs, his butt, and his guts. He writhed in the dust, covering his head with his arms. He had grown so fat I couldn't feel any bones in his body. He used to be all spine and muscle, moving with the force of a tornado, his eyes bright with spirit. For twenty-eight years, he had been my pride, my lost and found son. The great earthquake did not destroy him, nor the aftermath of the Cultural Revolution. But money and sex gobbled him up and spat him out as cow dung. I kicked and punched. I wanted to make him scream in pain. I wanted to scream in pain. Who would give back my son? Who would give me back my old Beijing, my old country?

Someone screamed, "*Call a cop!*"

Blood spurted from the scar on his thinning scalp, the scar made from the fallen beam twenty-eight years ago. He had been covering it carefully with his hair, and I had forgotten how long and deep it was. Now the reopened wound gaped at me like a hungry mouth.

The ground shook violently under me. There was the familiar muffled roar from the earth's belly, the violent swaying of the sky, the sound of the buildings collapsing, the most terrifying silence as the dust rose slowly like a giant mushroom, like the atomic bomb in Hiroshima, only this one was three thousand times bigger and darker…

I pulled him up from the bloodied street.

"Let's go home, son," I said. "Let's go home."

In Memoriam

"I went to the Classical master, though. He was an old crab, he was."

"I never went to him," the Mock Turtle said with a sigh. "He taught Laughing and Grief, they used to say."

"So he did, so he did," said the Gryphon, sighing in his turn; and both creatures hid their faces in their paws.

Lewis Carroll, *Alice's Adventures in Wonderland*

Where to begin?

Every Sunday from 1963 to 1967, I had lunch not at my parents' home but in the house of the novelist Marta Lynch. She was the mother of one of my schoolmates, Enrique, and she lived in a residential suburb of Buenos Aires, in a big villa with a red-tiled roof and a flower garden. Enrique had discovered that I wanted to be a writer, and offered to show his mother some of my stories. I agreed. A week later Enrique handed me a letter. I remember the blue paper, the wobbly typing, the big, ungainly signature, but most of all I remember the overwhelming generosity of those few pages and the warning at the end: "My son," she wrote, "congratulations. And I pity you more than you can know." Only one other person, a Spanish teacher at school, had told me that literature could be so important. Together with the letter was an invitation to lunch on the following Sunday. I was fifteen.

I hadn't read Marta's first novel, a semi-autobiographical account of her political and amorous involvement with one of the few civilian presidents who came to power after Perón's ousting. It had won an important literary prize and procured for her the kind of fame that made journalists ring her up for opinions on the Viet Nam War and the length of summer skirts, and her large, sensuous face, made dreamy by big eyes that seemed always half closed, appeared every other day in a magazine or a newspaper.

So every Sunday, before lunch, Marta and I sat on a large flowered couch and, in an asthmatic voice that I thought breathless with excitement, she talked about books. After lunch, Enrique, I, and a few others—Ricky, Estela, Tulio—would sit around a table in the attic and discuss politics, the

Rolling Stones complaining in the background. Ricky was my best friend, but Enrique was the one we envied because he had a steady girlfriend, Estela, who was then twelve or thirteen and whom he eventually married.

I have found that in Canada the idea of a group of teenagers earnestly discussing politics is almost inconceivable. But to us, politics were part of everyday life. In 1955 my father had been arrested by the military government that had overthrown Perón, and as coup followed government coup we grew accustomed to the sight of tanks rolling down the street as we walked to school. Presidents came and went, school principals would be replaced according to party interests, and by the time we reached high school the vagaries of politics had taught us that the subject called Civic Education—an obligatory course taught in school on the democratic system—was an amusing fiction.

The high school Enrique and I attended was the Colegio Nacional de Buenos Aires. The year we entered, 1961, a genius in the ministry of education had decided that a pilot scheme would be tested here. The courses, instead of being taught by ordinary high-school teachers, would be in the hands of university professors, many of whom were writers, novelists, poets, as well as critics and arts journalists. These teachers had the right (were in fact encouraged) to teach us very specialized aspects of their subject. This didn't mean that we were allowed to overlook generalities; it meant that, besides acquiring an overview of, say, Spanish literature, we would spend a whole year studying in great detail a single book, *La Celestina* or *Don Quixote*. We were extremely lucky: we were given essential information and were taught how to think about particulars, a method we could later apply to the world at large and to our own agonizing country in particular. Discussing politics was unavoidable. None of us thought that our studies stopped at the end of a textbook.

I've mentioned that prior to Marta Lynch's encouragement, one other person had told me that literature was a serious activity. Our parents had explained to us that artistic endeavours were not truly valid occupations. Sports were good for the body, and a little reading, like Brasso, gave one a nice shine, but the real subjects were mathematics, physics, chemistry, and a pinch of history and geography. Spanish was lumped together with music and the visual arts. Because I loved books (which I collected with miserly passion), I felt the guilty shame of someone in love with a freak. Ricky, who accepted my quirk with the magnanimity of a true friend, always gave me books for my birthday. Then, on the first day of our second year of high school, a new teacher walked into the classroom.

I will call him Rivadavia. He walked in, barely said good afternoon, didn't tell us what the course would be or what his expectations were, and, opening a book, began to read something that began like this: "Before the door stands a doorkeeper on guard. To this doorkeeper there comes a man from the country who begs admittance to the Law. But the doorkeeper says that he cannot admit the man at that moment…" We had never heard of Kafka, we knew nothing of parables, but that afternoon the floodgates of literature were opened for us. This was nothing like the dreary bits of classics we had had to study in our grade five and six readers; this was mysterious and rich, and it touched on things so personal that we would never have acknowledged they concerned us. Rivadavia read us Kafka, Cortázar, Rimbaud, Quevedo, Akutagawa; mentioned what the new critics were reviewing and quoted from Walter Benjamin and Merleau-Ponty and Maurice Blanchot; encouraged us to see *Tom Jones* even though it was rated R; told us about having heard Lorca recite his own poems one day in Buenos Aires "in a voice full of pomegranates." But above all, Rivadavia taught us how to read. I don't know if all of us learned—probably not—but listening to him guide us through a text, through the relationships between words and memories, ideas and experiences, encouraged me towards a lifetime of addiction to the printed page from which I have never managed to wean myself. The way I thought, the way I felt, the person I was in the world, and that other, darker person I was all alone by myself were for the most part born on that first afternoon in which Rivadavia read to my class.

Then, on June 28, 1966, an army coup led by General Juan Carlos Onganla overturned the civil government. Troops and tanks surrounded the government palace, only a few blocks away from our school, and President Arturo Illia, old and frail (cartoonists portrayed him as a tortoise), was kicked out into the streets. Enrique insisted that we organize a protest. Dozens of us stood on the steps of the school chanting slogans, refusing to go to class. A few of the teachers joined the strike. There were scuffles. One of our friends got his nose broken in a fight with a pro-military group.

In the meantime, the meetings at Enrique's house continued. Sometimes we were joined by Estela's younger brother; sometimes only Enrique and Ricky attended. I became less interested. On a few Sundays I left after lunch with some uneasy excuse. Marta Lynch published several more novels. She was now one of the best-selling authors in Argentina (which did not mean that she was making any money), and she longed for some success abroad—in the United States, in France. It never happened.

After graduation, I spent a few months at the University of Buenos Aires studying literature, but the plodding pace and the unimaginative lectures made me sick with boredom. I suspect that Rivadavia and the critics he had introduced us to had spoilt my enjoyment of a straightforward course: after being told, in Rivadavia's thundering voice, of Ulysses' adventures through a Borges story, "The Immortal," in which the narrator is Homer, alive throughout the ages, it was difficult to listen for hours to someone drone on about the textual problems in early transcriptions of the Odyssey. I left for Europe on an Italian ship in the early months of 1968.

For the next fourteen years, Argentina was flayed alive. Anyone living in Argentina during those years had two choices: either to fight against the military dictatorship or allow it to flourish. My choice was that of a coward: I decided not to return. My excuse (there are no excuses) is that I would not have been good with a gun. During my European peregrinations, I kept hearing, of course, about the friends I'd left behind.

My school had always been known for its political activities, and throughout history many notable Argentinian politicians had come from the same classrooms in which I had sat. Now it seemed as if the government had specifically targeted not only the school but my schoolmates. News about them began to trickle out, month after month. Two friends (one had taught himself to play the oboe and gave impromptu performances in his room; the other had observed that those performances were "more boring than dancing with your own sister") were shot dead at a petrol station just outside Buenos Aires. Another friend, aged sixteen—whose name now seems to have vanished with her and who was so small she seemed to be about twelve when I last saw her—was gunned down in a military prison. Estela's brother, barely fifteen, disappeared one afternoon on his way to the movies. His corpse was delivered, inside a mail bag, to his parents' doorstep, so badly mangled it was hardly recognizable. Enrique left for Spain. Ricky escaped to Brazil. Marta Lynch committed suicide. She shot herself in the kitchen while a taxi waited outside to take her to an interview at a radio station. The note she left read simply, "I can bear this no longer."

A few years ago I found myself in Brazil on a stopover. Back in Buenos Aires, one of my brothers had run into Ricky's mother, and she had given him Ricky's address in Rio, which my brother then forwarded to me. I called him. He was now married, with kids, and teaching economics at the university. I kept trying to understand what had changed in him because he didn't look old, merely different. I realized that everything he did now seemed slowed down: his speech, his gestures, the way he moved. A certain flabbiness had overtaken him; little seemed to excite him.

He had made a home in Brazil now—and though his wife, his children were Brazilian, it was still a foreign country. He told me that in exile, as he called it, a number of refugees had set up "memory groups." Memory groups, he explained, were in charge of recording political crimes so that nothing might be forgotten. They had lists of names of torturers, spies, informants. The Commission on the "Desparecidos" in Argentina, set up by President Alfonsin in 1983 to investigate the thousands who disappeared during the military dictatorship, later recorded the testimony of the surviving victims. The memory groups kept records of the victimizers in the hope that one day they would be brought to justice. I suspect that some of Ricky's despondency came from the fact that he foresaw the outcome of the trials Alfonsin had promised to hold: a few sentences, a few reprimands, and then the general amnesty proclaimed in 1991 by the new president, Carlos Menem.

I mentioned how extraordinary it seemed that our friends, our school, had been a target of the government. Ricky said that the military had depended on informants—that inside the school there were those who provided the torturers with details about us: our names, addresses, character descriptions, activities. I agreed that there were those who had always publicly supported the military, but, I said, there was a fair distance between waving a pro-military banner and actually collaborating with torturers.

Ricky laughed and said that I obviously had no idea of how those things worked. The military hadn't depended on a group of kids chanting things like "Homeland, Family, Church." They needed intelligent, resourceful people. Such as Rivadavia. Ricky said his group had solid proof that for several years Professor Rivadavia had passed on to the military government detailed information about us—his students. Not simply our names, but careful notes on our likes and dislikes, on our family backgrounds and school activities. He knew us all so well.

Ricky told me this a few years ago, and I have never stopped thinking about it. I know he wasn't mistaken. In my mind, I have three options:

I can decide that the person who was of the utmost importance in my life, who in a way allowed me to be who I am now, who was the very essence of the illuminating and inspiring teacher, was in fact a monster and that everything he taught me, everything he had encouraged me to love, was corrupt.

I can try to justify his unjustifiable actions and ignore the fact that they led to the torture and death of my friends.

I can accept that Rivadavia was both the good teacher *and* the collaborator of torturers, and allow that description to stand, like water and fire.

I don't know which of these options is the right one.

Before saying goodbye, I asked Ricky if he knew what had become of Rivadavia. Ricky nodded and said that Rivadavia had left the school and entered a small publishing company in Buenos Aires, and that he wrote book reviews for one of the major Argentinian newspapers.

As far as I know, he is still there.

India

For some days that part of Bombay had been tense. Every street was utterly silent and still.

In one direction there was the estuary flowing into the Arabian Sea, over which a monstrous flyover, one and a half kilometres long, had been built to carry the six-lane highway. Close by and far off, countless high-rise blocks lifted their heads up to the sky. In the opposite direction was a vast, dense slum—an ugly, impermanent human colony made from such things as asbestos, polythene sheets, beaten tin, tiles, bamboo, and tarpaulin. The inhabitants were all "no work–no pay" day labourers, poorer than poor. However, as Bombay was the city of gold, people from all over India had come to settle there in search of work and food. Most of them were Muslims.

Far from the slum was the three-storey home of Sumitra Talwarkar. With apartment houses on all sides, it might almost miss the eye, though there was a lot of open space around it. On many occasions, promoters had been around, wanting to demolish it and put up a huge high-rise building. They would pay handsomely and offer three flats of fifteen hundred square feet each. Sumitra and, in particular, her husband, Dibakar Talwarkar, would not agree. He was a man of a different kind of temperament, not to be shaken by the promise of unlimited profits.

The house had been built by Dibakar's grandfather sixty years before, so it was some fourteen years older than India's independence. Whereas the Bombay metropolis is marked by spectacular architecture, there was nothing splendid or showy about this residence. However, if this home, pervaded by the joys and sorrows, the dreams and memories of four generations, were demolished and a high-rise constructed of flat on top of flat in a suffocating environment like a pigeon-coop, people from regions of India from Assam to Kerala would become neighbours, producing a din of rowdy, excited, and agitated cries in various languages, and the Talwarkars would have no real identity of their own. And so Dibakar was unable to accept the offer. The unrestrained pursuit of wealth in the city of Bombay could have made him the master of twenty or thirty million rupees with no effort at all, but putting his house into the hands of promoters would mean the extinction of his family history. He did not want that. He had immense pride in his family.

A short time had passed since evening had fallen.

Sumitra was sitting beside the window in the huge bedroom on the second floor, frightened and anxious. At that moment, there was no one else in the house. They had a cook, a Marathi Brahman called Dhumal, who lived a considerable distance away. He had left after preparing the evening meal in the afternoon and would not be there again until the next morning at about nine—if the buses and trains were still running.

The house had two other domestic staff: a woman and a man. But the whole area where they lived had been cut off by terrible riots for the past few days and transport had been brought to a stop, so how could they come to work? Sumitra's only support was Dhumal, and who could say how much longer he would be able to keep working?

This year Sumitra had turned fifty-three. Although her complexion was no longer bright and fair, she was still quite beautiful for her age. Only a few days before, she had been vibrant and cheerful, always effervescent and full of life. But right now she was like a stone sculpture with thick, dark blotches all over her face. In a moment her well-being had been destroyed. It was as though all the joy and optimism had been sucked out, leaving her only a withered shell.

A photograph of Dibakar with a garland of jasmine draped around the frame sat on the large bed in the middle of the room. Sumitra would give money to Dhumal, and each day when he came to work, he would bring a new garland. The newness of the frame suggested that the photo had been in it for only a few days.

A wardrobe stood against the wall. Also in the room were a divan and a couple of sofas, along with a dressing table, a telephone, a colour television set, and an air cooler. An expensive carpet covered the floor.

The Babri Mosque in Ayodhya had been destroyed the previous month. In reaction to that, there had been a series of bomb blasts in Bombay, and then riots had broken out spontaneously. They were continuing, with killing, arson, and uncontrolled looting. The riots were horrific, spreading from one part of the city to another like a forest fire, and the great metropolis was now ablaze.

Sumitra's husband, Dibakar, had been an important officer in a nationalised bank. At the time of the Bombay blasts, he had gone to the stock exchange for some reason or other. His body was blown to bits in an explosion, and he was identified by his topaz ring, his teeth, and his right foot. One could tell from his photograph that he had been a handsome, serious sort of man. His last rites had been performed just a few days before.

Their only daughter, Madhuri, lived in Canada with her husband, who was a professor at the University of Toronto. The couple had become Canadians and set up home in Toronto. They had been unable to come to Bombay when her father died as Madhuri was in a maternity home at the time, intending to return home after the birth of her baby. When her father was no more, she was not happy about her mother's living alone in Bombay. She had a different view of life: the world did not stand still; things changed with the speed of lightning. What Bombay was for people these days was also true of Toronto, Melbourne, Tokyo, or London. Passionate family pride was merely sentiment. Madhuri wanted to sell the house in Bombay, end the connection with India forever, and take her mother with her to Canada.

The daughter's argument was very reasonable. At this moment, when murderers had laid claim to Bombay and people were no longer people but went about in gangs like crude primeval brutes stalking their prey, it was good that Madhuri should not travel there. Sumitra had also forbidden it. There was poison in the air of Bombay. Let the city return to normal and the minds of men be rid of thoughts of slaughter, and then Madhuri could visit. Let the two women discuss things cool-headedly and then make a decision.

Madhuri spent every moment in great anxiety, and she rang her mother at least once daily, even at night. Sumitra explained to her daughter that her area was safe and that there was no reason for worry. She was all right.

Sumitra's father's home was in Nagpur. Dibakar had been his parents' only child, and they had always been residents of Bombay; his aunts lived in Kolapur. Daily, someone or other of Sumitra's family would phone from Nagpur, and Dibakar's aunts would call from Kolapur, wanting Sumitra to leave Bombay and stay in Nagpur or Kolapur for as long as the turmoil continued. Sumitra gave them the same answer that she gave to her daughter, assuring them that there was no cause for worry. If things took a bad turn, she would let them know. For the moment, she said, nobody should come to Bombay.

The Talwarkars had been long-time residents of this area, and everyone held them in high regard. Some of their acquaintances in the neighbouring high-rise flats also rang Sumitra to enquire about her, saying that should she have any difficulty at all, she could stay with them. She thanked them all and told them that as yet she had experienced no kind of difficulty.

Sumitra looked through the window towards the distant flyover. The street lights had come on, and countless lights were burning in the surrounding houses as well. There were variously coloured neon lights on the tops of the distant skyscrapers, and the eye was dazzled by the innumerable coloured advertisements. But hardly anyone was about to take notice of them.

This city simply did not stop for a moment, but kept running breathlessly, always busy, always noisy. But now it was all deserted.

At other times there would be a stream of traffic on the flyover and swarms of people. Today just one or two vehicles appeared, moving furtively and disappearing in an instant, and virtually no people were to be seen either.

At this hour, on the Arabian Sea beyond the flyover, there would be a great many trawlers. Having fished in the ocean for the whole day, the flotillas would be returning now. But today no trawlers were to be seen. Had any of them even gone out?

The lights of the flyover and the skyscrapers and the multicoloured sparkling of the neon advertisements gave the sea an enchanting look. The lights—neon ones, too—continued to shine even after the outbreak of the riots. But the sea now looked quite ghostly.

Nothing had happened yet in Sumitra's neighbourhood, but terror was being borne on the wind. Since the outbreak of the riots, she had seen a few people going out during the day for one reason or another, but once evening had fallen, everywhere was deserted. People would return to their homes as quickly as possible.

The whole scene was familiar—the estuary, the highway and the flyover, the skyscrapers, the sea—and Sumitra watched it all, self-absorbed, as countless memories of her thirty-three years of married life with Dibakar kept coming back to her. They seemed like recollections of a previous life. She was unaware of the tears rolling down her cheeks.

Suddenly the silence was shattered by a roar, the drawn-out, unceasing bellow of a great many people all shouting and screaming together.

Startled and terrified, Sumitra looked this way and that, trying to ascertain the source of this fearsome sound. In an instant she saw a frenzied mob hurrying along the road that came down from the highway and ran only three or four hundred feet to the right of her house and around to the back of it. Each person carried some kind of deadly weapon: iron bars, spears, unsheathed swords, huge curved choppers, guns. Some carried tins of petrol. Most of them were wearing shorts and singlets or T-shirts. All had looks of mindless cruelty. It was as though an army of butchers had poured out of a hole in the earth.

An icy shock ran up Sumitra's spine; she trembled uncontrollably from her head to her toes, and her heart beat a continual tattoo. Her whole body became tense.

The hooligans had turned to the right and rushed behind Sumitra's house. She could no longer see them from where she was sitting. Their intention was obvious, but what part of this area would they assail? Whose blood were they running to let? Whose homes would they reduce to ashes? None of this was discernible.

The wild yelling of the thugs could be heard even though they themselves could not be seen. For quite a while, Sumitra remained seated, unmoving, benumbed. Suddenly she remembered the other room at the back of the house; if she went there and stood at the window, she would be able to see this armed force. She might also see where they were going.

Then she wondered why she was worrying so much about it all. Did she need to? After Dibakar's body had been blown to bits in the bomb blast, her world had collapsed. Why should she worry herself about anything that happened in the rest of the universe? Whatever the thugs were going to do, let them do it. But just then some inner being started to take firm hold of Sumitra's throat, and her head was pierced by a thousand darts. It seemed that there was no longer any air in this city beside the Arabian Sea, as though all of it had passed away and she could not get her breath back. She felt a mixture of agitation, fear, and panic—a feeling intense and unbearable. She could remain sitting there no longer but stood up, unaware of herself. As though being pushed, she allowed herself to be taken to the back room.

The window was open, and grasping the grille with both hands, she looked out. By this time the brutes were quite a long way off and approaching the slum. Their aim was now apparent.

Their screaming did not let up, but because of the distance it was faint.

Then, in a flash, the hooligans threw flaming torches at the slum. It was quite likely that they had already splashed petrol, and the flimsy homes that people had made from polythene, tarpaulin, the light timber of packing cases, and other kinds of highly flammable material all went up in an instant. The millions of tongues that leaped from the fire spread in all directions, and the sky above turned red.

The vast slum was swallowed up by fire. For the sake of their lives, people of all ages—the elderly, the young, small children—came pouring out like terrified mice. They seemed stupefied as they ran breathlessly, chased by the killers. The whole area was pervaded by their cries of distress and the exultant cries of the murderers, by the sound of gunfire, and by the inferno. In just a few seconds the place had become a slaughter field.

Because of the dark and the distance, it was not possible to see clearly, but Sumitra could tell that the powerful blaze covered an enormous area. The murderers struck with their iron bars the heads of any who tried to flee. Some people had sharp daggers or spears rammed right through them. Others had swords brought down on their necks. There were fountains of blood, and bloodied bodies were strewn everywhere.

Every day, Sumitra read the detailed reports of the riots in the newspaper and saw the pictures of burnt houses and rows of dead bodies. But they were only pictures, taken by press photographers. Some days back, the papers also presented pictures of the bomb blasts. Dibakar had been killed in one of those explosions. Pictures were published of the mutilated or headless bodies of a few hundred people, of corpses without limbs. They, too, were only photographs, inanimate and lifeless. Yet they were horrible.

However, Sumitra had never seen anything as appalling as that which now beset the distant slum. The sight was gut-wrenching, and she felt as if her every nerve and sinew were being twisted and ripped apart. Her eyes bulged in horror, for before them was a living nightmare, her whole world run amok, and she was unable to remain standing any longer. As she staggered away from the window, she suddenly noticed something else.

Right at the back of her house ran a narrow offshoot of the estuary. There was not much water in it; at most it was waist deep. Beside it were a few tall coconut trees and dense mangroves. Beyond that, on a bare stony mound, were some dry weeds and three or four sickly looking, nondescript trees. The slum was quite a distance beyond the mound.

Sumitra saw a middle-aged man holding a young woman close to his chest and running breathlessly and frantically over the top of the mound. Apparently, they were fleeing from the blazing slum.

The young woman, it seemed, could run no further. All her strength and stamina had been exhausted, and she stumbled aimlessly. Had the man not been dragging her, she would have collapsed long before. The man was desperate to save himself and her.

They had walked down the slope of the mound and were about to enter the mangroves when a group of eight or ten men could be seen reaching the top of the mound. The men were armed and frightening. As the gang of assailants looked all about, Sumitra could guess whom they were after.

The middle-aged man glanced back and saw the men on the top of the mound. He pulled the young woman close to him and disappeared among the mangroves.

The predators did not give up. Looking about carefully, they walked down the slope of the mound, probably guessing that the man and the young woman were somewhere on that side. They would not leave without looking everywhere, reluctant to let their prey go so easily.

Sumitra's heart missed a beat. She felt as though the entire universe were rapidly going dark. If this party of butchers were able to catch the middle-aged man and his young female companion, the instant result would be blood-smeared corpses. Sumitra could no longer think—her mind had become completely numb—nor could she move from the window, feeling as though someone had nailed her feet to the floor.

The greatest element of danger lay in the fact that the mangroves were not particularly dense. If the group of rioters got any closer, they would catch sight of the two fugitives.

What could Sumitra do? What should she do? The power of thought had earlier deserted her, and she just went on watching—unblinking, benumbed, and helpless.

The man's eyes were on the thugs. He could hardly be unaware of their intentions. He must also have realised that he and the girl would not be able to remain hidden among the mangroves for very long, as they would be seen by their pursuers. They would have to make a last desperate bid for survival.

With the young woman enveloped in his arms, the man went down carefully, one step at a time, to the estuary. He stooped as close to the water as he could to avoid being seen, crossed the estuary, and climbed up on the opposite bank, where some coconut trees, thickets, and mangroves grew. But once the pair had passed through all of that, they were seen by the rioters, who cried out jubilantly. Their pursuit had not been in vain! Waving their weapons above their heads, they ran down towards the estuary while the middle-aged man and the young woman tried to flee.

On all four sides of the compound of Sumitra's house was a wall. The man and the young woman approached the back wall and stopped there. Quickly they went to their left to the end of the wall, and then turned right, where they found another wall. They had not seen this from the other side of the estuary.

By now the armed gang had stopped at the estuary. They looked around for a few moments, their excitement apparently dampened. Maybe they thought that there was no point in wasting so much energy on only two people. If they went back to the slum, they would have easy access to much more prey. Somewhat crestfallen, they went back through the bush and started to climb the mound.

In her heart, this is what Sumitra had wanted. She had been quite unable to think of these two people being murdered before her eyes. Slowly, she started to feel that the air had come back to Bombay, and again she breathed deeply.

The distant slum was engulfed in frenzy. There was fire, there was slaughter, and there were cries of anguish.

Sumitra was going to her bedroom when she thought of the man and the young woman who were now beside her house, where there was a long alley running towards the highway. There were rioters not only at the slum, but in other places as well. What if one of them came across the man and the young woman? She was concerned about where they would go, and anxious, too. The two of them entered the alley to find only the boundary wall of Sumitra's compound.

She decided to go to a second-storey room on the other side of the house, from where the alley could be seen. The alley was unsealed as the Corporation had never bothered to do anything about covering it with pitch. Tall grass and weeds were growing on either side of it, and a narrow track beaten by footsteps ran down the middle.

Sumitra went to the window and was surprised by what she saw. The boundary wall on this side was not so high, and the man had somehow managed to get the young woman over it and into the compound. Now he had climbed to the top of the wall in order to get himself inside.

Sumitra called out, "Hey! What are you doing in here?"

The boundary wall was quite far from the house itself, and they did not hear Sumitra. In the meantime, the man had got over the wall. He picked up the young woman and sat her against the thick trunk of a big rain tree. Exhausted and not able to remain upright, the girl leaned her head on the man's shoulder after the stress of so much running and such intense fear.

It was obvious that they felt they had found a refuge. Sumitra could not decide what she should do. There was no one in the house but herself. Was it possible she could be harmed by a terror-stricken middle-aged man and young woman, especially in this well-protected area?

She did not take her eyes off the two strangers, who were breathing freely after their escape from the jaws of certain death. But how long would this respite last? They could not stay in her compound forever, and murderers roamed places beyond the distant slum. For some days now, she had felt that such people were all around her, so if the man and the young woman left her compound and tried to go anywhere, knives, choppers, and spears would make mincemeat of them in no time.

Obviously beside himself, the man was looking this way and that. Suddenly his eyes met Sumitra's, and immediately he pressed his hands together and seemed as though he would say something. Nothing was clear, except for the pitiable perplexity on his face.

There was a tuft of whiskers on the man's chin. He wore a long, loose-fitting shirt; the young woman wore a shaiwar and kameez and a light scarf. It was easy to guess their community from their appearance and dress. Up to this point, Sumitra had not considered this. Seeing these hounded, panic-stricken people had eclipsed her powers of thought, and now the first thing to cross her mind was that members of their community had been responsible for the explosion that had killed her husband a few days back.

Any compassion or pity she may have had for the man and the girl evaporated in an instant. The blood rushed to her head, and she seethed in indignation, in anger, in malice, in hatred, in an unbearable animosity, and if she lost her discernment between good and evil, there was no telling what she might do. Suddenly there came the sounds of a commotion in front of the house. Many people were calling out in Marathi, "Sister! Sister!"

What group of men was this? Alarmed, Sumitra watched the man and the young woman for a few moments, then left the room and went to the end of the passage, where the stairs led down. The ground-floor door leading outside was locked, and the folding grille gate in front of it was kept locked for security. Outside the door, in front of the house, was a garden, through the middle of which a narrow, pebbled path led to an iron gate leading onto the road. Since the riots had broken out in Bombay, this gate was also kept locked from the inside. When her domestic staff came, they would call to Sumitra from outside, and once she had seen them, she would undo the locks.

Through the grille of the folding gate, Sumitra saw the excited faces of many men, all of whom had in their hands a variety of deadly weapons. They were a gang of the same mob that had raided the slum. Many faces were familiar. She even knew the name of one them—Sadashiv Sathe— and a little about him: he was a local political leader.

"What do you all want?" Sumitra called.

Sadashiv's companions cried out in confusion. He stopped them and said, "Many packs of dogs from that slum at the back are running about. We've not been able to catch them all, so we're going from house to house. Has anyone got into your house?"

Sumitra's face set hard and her eyes blazed. Her nervous system was on edge, and flashes of Dibakar came to her mind. His body had been so destroyed in the blast that he was unrecognisable. Sumitra was not taken to identify him; she could not have suffered the sight. But in the next moment, before her eyes appeared the terrified form of the fugitive in her home. Instantaneously his face was replaced by that of Dibakar. Then again the other man. They alternated, then merged. Ultimately, the panic-stricken face of the fugitive remained before her.

Sadashiv Sathe kept urging her, "What's the matter, Sister? Why don't you say something?"

Sumitra answered, "You can see that the house is locked. How could anyone get in?"

"It's locked on this side. And at the back?"

"It is locked there, too."

"Be careful. We'll check on you from time to time." Sadashiv and his gang left.

For some moments after that, Sumitra stood there, her eyes shut while she held the grille gate and regained her composure. Then she closed the door and went to the back of the house. There, too, the door was bolted and the folding grille door was locked. She undid the locks, walked straight to the rain tree, and looked at the middle-aged man and the young woman. From the second storey, she had not seen much. Emaciated, the man had sunken cheeks, shadows under his eyes, and a prominent Adam's apple; thick veins protruded from the backs of his hands, and his skin was flaky. His hands were pressed together, in respect.

With a pallid face, the girl was also sickly. She no longer sat with her head on the man's shoulder, but was slumped. Fear filled her dim eyes.

Sumitra asked, "Why have you come into this place?" then wondered how such an absurd question had left her mouth. Didn't she know why?

The man started weeping loudly, and his face became twisted. In a voice of confusion and distress, he answered in Hindi, "If we hadn't come in, they'd have finished us off, Mother."

"What is your name?"

"Jahirul Haq, Mother."

Sumitra pointed to his companion. "Who is this?"

"She is my daughter-in-law," Jahirul replied. "My son's wife. Her name is Amina."

The hullabaloo of the rioters came, it seemed, from close by. In fear Jahirul said, "Mother, we are left under the open sky. Here there are two or three tall buildings. If anyone from there should see us…" He broke off, unable to go on. He swallowed a few times, his Adam's apple bobbing up and down in his worry and fear.

Sumitra understood what he meant. But she was also reminded that she was the daughter of a devout Brahman family, and that with due concern for lineage, character, horoscope, and so on, she had married into another orthodox Brahman family. She had inherited all the traditions and sacraments of the Brahmans, and when she came into the house of her father-in-law, she practised them even more rigorously.

Jahirul lowered his voice and said, "What will happen to us will, of course, happen, but we are putting you to great trouble, Mother."

Sumitra had not thought of this, and it startled her. The hooligans were nearby. They had already come looking once. If anyone should see Jahirul and the girl and report them, the consequences would not be at all pleasant. The two had come into her house, but she had not reported it. If the rioters got wind of that, they would not spare her. There would be hell to pay for such a misdemeanour.

Helpless, Sumitra said, "Come." Amina hunched as she sat, and Jahirul helped her to her feet. Sumitra now saw that the girl was pregnant and nearly due to have her baby.

Sumitra stared at her, dumbfounded. Finally she said, "What a state you are in!"

Jahirul said, "Yes, Mother. The girl is to be a mother."

Sumitra wavered for a moment, but then cast all hesitancy aside and said urgently, "Come with me." She took them both inside and shut the back door.

The ground floor was almost empty. On the first floor were a kitchen, dining room, guest room, and the like. Sumitra had her room on the second floor.

She went into a room in a corner of the ground floor, switched on the light, and said, "Sit down."

In the room were a small bed, two or three chairs, a steel almirah, and three or four cane stools—all old and last used long ago.

Jahirul and Amina sat on the floor, cowering. Sumitra noticed that the girl's eyes were half closed and that she was breathing heavily, finding it difficult to get her breath. Sumitra said to Jahirul, "Not on the floor. Let your son's wife lie on the bed."

Jahirul looked at her, stunned. Sumitra had not only given them shelter in her house but had instructed Jahirul to have Amina lie on the bed. He could hardly believe what he had heard.

"What's the matter?" Sumitra asked. "Didn't you hear me?"

"Yes, Mother—" Flustered, Jahirul took Amina by the hand and helped her to lie down. He then sat back on the floor.

Pointing to where the slum was burning, Sumitra asked, "You used to live over there?"

"Yes—"

"Who else do you have?"

"I have two sons and my wife." Looking at Amina, Jahirul went on, "This girl is my elder son's wife. The younger boy isn't married."

"Where are your wife and sons?" Sumitra asked.

"Once the house was set on fire, we had to run where we could for the sake of our lives. Only the Almighty knows if they have survived."

Sumitra said nothing.

Referring to Amina, Jahirul went on, "The girl hasn't got the strength to run in her condition. All I know is that we were chased by the killers and then found ourselves in your house."

Gradually it came out that Jahirul's family hailed from Muzafarpur, in Bihar. Among the poorer than poor, they did not have the smallest amount of land of their own. They had worked the fields of others, digging and ploughing, sowing the seed, harvesting the crop, and storing the grain in the landowners' warehouses, yet the payment they received could barely fill their bellies twice a day. Moreover, agricultural work lasted only four months in a year, and they had great trouble getting through the remaining months. They had survived by doing all sorts of things to eke out a living.

Jahirul had heard there was a lot of work in Bombay. No one remained idle there, and money floated about on the breeze. He considered for a month whether or not they should go there. Then, in great distress, he took the hand of his wife and, with their two sons, boarded the train to Bombay.

Bombay did not disappoint them. It was true that it had much wealth and abundant job opportunities. Many factories operated within a hundred-mile radius of the city, and there were huge building complexes with thousands of flats under construction.

Jahirul and his two sons, Rashid and Jamal, got labouring jobs with a large construction company. What the three of them earned together could not have been dreamt of in Muzafarpur. However, prices were also high in Bombay. Rice, dal, vegetables, fish, and meat were all very expensive. The family's greatest problem was finding a place to lay their heads. Given the high cost of living, people like Jahirul had no choice other than to live in slums or makeshift accommodation. And so the family had lived for a few years in the slum. They had also been able to put away a little money in a post-office account.

Everyone has some sort of dream. Big men have big dreams, and little men like Jahirul have little dreams. Having saved some money, he had had his elder son married two years before. Now he would have grandchildren, and his house would be filled with new descendants. His dream had been approaching fulfillment until today, when, in a moment, it had all come to an end.

Sumitra's heart ached as she listened.

Lying on the bed, Amina had been uttering faint cries. Now she started to make a sound like weeping. Jahirul looked at her and said, "Running so far and climbing that mound has caused her great distress. If she can rest for some time, she'll be all right."

Sumitra said nothing.

Jahirul then asked, "Mother, would you be so kind as to keep an eye on her? I know that she'll have nothing to worry about with you nearby. I have to leave now."

Sumitra was shocked. "You can't go out now! With what's going on out there, you'll be in tremendous danger."

"Mother, things have now been made good for the girl. But I have no idea where my two sons and their mother might be, or which way they have gone. I can't rest until I've found them." As he pressed his hands together, it was clear that his heart was breaking. Mother must not stand in his way. Once he had found his wife and sons, he would come back with them as quickly as possible.

Jahirul would not be stopped. He stroked Amina's head once and ran out of the room.

In distress and sadness Amina cried out, "Father! Father!"

Jahirul seemed not to hear her. Sumitra followed him to the back door of the house. She was anxious and afraid. What the man had set out to do could achieve only one thing: death. She called to him, "Listen! Listen!"

Jahirul did not look back. Like a man possessed, he ran off across the open space at the back of the house, scaled the boundary wall in a flash, and was out of sight.

Sumitra remained there stock-still for some time. Then she locked the folding grille gate, fastened the bolts on the leaves of the door, and went back to the corner room. Amina was lying on her side, gazing in distraction. In a lifeless voice she asked, "Couldn't you stop him?"

Sumitra slowly shook her head. "No, I couldn't."

Amina asked nothing more. By the cruel hand of fate, everything had been lost, and she remained silent. But that was only for a few moments, and then she started to cry again; she clenched her teeth in an endeavour to overcome the intense pain, her face grimacing.

Anxiously Sumitra leaned close to her and asked, "Are you in great pain?"

"Yes—" Holding her hand to her stomach, Amina said, "It's terrible pain. I feel as though my insides are being ripped out."

For Sumitra, so much had happened in the last couple of weeks, all of it dreadful and terrifying. There had been the explosion and her husband's death. Then came the riots. Her life had been turned upside down. But never before had she been in such danger. She could not think of what to do with Amina.

From the look of the girl, it seemed as if her baby would be born in a mere day or two, and yet no one of her own was with her. With the outbreak of the fire, her husband, brother-in-law, and mother-in-law had fled—goodness knew where. It was not certain if they were even alive. Now her father-in-law had placed responsibility for her in Sumitra's hands and had gone off in search of his family. And his death, too, was all but certain.

Sumitra's head felt foggy and heavy with worry. The domestic staff would come back tomorrow, and she would be in terrible trouble should they see Amina. The biggest problem would be with Dhumal, who was a strict, orthodox Brahman. She did not dare to think of what he would do if he saw Amina. But tomorrow's worries belonged to tomorrow. Sumitra's benumbed mind seemed not to be working, yet she now felt that there was an urgent need to call a doctor. She had some kind of pain-killing tablets, but whether or not it was right to give them to a pregnant woman she did not know. It might even be very harmful.

Suddenly Sumitra thought of Shalini Kulkarni, a doctor and her friend from childhood. They had lived in the same neighbourhood in Nagpur, and they had gone to the same school and the same college. Sumitra had studied arts and graduated with honours in history; Shalini, after completing a science degree, had gone on to medical college. After becoming a doctor, she had accepted a position at a private hospital in Bombay. She had not married. At first she stayed in the hospital quarters, and a few years later, she bought a big flat in Andheri East, from where she commuted to the hospital.

On account of her marriage, Sumitra also had moved to Bombay. The relationship between the two friends remained as close as it had been in their younger days. Because Shalini was busy with her patients at the hospital, she could not visit Sumitra as often, and being bound up with her family made it impossible for Sumitra to go to Andheri regularly. Nevertheless, they kept in touch by telephone.

If Sumitra described her problem to Shalini, the doctor would surely come straightaway. It was quite unlikely that the rioters would impede a doctor's car. Shalini was quite intrepid and sagacious and would surely be able to talk her way past the hooligans.

Amina was becoming more and more restless on the bed. How old was she? Nineteen or twenty? She was much younger than Sumitra's own daughter. Watching her, Sumitra was moved and said compassionately, "Try to persevere. I'll be right back." She quickly left the room and went upstairs to her bedroom on the second floor. She picked up the phone, dialed it, and heard the voice of Shalini's full-time maidservant, Renu. Recognising Sumitra's voice, Renu said in Marathi, "Sister, I heard that there's trouble over your way."

"Yes," Sumitra answered curtly. "Is Shalini at home or at the hospital?"

It seemed that Renu had not heard the question. Sounding very concerned, she went on, "There's been such a lot of killing. Slums have been set on fire—"

Sumitra sharply interrupted her. "If Shalini is there, put her on the phone."

Renu sounded startled by this. "But Sister is not in Bombay," she said.

"What? I was talking with her only three or four days back. Where has she gone?"

"She's gone to Delhi for some urgent work for the hospital."

It was as though the sky had shattered over Sumitra's head. After a stunned silence of a few seconds, she asked, "When will she be back?"

"Tomorrow."

There was some hope then. Until tomorrow Sumitra would have to rely on her own resources to nurse Amina and to keep her comfortable. "Tell Shalini to call me as soon as she gets back. It's very urgent. You won't forget?"

"Of course not. You—"

Sumitra hung up before Renu could say more, intending to go back to Amina. She got as far as the door when she was stopped by the ringing of the phone. She went back and picked it up. It was Mr. Kapadia, a businessman who lived in a neighbouring high-rise and was quite close to Sumitra's family. Seeing that riots had started in their area and that armed hooligans were noisily making their presence felt, he was very concerned about Sumitra and wanted to know if any of them should go to her house and spend the night.

Sumitra suddenly had a vision of Amina's face. She thanked Kapadia and said, "There's no need at present. If there is, I'll let you know."

No sooner had she put the phone down than it rang again. This time it was Mahesh Patil, another local resident. He had much the same thing to say. He and his wife wanted to go to Sumitra. She thanked him, too, and hung up. As she left the room and started going downstairs, she worried that the phone would not stop ringing. The people in this area were concerned about her well-being, all of them wanting to help her. But once riots had got underway, who could say how long it would take to quell them?

When she returned to the corner room, Sumitra saw that Amina was in control of herself and that her crying had stopped. Her hand on her stomach, she watched Sumitra anxiously.

Sumitra asked, "Has the pain got any better?"

"Yes," Amina replied in a weak voice.

"Has it been that bad before?"

"Yes—"

"Have you seen a doctor?"

"Yes—"

Amina told her that she and her husband had gone to the hospital that week.

Now Sumitra quickly thought about what would have to be done. Tomorrow morning Dhumal would arrive. Then, if the trains were running, the other domestic staff would be there. Amina would have to be kept out of their sight. That was one thing.

Another thing was Jahirul. Who could say when he would return, or if he would return at all? If he did not come back, it was extremely important that Amina be kept somewhere close to Sumitra during the night. She would have to attend to the girl if the pains returned. What a predicament Jahirul had got her into!

But how could Sumitra keep the girl close to her when she was on the second floor and Amina on the ground floor? Sumitra would not know if the girl were having any trouble. There was one solution: she could put Amina in the small room next to her bedroom. Then she could get up during the night and look in on her from time to time. Moreover, when Dhumal and the others arrived in the morning, they would not be able to see Amina. The domestic staff would not go to the second floor unless they were called there. Of course, there was the matter of cleaning the rooms, and for that, a girl named Durga would go upstairs. Sumitra would have to tell her tomorrow that there was no need to clean the second floor.

It seemed that there was a generally satisfactory solution to her enormous problem, but suddenly another difficulty arose: how could she take Amina up to the second floor? A room upstairs housed the images of the Beneficent Ganesh and Lord Vishnu. The Talwarkars were devout Brahmans, and in this family, daily worship had been offered to these two deities for generations. Someone in the family had to do that; it was a family custom that could not be avoided even for a day. As long as Dibakar had been alive, he had performed the worship. Now the responsibility was Sumitra's. But how could she take Amina where the two images were installed? The sanctity of the place would be polluted, and the souls of orthodox Talwarkar ancestors dwelling in heaven would be outraged. The orthodox Brahmanical values of the families of her father and father-in-law—set as deep as the marrow in her bones—were restraining her with a hundred hands.

Sumitra stood there motionless for a few moments, and then it seemed as if something possessed her. Putting aside all those powerful, unavoidable, and innate beliefs, she said, "Amina, get up carefully."

Putting her weight on her hands, Amina obediently sat up. Sumitra said, "Come with me. Now."

Amina asked no questions, but silently followed Sumitra out of the room. With the weight of the child inside her, however, she had a terrible time getting up the stairs. Sumitra noticed that she was not able to walk easily and that she sometimes reeled. If in this condition Amina should collapse, she could do herself serious harm, and Sumitra would be drawn into even deeper trouble. She hesitated for just a second, then put her arm around Amina and helped her up the stairs. The worship room was at one end of the large hall, and there the images of Ganesh and Vishnu were lodged. At the other end were two bedrooms, one smaller than the other.

As the women reached the second floor, Sumitra's eyes unconsciously turned towards the worship room. Just before evening every day, she would go there to light the lamp and some incense sticks. The sticks had burnt down, but their sweet smell still wafted about.

Glancing at the two stone images, Sumitra inwardly prayed, "Forgive me." Then she crossed the hall and went to the small room beside her bedroom. It was furnished with a bed, almirah, and dressing table and had a bathroom attached.

There was a total of sixty steps from the ground floor to the second floor, and having climbed so many, Amina was panting and struggling to catch her breath. Sumitra sat her down carefully on the bed and said, "Now rest for a while." She indicated a door and said, "That's the bathroom. Have a rest, then go and wash your face and hands."

Amina nodded her head like an obedient girl. "Yes."

"There's a towel there, and soap. Everything's there."

"Yes."

Sumitra then asked, "When did you eat?"

Amina replied, with her head down, "At midday."

"You've not eaten for a long time. You must be very hungry."

Amina did not answer.

It seemed to Sumitra that the girl became diffident at the mention of food. Sumitra said nothing more; she would bring her something to eat. As she walked towards the door, Amina called after her, "Mother—"

Sumitra stopped. "What is it?"

"Father has not come back with any news of my mother-in-law and their two sons."

It was clear to Sumitra that carrying this child was giving the girl no end of pain, and in addition to that, she was suffering from worry over her loved ones. Sumitra could not think of what to say.

Then Amina asked, "Will Father not come back, Mother?"

This was Sumitra's fear, too. If Jahirul had gone back to the burning slum to look for his wife and sons, a blow from a chopper, a thrust from a knife or spear, or a bashing with a lathi would have turned his body into a bloody lump of flesh by now. But she could hardly say that to Amina. She replied that it was not certain who had fled where after the slum had been set on fire and that it would take some time for Jahirul to find his wife and sons. Encouragingly she said, "Of course he'll come back. Don't worry." Sumitra stayed there no longer.

The kitchen was on the ground floor, beside the dining room. Dhumal had left Sumitra's evening meal in a hot box. She hesitated for a moment. She had held Amina close to her as she had helped her upstairs, and the girl's touch was on her blouse and sari. Could she handle foodstuffs in those clothes? She put her uncertainty aside and took a plate of food and a glass of water up to Amina's room. She then drew up a side table, placed the food and water on it, and called, "Amina—"

Amina was lying still, looking through the window to the distant ocean. Slowly she sat up.

The telephone rang in Sumitra's bedroom. It was sure to be some concerned friend. Hurriedly she said, "Eat now. I'll be right back."

The ring suggested that it was a long-distance call. Sumitra picked up the receiver and heard the voice of her daughter, Madhuri.

"Mother, what's it like in Bombay today?"

"Much the same."

"No disturbance in your part then?"

Sumitra stopped herself from answering. What had happened that day was still going on, and who could say what worry and anxiety it would cause Madhuri if Sumitra told her all about it. Moreover, Madhuri would be extremely worried if Sumitra mentioned the matter of Amina.

"No," Sumitra replied. "Nothing's happened here."

"I've told you before, Mother," Madhuri said, "there's no need for you to stay in Bombay. We'll be there within a couple of months. Then we'll sell the house and bring you back with us."

"All right. Come here first, and then we'll see about everything."

Madhuri's daughter had been born only about a month before. Whenever Madhuri called, Sumitra wanted to know about her granddaughter. Today she also inquired how Madhuri was nursing her and offered her daughter some advice. Then she asked about Madhuri and her husband. "You and Rajdip are well then?"

"Yes," answered Madhuri. "Don't worry about us. You just take care of yourself."

After speaking with her daughter, Sumitra went and sat on the chair beside the window facing west—toward the highway, the sea, and the fishermen's colony. She felt terribly tired. Her concern for Amina weighed on her mind like a heavy stone.

The room's southern and northern windows were also open, but Sumitra's eyes were on the sea. Lost in thought, she wondered what she should do. Amina's touch was on her clothes; would she be purified if she took them off and had a bath? Then it occurred to her that there was no certainty the night would pass without disturbance. Amina's pains could come back, and in nursing her, Sumitra would have to touch her again. How was it possible to have a bath every time she touched the girl? She put off for the moment her thoughts about washing.

Suddenly her gaze was drawn to the northern window. There was a burst of fire in the distance, and shouting and screaming accompanied the reddening of the sky. The riot had spread there, too.

After sitting silently for a little while, she got up. Amina was alone in a strange place. Moreover, the girl must be constantly fraught with worry about her husband and his family. Sumitra felt that she should stay by her.

When she went into the next room, she saw Amina sitting silently, her food untouched.

"Hey, what's this?" Sumitra said. "You haven't eaten anything. It's not good to have an empty stomach. Now eat up."

Amina's lips were trembling, and tears were welling up in her eyes. In a dull, choking voice, she said, "I don't want to eat. Father still hasn't come with the others?"

Sumitra tried to encourage her as she had before. "He'll come, he'll come. Now you eat something."

After much persuasion, Amina ate a little. Then she took her hand from the plate and said, "I can't eat anymore."

Sumitra did not insist. "Go and rinse your mouth out, then come back and lie down again."

Like an obedient girl, Amina did as she was told. Sumitra asked her, "You haven't had any more trouble then?"

Amina slowly shook her head. "No, Mother."

"It's getting very late. You shouldn't stay awake any longer. Get some sleep. I'm just in the next room. I'll look in on you from time to time. You don't have to be frightened of anything."

"But—"

"What?"

"The gates are all locked. If they should come—"

"I'll keep an eye open. If they come, I'll let them in and bring them to you." She turned off the strong light and switched on the blue night lamp, picked up the plate and glass, and went out. In case Amina should call to her during the night, Sumitra left the door open. She would have to leave her own door open, too.

As Sumitra passed the dining room on her way to the kitchen, she stopped suddenly. She would usually leave the night's dirty dishes in the kitchen sink, and Durga would wash them the next morning. But this plate and glass bore the leftovers of a Muslim; how could they be taken into a Brahman kitchen? Not all the traditional precepts could be put aside overnight. Sumitra thought for a moment, then put the plate and glass in a corner of the hall. She then went back to her own bedroom, had a bath, changed her clothes, and returned to the first floor.

She took from the refrigerator some bread and cheese and placed them and a banana on a large tray, which she took back to her own room.

When she had finished eating, she lay down for a while, keeping her ear tuned to the neighbouring room. The uproar could still be heard coming from the north and the east; it seemed that the frenzy would continue throughout the night. Although she was lying down, she was unable to fall asleep. Her eyes were burning. Would Jahirul be able to return with his family from that distant place of slaughter? Although Sumitra knew that that was a remote hope, an empty dream, miracles did indeed happen in the world. She could not remain lying there.

She got down from the bed and stood by the window facing the sea. The highway and the roads nearby were all deserted, and there was nobody, not even any of the rioters, to be seen. She stood there for a little while and then went to the room at the back. The windows were open, and lights shone inside the compound on all sides throughout the night. Pressing her face against the window grille, she looked down. She narrowed her eyes and looked carefully, but there was not a sign of human life, let alone Jahirul and his family. She also looked through the windows of the two neighbouring rooms, but no one was to be seen from there either.

She went back to her bedroom and lay down again. Everything that had happened since evening finally took its toll on her; she could not take the pressure and felt drowsy. Very soon her eyes closed and she fell asleep. Suddenly a distressed cry from Amina sent her running in a fluster to the next room. She turned on the main light and saw Amina tossing and turning. Her lips were blue with pain and were wide open. Her breast heaved with her rapid, heavy breathing, and a sound like hiccups came from her throat.

Sumitra quickly went to her bedside. The girl grabbed her hand and, gasping for breath, said in great anguish, "I'm going to die, Mother. I'm going to die. My chest is bursting—"

Amina's distress was ten times worse than when she had been in the room on the ground floor. Perhaps it was time for her baby to come into the world. Feeling that a doctor should be called, Sumitra looked at the clock on the opposite wall. It was 3:27.

How much Shalini's going to Delhi had increased her difficulty! Nearby was Dr. Apte, an elderly woman, but she would not go out in the evening. No doctor anywhere in Bombay would come to this area so late at night. Who would risk his life to go to a place where people were being murdered and blood was flowing, where looting went on unrestrained and homes were being set ablaze?

Unable to think of how the girl could get relief from her pain, Sumitra felt completely helpless. Then flashes of events from thirty years ago came back to her.

She was carrying Madhuri then. After nine months, she was having spasmodic pains, just like Amina, and feeling as though someone were slashing her insides with a knife. She still had not forgotten that experience. The doctor had told her to sponge ice-cold water on her stomach every now and then to lessen the pain. That had given her some relief.

As Amina became more restless, Sumitra said, "I'll do something right now. Just bear with it for a few more moments." She freed her hand from Amina's grip and ran down to the first floor, took a bottle of cold water from the refrigerator, and went back to Amina's room. There was no sponge in the house, so she folded a towel, wet it, and slowly wiped it over Amina's stomach.

Amina kept shaking her head in pain, trying to endure it by clenching her teeth. When it became too much for her, she burst into tears.

With one hand on Amina's head, Sumitra said gently, "Don't cry. Don't cry. Everything will be all right." As she looked at this young, unknown Muslim girl lying beside her lap, images of Madhuri's face kept filling her mind. Like any mother, she had wanted her pregnant daughter to be near her when she had her baby. But there were problems with Rajdip's getting leave, so they could not travel to India. Sumitra guessed that before the birth of her baby, Madhuri also had trouble like Amina's. As she thought of her daughter, an immense affection for Amina started to fill her heart.

Towards dawn the pain had lessened, and Amina's eyes slowly closed. Silently, Sumitra got up. She would let the girl sleep for a while; if she slept, she would feel a lot better.

Sumitra returned to her own room and looked through the open window at the tinge of indistinct light in the sky. Morning comes late to Bombay, and the sun would not be up for a couple of hours yet. She could not stand any longer; her head was spinning and her temples throbbing. As she lay down on the bed, she prayed to Lord Ganesh and Lord Vishnu to keep Amina's pain from worsening before Shalini returned from Delhi; if she had to call another doctor, Amina would become public knowledge.

Sumitra had no idea of when she fell asleep. When she awoke, the room was full of sunlight, and immediately Amina's face appeared in her mind's eye. She tried to listen for any sound coming from the next room, but there was not the slightest one. Of course, if she were in pain, Amina would not be lying there silently but would have cried out and woken her long before. Sumitra got down from the bed and went into the adjacent room. The girl was sunk in a deep sleep.

It was Sumitra's long-standing practice to have a bath in the morning. She returned to her own room and went into the bathroom. When she had finished her bath, she went down to the kitchen. If she did not have a cup of tea at this time, she would not have the enthusiasm for anything. Dhumal would arrive at nine, so there would be quite a delay if she waited for him. She made this morning cup herself.

She lit the gas and made two cups of tea, one for herself and one for Amina. She took the tea and biscuits upstairs and saw that Amina had already woken up. Seeing Sumitra, she slowly sat up.

The girl seemed quite calm now. Sleep had greatly dispelled her fatigue and her restlessness, though her face still reflected her anxiety. Sumitra understood why.

She asked, "Is there no pain now?"

Amina shook her head. "No, Mother."

"Go and wash your face, and then come and have your tea."

When she came back from the bathroom, Amina silently picked up the cup of tea. She said, "Father and the others didn't come then, Mother?"

If Jahirul had not been able to return with his wife and sons last night, how would he be able to do so today? Had any of them survived? Sumitra did not mention her fears to the pregnant girl.

Sumitra gave her the same answer now as she had given the night before. "They'll come. Surely they'll come. They've probably been held up somewhere. Now drink your tea. I'll bring you some breakfast a little later." She picked up her cup and went into her own bedroom.

Dhumal arrived right at nine. He was about fifty and a somewhat stupid-looking fellow. Before the riots, he would wear an old-style Marathi dhoti and a short-sleeved shirt, but now he wore loose-fitting trousers with the short-sleeved shirt. He had been the cook at the Talwarkar home for twenty years. Sumitra opened the three locks and let him in. She asked, "What's it like over your way?"

"There hasn't been any sort of disturbance," Dhumal replied. "But the place is heating up. I heard last night that the trains would not be running over there."

"Even if they do run, you take two or three days off. Riots have broken out in these parts. Get the cooking done today as quickly as you can and go home."

"All right." Dhumal inclined his head. "I also heard that there was a lot of bloodshed over here. I came to save you trouble, even though I was very frightened on the way."

The house's domestic staff were very faithful and trustworthy. They were never absent from their duties unless it were unavoidable.

Sumitra was thinking about Amina. She said, "Cook a little extra, enough for a couple of days."

Dhumal nodded.

As she was going upstairs, Sumitra said, "Don't go up to the second floor unless I call you."

Dhumal would not go upstairs if he had no reason to, but on the rare occasions that he had gone up, there had been no objection. So why did Sumitra make specific mention of it today? No clear explanation was given, and he could not figure out why. He was quite taken aback, but he did not ask any questions.

Sumitra went up to the second floor and to Amina. She said, "My cook has come. You must not leave the room under any circumstances. Don't even make a sound. Just understand that if he should find out about you, there'll be terrible trouble. Will you remember?"

"Yes," Amina said in a weak voice.

Sumitra went out and shut the door behind her.

Dhumal left at half past eleven, after he had finished his cooking. By then there had been many phone calls from concerned friends. They all said much the same thing: they wanted either to take Sumitra with them or to come and stay with her. As before, she thanked them and said that if the need arose, she would contact them.

There was no sign of the riots abating. Shouts and screams continued to be heard from time to time, and gangs of hooligans ran about to the north, the east, and the south. There was hardly anyone on the roads. On the highway, it was like the previous few days, with the occasional car scurrying past like some timid animal. Now and then, a black police van would suddenly come into view and then disappear.

At about one o'clock, after she had fed Amina, Sumitra had her own lunch, and the question of touch did not enter her mind. As time passed, however, she became more tense. What if for some reason or other Shalini could not return to Bombay today? What if she stayed another three or four days in Delhi? There were many flights from Delhi to Bombay. But on which flight would Shalini come?

There was, however, one good sign. So far, Amina had had no more pain. But pain was the reality of pregnancy, and there would be no warning when it returned. Sumitra wondered whether or not to call Shalini's flat, but then she remembered that she had spoken to Renu. Shalini would certainly get in touch with her as soon as she got back.

At about half past three, Amina's pains began again. Anxious and worried, Sumitra was just about to apply more cold water when Shalini called.

"I got back from Delhi just this minute. Renu told me I should call you as soon as I got in, that it was particularly urgent. What's the matter then?"

Sumitra gave a detailed explanation.

Shalini spoke urgently. "The girl must not be kept at home. She could deliver at any time, and that will be a real problem for you. I'll bring an ambulance right away."

Shalini arrived within forty minutes. She had brought not only an ambulance but also two stretcher bearers and a nurse.

Worried, Amina said to Sumitra, "I don't want to leave you. Not for anything."

Stroking Amina's head, Sumitra indicated Shalini and said, "There's nothing to be frightened of: she is my friend, and an important doctor. Like me, she is another mother for you. You'll be fine if you go with her. Now off you go." Her voice was filled with emotion.

Amina was put on a stretcher and taken downstairs. Sumitra, Shalini, and the nurse followed.

"Let me know when the baby is born," Sumitra said.

"Yes, of course," said Shalini. "I think you'll hear something within a couple of hours. Her time's getting close."

They all went out onto the road. As Amina was being put into the ambulance, she clasped Sumitra's hand and said in a broken voice, "Mother, if Father comes—" She could not finish.

"If they come, I'll bring them to you," Sumitra said.

When the ambulance had gone, she went back inside. As she was locking the gate, her eyes strayed to the near and distant high-rises. There was an inquisitive face at the window of almost every flat in those buildings. Certainly they would all want to know everything about Amina later on: how did this girl come to Sumitra's house? how was she connected to Sumitra? why was she sent to hospital in an ambulance? And so on it would go.

Sumitra was disconcerted. Then she resolved that what she would say would be the truth. Whatever would be would be. She would be prepared for any eventuality.

At a quarter past eight that night, Shalini called. "Good news. Amina has a son. A perfectly normal delivery."

Jahirul had left the night before and had not come back, nor would he—of this Sumitra was certain.

A nineteen- or twenty-year-old girl without any family had given birth to her first child. What would be their future in India? Sumitra could see no answer to this question. She would have to think anew about Amina and her child.

Translation by John W. Hood

Hoʻokuʻikahi: To Unify As One

When asked by our Polynesian cousins from Aotearoa in the late 1970s where our meeting houses were, we could only answer that we had our heiau, but many hadn't been used for generations. That changed in August of 1991 as Hawaiians from across the state gathered at Puʻukoholā Heiau to celebrate the bicentennial observance of its consecration by Kamehameha the Great, the first aliʻi who unified the Hawaiian islands.

For Hawaiians, this celebration was a time of Hoʻokuʻikahi, of reconciling and reuniting the descendants of the great Hawaiian chiefs who stood at the ramparts of this last great temple estate. It was an ancient murmur whispering. It was a shout to assemble, for in retelling our past, we honor our forefathers. They live through us—in our songs and our stories, and in who we are.

The celebration intended to bring two clans together who historically had been torn apart, to support those in search of their cultural roots, to honor and affirm those who continue the practices of their kūpuna, and to invite all Hawaiians searching for a united voice to come together as one at this place.

Polynesians from across the Pacific journeyed to Puʻukoholā to support their kin, as Hawaiians came together there to honor and reclaim certain traditional protocols for the first time in seven generations.

The gods of our ancestors took many forms. From Kū is invoked the manifestation of Kūnuiakea. It was under his watch that the construction of the mighty heiau began. The heiau was erected to house another manifestation of Kū—Kūkāʻilimoku, Kū the grabber of lands.

This temple of state was to be called Puʻukoholā: the Hill of the Whale. Rocks were passed hand to hand along human chains stretching for miles, from sources great distances away, and brought to the Hill of the Whale.

Kamehameha and the great chiefs labored until the heiau at Puʻukoholā was completed. The walls rose up and the paehumu, the kapu enclosure; the ʻanuʻu, the tower; the haku ʻōhiʻa, the main sacred image; and the hale mana, the largest house of the luakini heiau, were put in place. All that remained to fulfill the prophecy was to consecrate the great heiau.

When Keōuakūʻahuʻulaʻs
descendants voyaged to
Puʻukoholā from Kaʻū in
August 1991 on the sailing
canoe Hōkūleʻa, *they
retraced their chiefly
ancestor's route.*

Ka Lae, Kaʻū, Hawaiʻi
Photograph by
Franco Salmoiraghi, 1991

*"It is really important
that we renew ourselves
at the seventh genera-
tion, because the lord of
makani, the lord of the
wind, is waiting to erase
your memories and
everything you hold dear,
at the eighth generation.
And who are you? You
are the eighth generation.
You can choose to be
anything you want. You
can let your legacy be
blown away. You can
forget things that are
Hawaiian. You have
been eating from the
buffet of the world. And
neglect the plate of your
ʻohana. Something's lost.
Something can be
gained—it is just right
there. You have family
who know how."*
SAM KAʻAI

*En route to Puʻukoholā,
Keōuakūʻahuʻula and
his escorts landed at
Hōnaunau for prayer
and offering at Hale o
Keawe, the house where
the sacred bones of high
chiefs once lay.*

Hōnaunau, Hawaiʻi
Photographs by
Franco Salmoiraghi, 1991

Kawaihae, Hawai'i
Photograph by
Franco Salmoiraghi, 1991

Among Kamehameha's Hawai'i rivals was his cousin from the Ka'ū district, Keōuakū'ahu'ula. He had been warring with Kamehameha for nine years, seeking absolute rule over the same lands and people of the island of Hawai'i. A lasting peace was not possible while both were living.

As the god Kūkā'ilimoku reigned, tradition dictated that the consecration of the newly built heiau at Pu'ukoholā required a high sacrifice. Keōuakū'ahu'ula submitted to his fate by accepting Kamehameha's invitation to Kawaihae. Keōuakū'ahu'ula answered Kamehameha's summons to Kawaihae, knowing the time had come for him to answer for his transgressions. By accepting his fate, he saved his Ka'ū people from invasion and annihilation.

En route, Keōuakū'ahu'ula and his escort made their last stop at Kīholo Bay, at a pond called Luahinewai. There, he bathed and performed the ritual 'ūmu'o, which made him an imperfect sacrifice. It was a sign that Keōuakū'ahu'ula knew he would die. It was his final act of defiance toward Kamehameha.

Watching from the hill at Pu'ukoholā, the forces of Kamehameha and his armies of Kona and Kohala saw Keōuakū'ahu'ula and his men sail into the bay. Only one chief, Kamehameha, could fulfill destiny and unite the islands into one nation. As the canoes from Ka'ū approached the landing, Keōuakū'ahu'ula stood and cried out to Kamehameha, "Here I am!"

"Stand up and come forward that we may greet each other" was Kamehameha's reply.

As Keōuakū'ahu'ula stepped ashore, a swift thrust of a spear from Ke'eaumoku, Kamehameha's father-in-law, took the Ka'ū chief's life. All those on the canoe were killed as well. The body of Keōuakū'ahu'ula was prepared in the older heiau, Mailekini, just below Pu'ukoholā, and then taken up to the altar to be offered to the god Kūkā'ilimoku. The sacrifice of this chief made the consecration of this temple complete.

Bitter was the loss of Keōuakū'ahu'ula to the Ka'ū people, and that bitterness has flowed down through the veins of seven generations. In Hawaiian tradition and in many other native cultures, spiritual completion occurs when the seventh generation hands down its knowledge of all things inherent and sacred to their children. Now, the eighth generation comes, seeking to staunch the flow, heal the wounds, and serve as a symbol of unification....

Symbolically, rebuilding this place and retelling its story through commemorative events since 1991 continues to be life-changing for those who participate. Researching the history, recruiting participants, and making implements in the traditional manner challenges us to reclaim and recommit ourselves to being courageous.—Adapted from *Ho'oku'ikahi: To Unify As One*, a film produced and directed by Meleanna Aluli Meyer and written by Meyer with John Keolamaka'āinana Lake.

Kawaihae, Hawai'i
Photographs by
Franco Salmoiraghi, 1991

Kawaihae, Hawaiʻi
Photographs by
Franco Salmoiraghi, 1991

"Reconciliation between the people of Kaʻū and Kohala became an open invitation to all Hawaiians to participate in a solemn occasion requiring serious practice, dedication, pule without censure, attention to authentic learning and protocol, and faith in our ancestors to guide the process."

JOHN KEOLAMAKAʻĀINANA LAKE

Kawaihae, Hawai'i
Photographs by
Franco Salmoiraghi, 1991

"*We are planning for those generations who are coming and preparing all this so that they have a foundation when they arrive.*"
HALE MAKUA

Hōnaunau, Hawaiʻi
Photograph by
Franco Salmoiraghi, 1991

Puʻukoholā,
Kawaihae, Hawaiʻi
Photograph by
Franco Salmoiraghi, 1991

Two hundred years ago, the forces of Kameha-meha and the armies of Kona and Kohala waited at Puʻukoholā, watching from the hill. They saw Keōuakūʻahuʻula and his men sail into the bay. As he approached the landing at Kawaihae, he stood and said, "Here I am."

"Stand up and come forward that we may greet each other," was Kamehameha's reply. The sacrifice of this chief made the consecration of Puʻukoholā complete.

Puʻukoholā,
Kawaihae, Hawaiʻi
Photograph by
Franco Salmoiraghi, 1991

*Now two centuries later,
a canoe again lands at
Kawaihae. And this time,
those it bears are wel-
comed and asked to
hoʻokuʻikahi—to come
together as one—to unite
the peoples of Kaʻū and
Kohala and assist all
Hawaiians in unifying
as one.*

Kawaihae, Hawaiʻi
Photograph by
Franco Salmoiraghi, 1991

"It not about being
warlike; Nā Koa is about
being courageous enough
to look at your spirit."
SAM KAʻAI

Nā Koa (Warriors),
Puʻukoholā,
Kawaihae, Hawaiʻi
Photographs by
Franco Salmoiraghi, 1991

"Part of the mission of Nā Koa is the vision to preserve our culture. Every one of the members has committed to preserving it for seven generations. Might not be in our lifetime, but it's gonna carry on by teaching our families and our friends about the culture and also the history of the heiau that we protect."
JOHN ROBERTS

*The descendants
of Keōuakūʻahuʻula and
Kamehameha proceed
together up the hill to
take part in ceremonies
at the heiau. The god
Kū presides over the
ceremonies.*

*The life that is being
renewed at this place
through these ceremonies
binds us one to another.*

Puʻukoholā,
Kawaihae, Hawaiʻi
Photographs by
Franco Salmoiraghi, 1991

"The death of one takes place, and the birth of a nation takes place on this particular ground. Let's use it as a living place."
JOHN KEOLAMAKAʻĀINANA
LAKE

"Puʻukoholā is a temple of state. Our nation was built here. This is where Kamehameha started his campaign for sovereignty. Two hundred years later, we have come back to Puʻukoholā. It gives us an identity—a cultural, historical, political, economic, and social foundation."
JOHN KEOLAMAKAʻĀINANA LAKE

Puʻukoholā,
Kawaihae, Hawaiʻi
Photographs by
Franco Salmoiraghi, 1991

For Hawaiians, this is the
time of hoʻokuʻikahi, of
reconciling and reuniting
the descendants of the
great ancient chiefs who
stood at the ramparts of
this last great temple of
state, built two hundred
years ago. It is at Kawai-
hae at Puʻukoholā that
we unify as one.

Pu'ukoholā became a place to gather, a rallying point that has inspired hundreds to return to Kawaihae every year since 1991, to reaffirm ancestral ties, to resume traditional protocols, to reclaim their cultural identity as Hawaiians, to make personal gifts and offerings of oli, *hula, lua, and nā mea Hawai'i. They come in search of renewal and are affirmed through their participation in ritual and ceremonies.*

"There is no ha'ina [last verse] to this song, it's like a puana [refrain] that keeps on going and going."
SAM GON

Pu'ukoholā,
Kawaihae, Hawai'i
Photographs by
Franco Salmoiraghi, 1991

Meditation #7: Prayer for Peace

May a bird kill a cannon
and a baby destroy a gun
May buildings banish missiles
and children stop tanks
May a mother's love bury bombs
and hand grenades
May palm trees and olive groves
overwhelm planes with their
beauty and bounty
May the rivers and the earth repel
all things that stain and sully them
May blood spilled flow back into the
veins of the innocent dead
May families rise up out of the ashes
to break bread once more
May love curl around the barren hearts of men
May the flowers of imagination bloom in their minds
May our wars be only of words, never of swords
May the gods we pray to be
without history, without names
without nations, without creeds
without religion
May I love you in laughter and grace all the
Days without end

GALSAN TSCHINAG

The Tamyrs: A Tale of Two Peoples _____

Translator's Note
      "The Tamyrs" (Die Tamyr) was published in 2002 in a German-language collection of short fiction called *Dew and Grass* (Tau und Gras). Written in oral narrative style, the story begins in 1922, after the Mongolian revolution and the overthrow—with the aid of the Soviets—of the Chinese occupation. Tribal warfare within Mongolia was intense. In the mountains separating China and Mongolia, two groups of refugees—Tuvans and Kazakhs, as the reader learns at the end of the story—engage each other in a battle. While the setting is historical, the story's theme is also topical: the relationship is precarious between the minority Tuvans and majority Kazakhs in the high Altai range of the western Mongolian province of Bayan-Ölgiy, which is the traditional homeland of the Tuvans. The province borders on the Russian Federation to the north and the People's Republic of China to the south.

    As the chieftain of the Tuvans, Galsan Tschinag works tirelessly to promote interethnic understanding and foster economic opportunities for both the Tuvans and the Kazakhs.

1

The story I want to tell you took place in the year that those on the outside call 1922. But here in our small corner of the world, it was again the Year of the Black Dog. As you know, that did not bode well for us. The land was in turmoil. Small tribal feuds were flaring up into all-out war, and more and more tribes were drawn into the fighting that spilled over the borders. Traditional ties between tribes were severed as some took one side and others took another. Rumors of war and invasion were rampant, causing suspicion and fear in everyone. The most vulnerable were the first to flee their homelands in panic; others followed, and soon mass migrations had begun in all directions.

    In midsummer of that year, during the early hours of the morning, fighting broke out on the Mongolian side of the precipitous peak of the Örmegejti glacier, separating China from Mongolia. At dawn, members of two tribes—or rather, two peoples—stumbled into each other in the dim light. Neither group could tell who the other was. The night before, each must have taken a different route up the glacier, and now in the half-light of dawn, they met on the descent. Men, women, and children were all alarmed, and in the panic each group decided that to defend itself, it should be the first to attack. So in a flash, everyone charged at one another. Nobody was prepared or armed for a fight, and because the people had only their bare hands, stones, and knives, it made the battle longer and more brutal. These people were poor, peaceful refugees trying to flee the bloodshed in their homeland, and suddenly they were in the midst of a life-or-death struggle with an unknown adversary. Such slaughter...

Someone was strangled here; another was clubbed to death over there. Many who became locked in battle tumbled off the side of the glacier, their arms and legs intertwined as though gripping one another in a final embrace. Their deaths were certain, as once they began sliding down the smooth, steep ice face, nothing could save them. Soon, many people were slaughtered. But still the dying called to those remaining, imploring them to continue the massacre and not to cease, even though the jaws of death were engorged.

A father called out to his two sons, placing on them the burden of his dying words: "Revenge! Get blood for blood. Destroy their tribe—destroy them all." Huddled behind a rock that jutted from the ice, his ten-year-old and twelve-year-old sons had been shaking in terror. But when they heard their father's dying words, their fear no longer held them back. The boys bolted from their mother's arms and charged, screaming. Their mother barely managed to restrain the younger one. His older brother entered the fray, and immediately two boys about his age rushed out of a trembling group of people to engage him. Only moments before, these boys had also been watching the slaughter from the protection of their mother's arms. Then their father had been killed, and he too had burdened his sons with his last command: "Revenge!" This single word had propelled his two sons forward. Their mother managed to restrain only her youngest son, and she watched in horror as her other two boys threw themselves furiously on the boy from the other tribe. All of them died.

When it was over, the survivors set about attending to their dead. The custom of one tribe was to strip the bodies and leave them on the open ice, to be eaten by vultures and foxes. In this way, they believed, the souls of the dead would be released. The other tribe's custom made the disposal of bodies more difficult. They dragged their dead to patches of hard ground, where they dug graves as best they could and piled rocks on the corpses to protect them from wild animals. While they were digging, survivors from the other tribe watched and shouted degrading comments on their burial custom. Both sides traded angry looks and threatening gestures. Their taunts and insults were like splashes of oil on fire, and hatred once more blazed up in their chests. Each group of survivors pursued the other with such murderous intensity that hatred bound them to one another for years into the future.

2

Time—which the aged regard as moving with magical swiftness—moves slowly for the young. For Schöödün and Botaj, time seemed nailed to the ground even though days and nights still took turns coming and going. Each boy was impatient to grow to manhood faster than the other, and their annoyance at the sluggishness of time became a cancer slowly eating away at their insides.

The reader will have guessed correctly that I am talking about the two boys who had watched their fathers and older brothers die and who had survived only because their mothers' arms had held them back. Faithful to the legacy of their fathers, each was burning for revenge.

Finally the day arrived when they had both grown into *dshigit*s, young men of battle-ready age. Each felt strong enough in body and mind to challenge the other to a duel or to force the other to issue a challenge, so that at long last he could fulfill his father's last wish: to spill blood for blood, to take revenge for what had happened on the Örmegejti glacier. To their dismay, challenging someone to a duel was not as easy as it had been in times past. The government had violently suppressed tribal feuding, and anyone trying to carry out a vendetta was harshly prosecuted. New rules were being enforced, and people had no choice but to obey them. The two young warriors could do nothing except wait—but at least time seemed to be passing more swiftly.

I should note here that in our part of the world, tradition did not allow vendetta killings to be undertaken by trickery or ambush. Anybody who violated that tradition was scorned as a coward.

Eventually, our two *dshigit*s became heads of families and fathered their own children. While this certainly hampered their plans, each consoled himself that in the end it would sweeten his revenge. For the time being, both behaved peacefully, did their chores, and lived their lives in pretty much the same way. When life was hard for one, it was equally hard for the other. Oddly enough, time and again they were faced with identical problems. Sometimes, they had to build a wall of rocks to shelter their herds, at other times to raft large logs down the river that one called Homdu and the other Kobda. Each secretly competed to show the other how strong and skilled he was, and as a result they were among the best workers in their nomadic settlements. Often, they were also charged with urgent communal jobs that needed to be done in their region, and sometimes had to work alongside one another, with no one else around.

One day they were working in the forest alone together, tasked with felling long, straight trees and dragging the trunks to the river. Each was on his guard, especially at night, when they lay head-to-head in their narrow tent. Both spent the first night wide awake, their eyes fixed on one another, their bodies ready to lunge and pounce. But each succeeding night, they slept longer and more deeply.

During this time, when they were supposed to float the logs down the river, an accident occurred. They had bound the huge, wet logs into a raft on which they stood, but in the rushing waters it proved to be unwieldy and too heavy. The force of the current slammed the raft into a rock, the ropes snapped, and the logs broke apart. Both men were hurled forward, but Botaj managed to hold on and keep himself from going into the river. Schöödün, however, was not so lucky. The crashing, foaming water rolled him over and flung him around before he sank from sight. Above him, Botaj saw what had happened. By sheer chance, he was able to reach over the side, grip the drowning man, and pull him up. The section of the broken raft holding the two men drifted onto a half-flooded island and came to a stop.

Shortly afterwards, Schöödün said to Botaj, "You are a *dshigit,* so you know that nothing except vengeance can redress the spilling of a father's blood, or erase the obligation that our traditions place upon us." Botaj was dismayed, but he had to admit that he himself was thinking the same thing.

3

In the Year of the Yellow Rabbit—that is, in 1939—both men, together with others their age, were drafted into the army. As if mocked by fate, they ended up in the same unit far away from home. Hundreds of rivers and thousands of ridges separated them from the blue backs of their mountainous Altai homeland.

One day Botaj said to Schöödün, "What are you glaring at? We're not in our remote corner of the country anymore, with its bloodthirsty customs frozen in time. Can't you see how all Mongolians here stick together like blood brothers, while only you and I behave like idiots? We look past each other like a ram and a billy goat—it's a disgrace. Everyone is a representative of the place he's from and must uphold its good name. Our home gave us everything we've ever had, and while we're not there now, it doesn't deserve to be shamed on account of our behavior. How about putting off our personal business, *dshigit,* until we've done our military service and gone home?"

Schöödün felt both ashamed and pleased. Botaj had expressed what he himself was thinking and suffering. Both men began trying hard to be respectful of one another. And for the six long years of their military service, they succeeded.

These two *dshigits* were assigned to guard the southern border. Skirmishes were frequent, and life in the army was hard. In the spring, it happened that our two men, along with a third man who was from the northern regions, lost their way in a sandstorm. Toward the evening of the second day, they came upon a spring in the middle of an oasis. It was almost buried by sand. But it had water. On seeing it, however, Schöödün yelled, "Stand back!" This was not just a warning but an order: he was the ranking soldier-in-charge, so he was responsible for his comrades' safety. They had just passed the carcass of a camel, and not far from the spring was also a dead horse. Thus, Schöödün suspected that the water was poisoned. However, the two other men seemed to have lost their senses. Along with their horses, they hurled themselves at the shining water. Schöödün seized the shoulders of the northerner, the man closer to the water, and tried to hold him back. But the man was a strong wrestler and shook him off, knelt down, and fell face-forward into the spring. Getting to his feet, Schöödün turned his attention to Botaj, who had not yet touched the water. Botaj fought as tenaciously as the first man but lacked his strength. Schöödün managed to shove him away from the spring, knock him down, and restrain him. Botaj went wild and called him a devious swine who only wanted Botaj to die of thirst. Schöödün was forced to listen to more accusations and insults, but he stood firm and held tight to the crazed Botaj. By then the wrestler, apparently having regained his sanity, stood back from the water. Schöödün ordered him to help restrain the raging Botaj. Panting and railing, Schöödün fell next to his comrades as they battled each other. He was struggling in more ways than one because, like the other two, he felt a great urge to fling himself at the shimmering water and drink. All at once, the wrestler clutched his belly and vomited. Schöödün jumped to his feet and began to curse the sky and the earth. When Botaj finally came to his senses, the other soldier lay dead. All their horses died as well. The following day, a search party found Botaj and Schöödün alive.

Sometime later, Botaj said to Schöödün, "I am not saying this because you are stronger in battle. Compared to you, I'm a weakling. But I am grateful to you." Embarrassed, Schöödün cut him short, though he appreciated what Botaj had said. For quite some time, Schöödün had felt sorry for having said harsh words to Botaj instead of thanking him for saving his life at the river.

Their interminable military service eventually came to an end. The discharged soldiers tearfully kissed their regimental flag. Botaj sobbed as he said to his countryman, "Comrade Soldier-in-Charge, do you think every-thing that has happened between us should be allowed to fade from our memories and be covered by the shadows of time?" Schöödün had no reply because he was wondering the same thing.

4

The two men returned home as victorious heroes and were greeted with enormous joy. At first, they went their separate ways. But it was not long before Schöödün unexpectedly appeared, slightly drunk, at Botaj's home. Botaj welcomed his guest in the traditional way, honoring him as though he were heaven-sent.

As they drank their tea, Schöödün asked his former comrade-in-arms, "Do you still have your father's dagger? Or at least a dagger from that time?"

Botaj paled, then said he did.

"Get it and come with me," Schöödün said and left the yurt. Botaj's mother, who had been devoted to her late husband and had sought to raise her son to respect the traditions of their elders, immediately stopped what she was doing. Her eyes were shining. Botaj's wife, who had been told the story of the vendetta by her mother-in-law, froze.

Schöödün went to the river. Botaj followed. It was late fall, and most parts of the river were low, but they went to a place where the water was deep and full of rocks. Schöödün produced a long, pointed dagger with a yellow horn hilt and said without looking at Botaj, "You go first."

Botaj did not move. He replied, "Why me? It's you who brought us out here."

"Wouldn't you have done this?" Schöödün asked.

"No, I wouldn't have," said Botaj.

All at once, Schöödün threw his dagger in a high arc into the river. Botaj did the same with his. Then they turned and fell into each other's arms.

"I knew it all along," Schöödün declared loudly.

Though stone-cold sober, Botaj was staggering. "The past has been buried once and for all, Brother. We have struggled and finally freed our-selves from our fathers' despicable tradition."

A wether was slaughtered. On the table, a bottle appeared next to the tea bowls. And then feasting began. Afterwards, Schöödün disappeared from the village but returned a few days later, leading five camels. He helped Botaj's family load their yurt and belongings onto the camels' backs and gather their herds, then took them to visit his family. Schöödün's mother received the guests with a bowl of milk. Botaj's mother took the first taste of the drink of honor.

Not only did the two men become *tamyr*s, brothers as if by blood, but their sworn brotherhood extended to their families. From then on, neither family would use the other's proper names. They used the solemn word *tamyr* instead: *tamyr*'s mother, *tamyr*'s wife, *tamyr*'s son, *tamyr*'s daughter, and so on.

The boy who was born into Schöödün's family the following year was given the Kazakh name Tölegen. The girl born a little later into Botaj's family got the Tuvan name Orsa, which the teachers at the progress school later changed to Rosa.

I am hesitant to give this story a cloyingly sweet, predictable ending. But I must tell the truth of what really happened. The *tamyr* people did become actual kin: Tölegen and Orsa married. While mixed marriages between Kazakhs and Tuvans were so few they could be counted on the fingers of one hand, this was one of them. It caused quite a stir, but what did that matter? Children were born, which was proof enough that there was nothing improper about this new kinship.

Translation by Katharina Rout

About the Contributors

Tony Birch writes fiction, poetry, and creative nonfiction. His story in this issue is from his collection of linked stories, *Shadowboxing,* which was short-listed for the 2006 Queensland Premier's Literary Awards. He teaches creative writing at the University of Melbourne and has worked as a writer and curator in collaboration with photographers, filmmakers, and artists.

Catherine Filloux has received numerous awards for her plays, including the PeaceWriting Award and Callaway Award, and is a co-founder of Theatre Without Borders. Her play in this issue premiered in 2004 at the National Asian American Theatre Company in New York City. The play received the Roger L. Stevens Award from the Kennedy Center Fund for New American Plays and the Eric Kocher Playwrights Award from the O'Neill Theatre. Her other honors include selection as a Fulbright senior specialist, Thurber playwright-in-residence, Asian Cultural Council grant recipient, and Heideman Award finalist.

Luis H. Francia is a poet, nonfiction writer, and journalist. He has published three collections of poetry, the latest being *Museum of Absences* (2004). His memoir, *Eye of the Fish: A Personal Archipelago,* won both the 2002 PEN Center Open Book and the 2002 Asian American Writers literary awards. He writes a monthly online column for Manila's *Philippine Daily Inquirer.* He lives in Queens and teaches at New York University.

Karen Gernant has collaborated with *Chen Zeping* on translations published in *Mānoa, turnrow, Conjunctions, Black Warrior Review, Words Without Borders,* and *Ninth Letter.*

John W. Hood has published several books on Indian art cinema and has translated Niharranjan Ray's *History of the Bengali People,* a volume of poems by Buddhadeb Dasgupta titled *Love and Other Forms of Death,* two novels by Buddhadev Guha, and six novels and two collections of short stories by Prafulla Roy.

Ann Hunkins is a poet, photographer, translator of Nepali, and former Fulbright grantee. She has been traveling to Nepal for twenty years. In 2006, during the Maoist conflict, she worked as an interpreter for the United Nations Office of the High Commissioner on Human Rights, interviewing torture victims, war-crime witnesses, and others. She lives in Santa Fe, New Mexico.

Wayne Karlin is the author of seven novels and two memoirs. He has received two fellowships from the National Endowment for the Arts, the Paterson Prize in Fiction, and the Viet Nam Veterans of America Excellence in the Arts Award. Professor of Language and Literature at the College of Southern Maryland, he edits the Voices from Viet Nam Fiction Series for Curbstone Press.

John Keolamakaʻāinana Lake is a kumu hula, chanter, and retired teacher from Saint Louis High School. His chant and dance education began in childhood under the tutelage of his grand aunt, Kaʻehukai of Lāhaina; other mentors included Edith Kanakaʻole, Maiki Aiu Lake, Mary Kawena Pukui, ʻIolani Luahine, and Henry Moʻikeha Pā. He is the kumu-in-residence at Chaminade University and the head of Hālau Mele, a Hawaiian arts academy.

Barry Lopez is an essayist and fiction writer. His works include *Arctic Dreams,* for which he received the National Book Award; *Of Wolves and Men,* a National Book Award finalist and recipient of the John Burroughs and Christopher medals; and eight works of fiction, including *Light Action in the Caribbean, Crow and Weasel,* and *Resistance.* His essays are collected in two books, *Crossing Open Ground* and *About This Life.*

Oren Lyons is a Faithkeeper of the Turtle Clan among the Onondaga people of western New York. He is a professor of American studies at the State University of New York at Buffalo and is the publisher of *Daybreak,* a national Native American magazine. He is the recipient of national and international awards, and for more than three decades has been a defining presence in the areas of international indigenous rights and sovereignty.

Alberto Manguel is a translator, editor, essayist, and novelist. He was born in Buenos Aires and raised in Israel, where his father was the Argentine ambassador. In 1982, he moved to Canada; he now lives in France, where he was named an Officer of the Order of Arts and Letters. He is the author of the novel *News from a Foreign Country Came* and the nonfiction books *The Dictionary of Imaginary Places* (coauthored with Gianni Guadalupi) and *A History of Reading.*

Julia Martin grew up in Pietermaritzburg, South Africa, and now teaches in the English department at the University of the Western Cape.

Chris Merrill is the author of the nonfiction book *Things of the Hidden God: Journey to the Holy Mountain* and the poetry collection *Brilliant Water.* He directs the International Writing Program at the University of Iowa.

Meleanna Aluli Meyer received her degree in design and photography from Stanford University and her master's degree in educational foundations from the University of Hawaiʻi. A recipient of numerous awards, she is an advocate for all things Hawaiian, and for justice and peace.

Māhealani Perez-Wendt is executive director of the Native Hawaiian Legal Corporation, a public-interest law firm responsible for groundbreaking achievements in Native Hawaiian law: access rights, Hawaiian Homes entitlements, ceded lands trust principles, and traditional and customary rights. She was the first Native Hawaiian board member of the Native American Rights Fund, a national law firm representing tribal governments in landmark cases throughout the United States, and is currently involved in a project to promote peacemaking outside the courts.

Katharina Rout was born in Germany. After she received a doctorate in medieval German literature, she immigrated to Canada, and she now teaches English and comparative literature at Malaspina University-College in Nanaimo, British Columbia. Her translation of *The Blue Sky,* a book by Galsan Tschinag, is the first English translation of one of his novels into English; it was published simultaneously in Canada (Oolichan Books) and the United States (Milkweed Editions). Her previous translations include *Seductions,* a novel by Marlene Streeruwitz, and *Love in a Time of Terror,* a novel by Ulla Berkewicz about the Arab-Jewish conflict.

Prafulla Roy is an eminent Bengali writer whose collected works are projected to run to more than thirty volumes. His most memorable writings are on the rural underclass and on Partition, the tragic consequences of which he experienced firsthand, when forced to leave his home in Dhaka to start a new life in Calcutta.

Franco Salmoiraghi has lived and photographed in Hawai'i since 1968. His photographs are featured in numerous books and periodicals locally and internationally, and his prints are represented extensively in private and public collections, including that of the Hawai'i State Foundation on Culture and the Arts.

Kazuko Shiraishi was born in Vancouver, Canada, and moved with her family to Japan in 1938. She is one of Japan's most prominent authors and performance poets, having published more than twenty books of poems and numerous volumes of essays on poetry, art, and music. Her awards include the Mugen Poetry Award, the Rekitei Award, the Bansui Award, the Takami Jun Award, the Yomiuri Literature Award, and the Purple Ribbon Medal from the Emperor of Japan.

Galsan Tschinag was born in Mongolia in the 1940s. An ethnic Tuvan whose name in his language is Irgit Shynykbioglu Jurukuvá, he was taught to read and write in Mongolian and was required to take a Mongolian name. Following a year of study at the university in Ulan Bator, he was chosen in 1962 to attend the University of Leipzig in the German Democratic Republic (East Germany). Returning to his homeland in 1968, he became a lecturer in German at the university in Ulan Bator. During the next eight years, however, he was branded an "unreliable element" for his outspoken opinions, denounced, and stripped of his position. As chieftain of the Tuvan, in 1995 he negotiated a land-claim treaty with the president of Mongolia that allowed his people to return to the High Altai. For sixty-three days, he led a caravan of extended families across deserts and mountains, back to their homeland. In addition to leading his people as a chieftain and shaman, he is the author of more than thirty books, and his work has been translated into many languages.

Yumiko Tsumura received a master-of-fine-arts degree in poetry and translation from the University of Iowa and is now a professor of Japanese and culture at Foothill College, in California. Her books of translation, in collaboration with her late husband, **Samuel Grolmes,** include Ryuichi Tamura's lifetime work, *Tamura Ryuichi Poems 1946–1998,* and two volumes of poems by Kazuko Shiraishi: *Let Those Who Appear* and *My Floating Mother, City,* all published by New Directions.

Wang Ping was born in China and came to the U.S. in 1985. Her works include the fiction collections *American Visa* and *The Last Communist Virgin;* the novel *Foreign Devil;* two poetry collections, *Of Flesh & Spirit* and *The Magic Whip;* and a cultural study of footbinding in China, *Aching for Beauty,* which won the 2000 Eugene Kayden Award for best book in the humanities. She is also the editor and cotranslator of the anthology *New Generation: Poetry from China Today.* She is an associate professor of English at Macalester College.

Yan Lianke was born in Song County, Henan Province, in 1958. He is the author of the novels *The Dream of Ding Village, The Joy of Living, The Sunlit Years, Solidity of Water,* and *Serve the People,* which was banned in China and later translated into French and Japanese. He has also published numerous collections of short stories and novellas, including *Years, Months, Days* and *Song of the Plow.* He is a member of the Chinese Writers' Association and is the recipient of numerous literary awards, the most prestigious of which have been the first and second Lu Xun Literary Prizes and the 2004 Lao She Award for literary excellence.

Reprint Permissions

The editors gratefully acknowledge permission to reprint the following:

"The Ice Is Melting in the North" by Oren Lyons first appeared in *Sacred Fire* 5 (2007). Reprinted by permission of the author.

"The Leadership Imperative: An Interview with Oren Lyons" by Barry Lopez first appeared in *Orion* (January/February 2007). Reprinted by permission of the author.

"The Return" by Tony Birch. From *Shadowboxing* by Tony Birch. Victoria, Australia: Scribe, 2006. Reprinted by permission of the author.

Eyes of the Heart copyright © Catherine Filloux. All rights reserved. Reprinted by permission of Playscripts, Inc. To purchase acting editions of this play, or to obtain performance rights, contact: Playscripts, Inc. http://www.playscripts.com or info@playscripts.com or 1-866-new-play.

"Wandering Souls" by Wayne Karlin first appeared in *War, Literature & the Arts* 18:1–2 (2005). Reprinted by permission of the author.

Excerpt from *'Onipa'a: Five Days in the History of the Hawaiian Nation*. Honolulu: Office of Hawaiian Affairs, 1994. Reprinted by permission.

"The Homecoming of an Old Beijing Man" by Wang Ping. From *The Last Communist Virgin* by Wang Ping. Minneapolis: Coffee House Press, 2007. Reprinted by permission of the author.

"In Memoriam" by Alberto Manguel. From *Into the Looking-Glass Wood* by Alberto Manguel. Toronto: Knopf Canada, 1998. Reprinted by permission of the author.

"Meditation #7: Prayer for Peace" by Luis Francia. From *Museum of Absences* by Luis Francia. St. Helena, CA: Meritage Press and Quezon City: University of the Philippines Press, 2004. Reprinted by permission of the author.

Ka Moʻolelo o Hiʻiakaikapoliopele

The Epic Tale of Hiʻiakaikapoliopele

Text by Hoʻoulumāhiehie
with Translation by Puakea Nogelmeier
Illustrations by Solomon Enos

This ancient saga begins with the goddess Pele's migration to Kīlauea and her spirit's search for a lover. The story details the quest of Hiʻiakaikapoliopele to find Pele's beloved Lohiʻauipo and bring him back to their crater home. Graced with a magical skirt and wielding supernatural powers, Hiʻiaka and her companions make their dangerous journey, facing supernatural foes, and cunning human ways. This engrossing account of love and lust, jealousy and justice, is replete with deities, demons, chiefs and commoners. This version by Hoʻoulumāhiehie was published as a daily series from 1905 to 1906 in *Ka Naʻi Aupuni*, one of the many Hawaiian-language newspapers in print in Hawaiʻi a hundred years ago.

Awaiaulu Press fosters community access to the extraordinary body of historical Hawaiian knowledge through the translation and publication of Hawaiian writings contained in over a century of Hawaiian language newspapers. The press fulfills a critical role in training and mentoring Hawaiian language translators to continue developing the vast cultural legacy found in Hawaiian-language sources.

NĀ KUA'ĀINA
Living Hawaiian Culture
DAVIANNA PŌMAIKA'I MCGREGOR

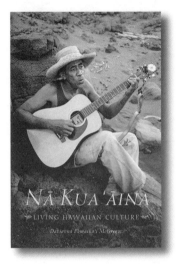

The word *kua'āina* translates literally as "back land" or "back country." Davianna Pōmaika'i McGregor grew up hearing it as a reference to an awkward or unsophisticated person from the country. However, in the context of the Native Hawaiian cultural renaissance of the late twentieth century, *kua'āina* came to refer to those who actively lived Hawaiian culture and kept the spirit of the land alive. *Kua'āina* are Native Hawaiians who remained in rural areas; took care of *kūpuna*; continued to speak Hawaiian; toiled in taro patches and sweet potato fields; and took that which is precious and sacred in Native Hawaiian culture into their care. The *mo'olelo* recounted in this book reveal how *kua'āina* have enabled Native Hawaiians to endure as a unique and dignified people after more than a century of American subjugation and control. The stories are set in rural communities or cultural *kīpuka*—oases from which traditional Native Hawaiian culture can be regenerated and revitalized.

Unlike many works of Hawaiian history, which focus on the history of change in Hawaiian society, particularly in O'ahu and among the ruling elite, *Nā Kua'āina* tells a broader and more inclusive story of the Hawaiian Islands by documenting the continuity of Native Hawaiian culture as well as the changes.

Davianna Pōmaika'i McGregor is professor of ethnic studies at the University of Hawai'i and a historian of Hawai'i and the Pacific.

2007, 384 pages, 36 illustrations, 5 maps
ISBN 978-0-8248-3212-4, paperback, $20

UNIVERSITY OF HAWAI'I PRESS
Phone 808-956-8255 or toll free 1-888-UHPRESS
Email: uhpbooks@hawaii.edu • Web: www.uhpress.hawaii.edu

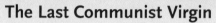